REINVIGORATING DEMOCRACY?

Reinvigorating Democracy?

British politics and the Internet

Edited by

RACHEL GIBSON and STEPHEN WARD
University of Salford

Ashgate

Aldershot • Burlington USA • Singapore • Sydney

Published by
Ashgate Publishing Limited
Gower House
Croft Road
Aldershot
Hampshire GU11 3HR
England

Ashgate Publishing Company
131 Main Street
Burlington, VT 05401-5600 USA

Ashgate website: http://www.ashgate.com

British Library Cataloguing in Publication Data
Reinvigorating democracy? : British politics and the
   Internet
   1.Politics, Practical - Great Britain - Computer network
   resources 2.Information technology - Political aspects -
   Great Britain 3.Internet (Computer network) - Social
   aspects - Great Britain 4.Democracy - Great Britain 5. Great
   Britain - Politics and government - 1997 -
   I.Gibson, Rachel II.Ward, Stephen, 1965-
   320.9'41'0285'4678

Library of Congress Control Number: 00-134479

ISBN 1 84014 793 8

Printed in Great Britain by
Antony Rowe Ltd, Chippenham, Wiltshire

Contents

List of Figures and Tables

List of Contributors

Yaman Akdeniz is a PhD candidate at the CyberLaw Research Unit, Centre for Criminal Justice Studies, University of Leeds. His thesis concerns The Governance of the Internet in Europe and he has published widely on legal issues and the regulation of the Internet. He is also the founder and director of Cyber-Rights and Cyber-Liberties (UK) (http://www.cyber-rights.org), a non-profit making civil liberties organisation set up in January 1997.

Stephen Coleman is Director of Studies at The Hansard Society for Parliamentary Government (see www.hansard-society.org.uk) and heads its *Parliament and the Electronic Media* programme. He lectures on Media and Citizenship at the London School of Economics and Political Science. Recent publications include *Parliament in the Age of the Internet,* edited with J. Taylor and W. van de Donk, OUP, 1999; *Electronic Media, Parliament and the People: Making Democracy Visible,* Hansard Society, 1999, and *Televised Election Debates*, Macmillan, 1999.

Richard Davis is Professor of Political Science at Brigham Young University, Utah, USA. He is the author of *The Web of Politics: The Internet's Impact on the American Political System*, Oxford: Oxford University Press, 1999, and co-author (with Diane Owen) of *New Media and American Politics*, Oxford University Press, 1998.

Rachel Gibson is a Lecturer in Politics at the European Studies Research Institute, University of Salford and visiting research fellow at the School of Social Sciences, Australian National University, Canberra, 1999-2001. She is currently involved in a number of research projects examining the impact of the Internet on politics, in particular, European political parties (with Stephen Ward). Other publications have included work on anti-immigrant parties in Western Europe and power distribution within political parties.

Paul G. Nixon is European project co-ordinator for CIRA, and a Senior Lecturer in Comparative Politics and Policy, at the University of Teesside. He has published a number of pieces on both political organisations usage of ICTs and policy related issues in Europe including:

'Transparency through Technology: A Comparative Study of Political Parties and their Use of the Internet' (with Hans Johansson) in B. Hague and B. Loader (eds), *Digital Democracy* Routledge, 1999, and 'Government and ICT's', in V. Koutrakou (ed), *The Government of the European Union,* by to be published in 2000 by Macmillan.

Janie Percy-Smith is Principal Lecturer at the Policy Research Institute, Leeds Metropolitan University where she is involved in a wide range of research relating to local governance and citizenship, urban policy and social exclusion. She is the co-author of *Local Governance in Britain,* (2000, Macmillan); editor of *From Exclusion to Inclusion. Policy responses to social exclusion* (2000, Open University Press); and editor of *Needs Assessments in Public Policy* (1996, Open University Press).

Jenny Pickerill is currently completing her doctoral thesis in the Department of Geography at the University of Newcastle-upon-Tyne. Her main areas of interest lie in the use of computer-mediated communication by groups to facilitate their political activities and in the study of the environmental protest movement, both within the UK and world-wide. Other research that she has been involved in includes a project examining the perceptions and use of e-commerce at Lancaster University.

Clive Walker is Professor of the Faculty of Law and Director of the Centre for Criminal Justice Studies, University of Leeds. He is the author of many articles in the fields of criminal justice, constitutional law and politics and media law. His recent book titles include works on failures in the justice system, *Miscarriages of Justice: A Review of Justice in Error,* Blackstone Press, 1999, and the impact of the Internet on court process, *Crime, Criminal Justice and the Internet,* Sweet & Maxwell, 1999.

Stephen Ward is a Lecturer in Politics, at the European Studies Research Institute, University of Salford. His research interests include environmental politics and policy-making and politics and the new media. His recent publications include *British Environmental Politics and Europe: Politics and Policy in Transition,* edited with Philip Lowe, Routledge, 1998, as well as a number of articles with Rachel Gibson on political parties and the Internet.

Mark Wheeler is a Senior Lecturer in Politics at the Department of Politics and Modern History, London Guildhall University. He is the author of *Politics and the Mass Media,* Blackwell, 1998, and has published articles in research journals such as *Democratisation and Convergence* concerning the impact of new ICTs on democratic practices and political communication. He is also a researcher for the British Screen Advisory Council.

Acknowledgements

The editors would like to thank the European Studies Research Institute at the University of Salford for their support of the workshop that led to this edited collection. Special thanks also go to Leslie Harris for her word processing skills and Janet Bell for her all round guidance, organisation and patience.

Rachel Gibson and Stephen Ward, March 2000, Salford.

List of Abbreviations

ABA	American Bar Association
ACPO	Association of Chief Police Officers
BNP	British National Party
CACTUS	Criminal Appeals Case Tracking User System
CAT	Computer Aided Transcription
CEC	Commission of the European Communities
CPGB	Communist Party of Great Britain
CPS	Crown Prosecution Service
CSMB	Court Service Management Board
DETR	Department of the Environment, Transport and the Regions
DTI	Department of Trade and Industry
DUP	Democratic Unionist Party
FITLOG	Foundation for Information Technology in Local Government
HTML	Hypertext Markup Language
ICTs	Information Communication Technologies
INSINC	National Working Party on Social Inclusion in the Information Society
ISPs	Internet Service Providers
ITAC	Information Technology and the Courts Committee
IWF	Internet Watch Foundation
JTG	Judicial Technology Group
LCD	Lord Chancellor's Department
LGMB	Local Government Management Board
MAI	Multilateral Agreement on Investment
NCIS	National Criminal Intelligence Service
NDP	National Democratic Party
NF	National Front
NGOs	Non Governmental Organisations
NII	US National Information Infrastructure
NSMs	New Social Movements
OECD	Organisation for Economic Cooperation and Development
PDVN	Parliamentary Data and Video Network

PFI	Private Finance Initiative
PITO	Police Information Technology Organisation
POST	Parliamentary Office of Science and Technology
PUP	Progressive Unionist Party
SDLP	Social and Democratic Labour Party
SEP	Socialist Equality Party
SLD	Scottish Liberal Democrats
SNP	Scottish National Party
SOCITM	Society of Information Technology Managers
SOLACE	Society of Local Authority Chief Executives
SPGB	Socialist Party of Great Britain
TTP	Trusted Third Party
UDP	Ulster Democratic Party
URL	Uniform Resource Locator
UUP	Ulster Unionist Party
UKIP	United Kingdom Independence Party
WWW	World Wide Web

Introduction

RACHEL GIBSON AND STEPHEN WARD

> It maybe that the era of pure representative democracy is slowly coming
> to an end... . Democracy and legitimacy need constant renewal. They
> need to be redefined with each generation... . Representative government
> is being complemented by more direct forms of involvement, from the
> Internet to referenda... . That requires a different style of politics (Peter
> Mandelson, quoted in *The Guardian,* 16 March 1998, p. 14)[1]

The rapid expansion of digital technologies are heralded as having
significant implications for the functioning of democracy in general and
political institutions in particular. This book is designed to focus on what
new Information Communication Technologies (ICTs) mean for key actors
in the UK political system, both from an internal perspective, but also with
regard to their external relations with the public. In doing so, its chief goal
is to move us away from the current highly abstract debate on the future of
politics in the digital age towards a more empirically grounded
understanding of the effects that the new media are having on the
organisations and institutions that play a major role in shaping government
and maintaining democracy.

The fundamental questions lying at the heart of the book relate to
broad issues about the health of democracy in the UK and the levels of elite
accountability and responsibility. Recently, notions of a democratic deficit
and a participation crisis in modern societies have arisen, centring on the
apparently declining relevance of our representative structures such as
parties and Parliament, and falling turnout at elections. Against this
background, new ICTs have been seen to offer a solution to such problems
given the reduction in time and space they offer for communication flows,
and the opportunities for interactive communication. By opening up the
communications process to more information and more voices, technologies
such as the Internet are seen as offering potential for bringing government
closer to the people, making it more responsive and relevant.

Rationale for the Book

This book addresses the question of how revolutionary new ICTs will be for government and politics, primarily in the UK, but with reference to the USA. As such, it takes an empirical approach to the question of application of new ICTs to key processes, institutions and organisations within the political system, notably the courts, Parliament, local government, parties, Whitehall bureaucracy and interest groups. How are these actors adapting to the new, faster and more interactive methods of communication and information storage introduced by the Internet in particular and by digital technology in general? What does it mean for their operation, structure and ultimately output? Will it lead to their wholesale transformation, more moderate reform and reinvigoration, or little perceptible difference?

The need to address such questions has become more pressing during the course of the past five years, given the many claims made for and against new ICTs as tools of governance in the 21st century. Some clearly foresee a bright future in which government becomes a faster, smoother, and less unwieldy deliverer of the goods and services. Equally, the opportunities for citizens to play an active role in their own governance is seen to increase, as the need for elected representatives are replaced by electronic or e-voting on policy referenda, and more inclusive on-line debates. Alternatively, there are those who envisage that the new technologies will offer new opportunities for state control. The joining up of government agencies into a more seamless web of information sharers, it can be argued, increases the possibilities for state monitoring and control of individuals. Further, while perhaps offering more outlets for citizen input, such scenarios seem fairly vague on the key question of agenda control - what questions are actually put to the public, and who is involved in such decisions?

Such visions are indeed speculative and futuristic and cannot be answered fully at this point. What is possible, however, is an identification of the chief forms of new ICTs most relevant for current political institutions, and assessment of how they are responding to the challenges and opportunities presented by the new medium. While the new digital technologies are not, as yet, mass media, during the past five years elite and mass level usage has grown significantly. Thus, such a study would clearly serve as a benchmark and timely point of reference for future research on government's use of the media. Was there a point at which big changes were possible and not undertaken, or were the technologies always seen to be of useful but limited value?

Aims of the Book

The goal of this edited volume is to examine the extent to which the new digital technologies, such as the World Wide Web (WWW), e-mail, and new database software, are being used within our major political institutions and organisations, and reflect on how far this is engendering significant change in their form and function. The book's primary focus, therefore, is the political system of the United Kingdom and those close to or at the elite level of policy-making, rather than the mass level. The decision to concentrate on those more proximate to the decision-making process is made largely because it is here that the most significant degree of activity and adaptation appears to be taking place. By 1998 almost all government departments, political parties, and a huge range of interest groups have established a presence on the WWW. In addition, many of these bodies, plus the courts, have established or are attempting to establish computerised internal communications systems that utilise e-mail, databases and new software packages to promote greater efficiency and dialogue. While public usage of the new media is growing, as the ever-expanding rates of Internet access reveal (Chapter 1), it is still a 'significant minority' medium, rather than a mass medium. Further, the demographic and socio-economic status of that minority make them highly unrepresentative of the public as a whole. It would appear that wider use of the Internet and e-mail by the poor, women, racial minorities, and older people is actually dependent upon government-based initiatives, perhaps in partnership with the private sector.

From a less practical point of view, the focus on established political institutions, organisations and the practice of government is needed to counter the technological determinism behind some of the more radical scenarios built around the move into the information-based digital era. According to these cyber sages, the new politics, characterised by its more transparent and accountable democratic form, emerges from the levelling of traditional hierarchies, such as Whitehall bureaucracy, national parliaments and mass parties. If one accepts that the new technology may indeed present the possibility of removing the 'middle' men in politics - the elected representatives, multiple layers of the Civil Service, political parties and other input channelling vehicles - it would seem naive in the extreme to suppose that these same groups would not fight back. In fact, in terms of resources and power advantages they would seem to be in the best position to adapt new ICTs for their own advantage, and to remove any potentially damaging impacts. Thus, from a theoretical point of view, one might expect the greatest activity to be taking place at the elite rather than the mass level within politics.

Despite this self-declared, more limited focus, it is clear that any study of technological innovation and government will inevitably be involved in exploring issues pertaining to the broader public and democratic society in general. While this book seeks to put the focus on institutions as the crucial conduit to the digital or electronic democracy of the future, the decisions made by the legislators, civil servants, judges, or local councillors on how, when and where to implement new communications mechanisms will, of course, be driven in part by perceptions of the articulated demands and needs of the citizens.

Of course it may be the case that some institutions and groups are responding more actively to the new ICTs. Certainly, within the political organisations sector, the more loosely structured new social movements would seem to have more to gain by embracing hierarchy-flattening technology than the Conservative Party for example. Equally, across institutional sectors, one might argue that Parliament and perhaps the courts would be more receptive to promoting the interactive properties of the Internet to allow more voices into the legislative and judicial process. The executive branch, however, with its more specialised implementing remit, would be less eager to the let the 'daylight' in. This edited volume allows us to assess whether such disparities are in fact beginning to emerge and if so, what this might mean, if anything, for the relative weight of these different actors in the political system of the future.

Overview of the Book

To answer some of these questions the book concentrates on the impact of new ICTs in three areas: (1) the formal institutional aspect of British politics, Whitehall and government bureaucracy, local government, Parliament, and the court system; (2) the impact of new ICTs on the more informal institutions of UK government - political parties and pressure groups and new social movements; (3) the policy responses of government and their attempts at regulating the Internet.

The editors' introductory chapter highlights the central themes of the book. It provides an overview of the development and use of the Internet and considers the debates surrounding the potential democratising or otherwise influences at two levels: the mass public, and the institutional and organisational. The various options presented range from erosion of established structures, to radical reform to no change.

Paul Nixon and Janie Percy-Smith's chapters consider the impact of new ICTs on central and local government, respectively. Nixon's analysis focuses on the content and implications of the Labour Government's White Paper on *Modernising Government* (Cabinet Office, 1999). It outlines the main proposals for the harnessing of government to new information and communication systems and assesses the implications for the 'logic' of government organisation. It argues that while this may eventually lead to significant reform within Whitehall and government agencies, one can question how far the citizen will gain democratically from moves towards 'joined-up' government. Similarly, Percy-Smith examines the role that new ICTs can play in current efforts to 'modernise' local government. Given their widespread presence on the Internet and the increasing number of on-line community-based initiatives, local authorities are sometimes seen as key innovators in the field of ICTs. The chapter provides a contemporary critique of the prospects for new ICTs to enhance democratic practices at the local level and concludes with a sobering assessment of the barriers and constraints that may prevent local authorities from utilising the new ICTs to their full democratic potential.

Both Stephen Coleman and Clive Walker discuss whether ICTs can promote better democratic citizenship through the utilisation of new media to facilitate greater communication, openness and participation in institutions. As Director of Studies at the Hansard Society, Stephen Coleman provides an inside assessment of developments within UK legislatures. The chapter notes that, comparatively, Westminster and MPs have been slow to use new ICTs for interactive purposes, although the new Scottish and Welsh Parliaments may be in better position to take advantage of the technology. In the context of the UK legal system, Walker analyses whether application of new technology is a positive benefit for the justice system. He asks how far on-line experiments actually effect legal decision-making and whether debate on the Internet differs from that of the traditional media. So far, whilst there is much hype surrounding new initiatives, the legal system has not offered much that is truly new in the sense of participation.

Use of the new media by UK political parties is assessed in the chapter by Rachel Gibson and Stephen Ward. They chart the parties' developing use of new ICTs and the role of public web-sites within party campaign strategy. The chapter indicates that although parties have not used the technology creatively, minor parties in particular have benefited from establishing a presence in cyberspace. The Internet with its decentralised structure and lack of editorial control would seem to give them a more equal footing than that enjoyed in traditional media.

Jenny Pickerill investigates the political implications of the use of the Internet and e-mail networks by pressure groups and New Social

Movements (NSMs), to aid campaigning, focusing on the environmental lobby, who are seen as one of the most active and enthusiastic users of the Internet. Using case studies and interview data, the author argues that pressure groups view the Internet as a useful communications tool with which to reach potential supporters quickly and efficiently, enabling them to compete more effectively with multi-national firms and government. Nevertheless, Pickerill argues that the new forms of activism promoted by the Internet need to be assessed alongside the benefits gained from more 'traditional' methods of campaigning.

Mark Wheeler and Yaman Akdeniz analyse debates surrounding the role of the state *vis-a-vis* the information society in general - essentially, can and should governments' attempt to establish regulatory frameworks to supervise the Internet. Wheeler centres on the area of e-commerce with specific reference to the 'virtual economy'. To make Internet trade viable, encryption methods are required to secure private data. Clearly governments are unwilling to allow exchanges to take place without the ability to check for illegal or dangerous content. As Wheeler notes, however, these controls have been met with resistance and such plans raise the spectre of an information elite with the potential for far greater control by government over its citizens.

Akdeniz's chapter takes the form of a critique of government efforts to police Internet content. In doing so it deals with broader issues of freedom of expression and privacy in the global information society, suggesting that national government sponsored initiatives rarely achieve their aim of controlling the pornographer or the racist but may lead to further erosions of fundamental human rights.

Given that the USA is regarded as one of the leaders of political Internet innovation (at least two years ahead of the UK), Richard Davis offers an overview of the US experience of the Internet and analyses whether the American experience holds any lessons for British politics. He argues that the new media has not and is not transforming American politics, nor will it in the UK. Hopes for direct or participatory democracy have been dashed as the established players have adapted relatively easily and now dominate the new media as they do the old media.

The final chapter by the editors draws together the debates from the various chapters. It identifies current trends in online political behaviour and the emerging patterns of institutional practice. Inter-organisational comparisons are then made in order to identify which actors and institutions in the political system are adapting more easily and creatively to the new media and why. Thus an overall assessment is produced on how far new

ICTs are likely to foster a different style of politics in the UK either by eroding or reinvigorating established political institutions.

Note

1. Peter Mandelson was at the time cabinet Minister without Portfolio. The report stems from discussions between Mandelson and Wolfgang Schauble of the German Christian Democrats (CDU) on visions for a millennial democracy. Such views were echoed almost exactly 18 months later by leading Labour Party pollster and electoral adviser Philip Gould, *The Times*, 15 November 1999, p. 17.

1 'Perfect Information, Perfect Democracy, Perfect Competition': Politics and the Impact of New ICTs[1]

RACHEL GIBSON AND STEPHEN WARD

In the space of little more than five years the Internet has gone from being the preserve of computer geeks and academics to being a world-wide media of central concern for political actors and government policy-makers. Even two to three years ago, it would be been rare to have found any mention of the Internet in the tabloid press, now the same newspapers have become Internet Service Providers (ISPs). Barely a day now goes by without the Internet either being declared the solution to a variety of social problems, low political participation and business competitiveness, or being held responsible for the promotion of pornography, racism and violence. Nevertheless, despite its rapid expansion, the majority of the UK population do not yet have access to the Internet; a sizeable minority have declared no interest in using it; and 1.6 million of the British public claim never to have heard of it. Perhaps not surprisingly, speculation about its impact therefore ranges from the wildly utopian to the hugely pessimistic.

This opening chapter seeks to place in context some of these claims by providing an overview of the development of the Internet in the UK and analysing some of the scenarios concerning the potential impact of ICTs at two levels:

- the mass level – centring on public use of Internet for political participation;
- the systemic level – focusing on the potential of the Internet to reform our political institutions and produce new styles of democracy.

What are New ICTs?

The claims for the new media's transformative effects on our political worlds are premised in the properties that distinguish them from that which came before. Therefore what exactly do we mean when we refer to new ICTs and how are they so different from previous forms?

New ICTs, broadly speaking, constitute forms of digitised information flow, whereby data, be it text, sound or moving real-time images are compressed into a series of zeros and ones and transmitted via airwaves, underground cable and overland networks (Graham, 1998). This technology had its first and most widespread usage in the shape of the Internet, an international network of computers connected to one another that started in the 1960s in the US Defence Department. For a period of over 20 years the Internet remained a largely elite and private mode of telecommunications, used and developed primarily by academics and government bodies (Streck, 1999). Transformation occurred in 1989 with the development of the graphic interface to the Internet, the WWW and the browsers (Mosaic in 1992 and its more sophisticated successor Netscape in 1994). With these developments the Internet became more easily accessible, as did its other applications such as e-mail and use-net. Thus, what emerged was a newer and faster technology that merged telecommunications facilities with mass media publishing.

Given that existing ICTs such as television and the telephone are beginning to move to digital mode and open the possibility of convergence with the Internet, it is becoming more difficult to draw a line around the specific forms of new ICTs. What constitutes the old media and what the new? While this book recognises that an Internet-based media and telecommunications system, accessible via television, may be the next and most influential generation of new ICTs, the focus here is mainly on the existing forms and those most useful for elites, i.e. the Internet, video conferencing and e-mail.

What is Different about New ICTs?

While uniting a number of different applications, new ICTs have generally been distinguished from their predecessors by the following properties (Abramson *et al* 1988; Bonchek, 1995; Wheeler, 1997):

• they greatly increase the volume and speed of information that can be sent;

- they allow for changes in the style and format of message sent through combining print and electronic communication;
- they decentralise control over the content and timing of messages sent and received;
- they greatly expand interactivity.

On one level, these innovations simply relate to an expansion of the existing capabilities of the old media and telecommunications methods: digital communication speeds up and expands the communication already taking place via analogue television, radio and the telephone. On another more social level, however, they represent a fundamental shift in the mechanism of mass communication. The increases in volume and speed make possible the transfer of far larger amounts of data in a much more immediate way across great geographic distances. In addition, since the development of the WWW in the early 1990s, one can add that new ICTs also innovate in the form of the message sent by combining text-based, audio and visual media into one. As well as overcoming barriers of time and space in information flows, however, this expanded bandwidth also introduces opportunities for much greater user control and decentralisation of media ownership in the communications process.

In the traditional print and electronic media, while there is competition between individual producers of information be they the broadcast networks or newspapers, owing to limited bandwidth or high production costs production of news is centralised in the hands of a few corporate actors. Given the relatively unlimited space accorded to new ICTs such as the Internet, however, and the low cost of production (a computer and an Internet access account), individual consumers can now become publishers of the news, alongside these corporate giants. In addition, as a consumer of news the individual is required to exercise greater initiative in the information-gathering process. Rather than being presented with a pre-packaged edited version in the shape of a daily newspaper delivered through the door or the evening news broadcast on radio and television, the Internet user has to actively search out the information they want. They can then edit and collate their own news sources.

The Impact of ICTs at the Mass Level

At the mass level, new ICTs are seen as presenting significant opportunities and also challenges for expanding public participation in politics. Some argue that the new ICTs, because of the unique features outlined above, will widen the numbers involved in political participation and deepen the quality of that participation. From a rational choice perspective, new ICTs could significantly lower the barriers (costs) to participation for individuals from more marginal and excluded groups. Political activity such as information gathering, joining organisations or directly contacting political institutions and organisations could become far easier and quicker (Street, 1997; Percy-Smith 1995; Mulgan and Adonis, 1994). Further, it is argued that as technological development takes place, access, in terms of the educational and financial resources necessary to engage in the process will diminish. The arrival of set-top boxes and Internet TV will allow the house-bound, such as the elderly, single parents and the disabled, to participate more easily from their homes. The introduction of cheaper computer hardware and Internet connections, along with the introduction of public access in libraries and other public facilities, could help to overcome the exclusion of lower income individuals and families.

The Internet could also deepen citizen involvement by allowing more regular participation and more accountability in political decision-making. Rather than just being able to vote periodically, citizens could be offered considerably more direct opportunities to engage with the political process through electronic referenda, citizen juries, on-line discussion and debate foras with politicians. Engaging in such activities may in itself serve to increase political interest, and stimulate a positive orientation toward participation. Such electronic initiatives, it is argued, will lead to more accountable elites and new communities of interest that in turn will increase the efficacy of participants and encourage further activism (Rheingold, 1995; Rash, 1997).

The contrary and more pessimistic view is that new ICTs will not increase participation, but may well narrow and trivialise it. Critics argue that the optimists have forgotten the financial costs and skills required to use the technology. The costs of going online are likely to remain beyond the poorest in society for some time and simply providing public access points is not equal to having unlimited access at home. Similarly, the socially excluded are also those least likely to have the skills and training to use the technology. Hence, the introduction of new ICTs into the political process could quite easily further strengthen the position of advantage of high socio-economic status (SES) groups within society. In short, the people who already participate the most will gain the most.

Pessimists are equally, sceptical of the ability of electronic forms of participation to produce meaningful political deliberation. They contend that the individualistic push button mode of participation will render participation less meaningful and erode citizen interest, making collective action harder and elites less accountable (Lipow and Seyd, 1996; Street, 1997; Barber *et al*, 1997). Electronic participation through referenda and the like may become no more than the registering of individual preferences (McLean, 1989). While citizens may have access to large amounts of information on-line, they may either become overloaded and switch off, or not use it and insulate themselves from alternative opinions by only selecting a narrow range of on-line information sources. As Shapiro has noted this raises the possibility 'that many people may be inclined to use their new power over information to reinforce existing political beliefs rather than to challenge themselves' (1999, p. 25).

Although it is too early to make definitive judgements about the impact of the technology at a mass level it should be possible to detect some trends towards the digital future. At a minimum, if the optimists are right at least three criteria will need to be fulfilled: rapidly increasing usage so that the Internet is on its way to becoming a mass medium; a narrowing of reduced SES usage differences; indications that the mass public are using/are interested in using the WWW for political purposes.

The Growth of the Internet: Towards a Mass Medium?

Internet usage rates in the UK have increased markedly since 1994 but the pattern of growth has been somewhat distorted (Figure 1). In the early years it grew relatively slowly by only 1 or 2 per cent per year. However, since autumn 1998 there has been a rapid uptake of Internet technology. The numbers claiming to use the Internet regularly have doubled in the space of six months from 11 percent in autumn 1998 to 22 percent by spring 1999. At the time of writing (late 1999), latest indications show that this has risen sharply again, to just under 30 per cent of the population, with overall potential access to the net rising to around 40 per cent of the UK population. If one adds on those with access to e-mail only, then some 60 per cent have the potential to use e-mail and/or the WWW according to Cabinet Office statistics.

If such access and usage figures are compared with other similar countries, then the UK is in the top quarter. However, it is well behind Scandinavian countries (Sweden was first European country where Internet penetration exceeded 50 per cent of the population in 1999) and the USA, but has favourable usage rates compared to Germany or France. As a result, it has been argued that the growth of the Internet in the UK resembles a somewhat similar pattern to that in the USA, but with the UK lagging around two years behind the USA in terms of Internet coverage.

Figure 1.1 Internet Users (percentage of population)

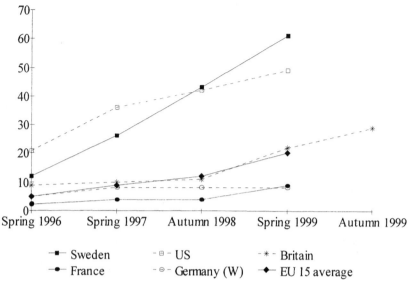

Source: *Adapted from Norris, 1999, p.20*

The best explanation for the sudden surge of growth was the introduction of 'Freeserve' by the Dixons retail group, which provided a no-charge service for connecting to the Internet and the resulting growth of competing ISPs. Within weeks of Freeserve being introduced 900,000 people had signed up.[2] By spring 1999 nearly all major ISPs had scrapped subscription and joining charges for Internet and e-mail use and a wide range of organisations including banks, supermarkets and newspapers were all offering Internet access. Nevertheless, the bare user statistics need to be treated with caution on a number of grounds. First, regular usage is often only defined as using the Internet in the last month. Daily users of the WWW comprise a much lower figure of around 10–15 per cent of the UK public. Second, there is a gap between access to the Net and actual usage of it. For example, it has been reported that although people are often given free introductory access when they purchase new computers, many fail to make use of it, or use it only for e-mail rather than surfing the Web.[3] Third, even though the costs of technology are falling in real terms, there is still a considerable barrier of the high costs of UK telephone calls for using the Internet. Repeated surveys have shown that people are reluctant to go on-line given the costs of calls and that even when they do, they are conscious of limiting their browsing time. Recent estimates indicate that British users spend only 17 minutes a day on-line, only one quarter that of their American counterparts.[4]

User Profiles

In terms of the profile of users, from the limited evidence available it appears that the UK follows the stereotypical pattern identified in more numerous American studies. Heavy Internet users tend to be predominantly male, middle class, in professional employment, with high educational attainment (degree standard and above) between the ages of 24–40 years old, residing in urban areas. In both the USA and Europe the work of Norris (1998; 1999; 2000) and Bimber (1998) over a three-year period (1995–1998), indicates that those accessing the Internet and using it for political purposes (either information seeking or contacting and discussion) had higher levels of political interest, knowledge, efficacy and were of higher socio-economic status (see also Chapter 10). Similarly, in the European context Gibson and Ward identified the key variable determining on-line political activity was one's pre-existing proclivity to engage in political debate off-line. Consequently, it was concluded that:

> The Internet is not galvanising hordes of previously apathetic individuals to become more politically involved; neither is it promoting a deepening divide between information rich and poor... . Indeed, if anything, it may lead to a deepening of political involvement as new modes of participation open up (Gibson and Ward 1999a, p. 17).

Nevertheless, important caveats have been offered in relation to these general trends that may provide hope for supposedly democratising potential of new ICTs. First, the greater proportion of younger users (18–29 year olds) relying on the Net for news. Such a trend could lead to greater political involvement amongst this traditionally disinterested group. Second, in the USA at least, Bimber (1998) detected that general levels of civic engagement and propensity to vote actually increased among those with Internet access, regardless of SES. Third, as many of the surveys point out, uneven profiles may level out over time as access increases. As a result, some of these demographic imbalances may be relatively short lived, others more enduring. Although income and class disparities appear as yet stubbornly ingrained, evidence is already emerging that the gender and age distinctions are being eroded. More women and older people have moved on-line since 1998 and surveys are now showing that the number of women on-line in the UK is nearing 40 per cent.[5]

Although overall usage of the Net is growing, political activity on-line remains a minority interest. The Internet is currently reliant on citizens actively seeking out and visiting sites. Simply because (political) sites are available does not mean that they will be used. Independent evidence indicates that most people do not go on-line for politics and are relatively conservative in their choice of sites. Sport, sex and shopping remain the commonest areas of interest on the WWW. Perhaps even more interestingly, the same studies suggest that while Internet surfers are spending more time on-line they are visiting less sites than two years ago.[6]

Although the Internet is growing rapidly it is still a long way from widespread penetration and there are considerable technological social and political barriers to be overcome before the Internet can claim to be a mass medium. It is already possible to see some of the financial and technical hurdles being tackled. Worries about the costs of the Internet limiting the potentials for e-commerce have led to British Telecom signalling a move to cheap rate Internet telephone calls.[7] Likewise, the technology itself is likely to become easier to use through the introduction of set-top boxes, key pads instead of keyboards, and more fundamentally the general convergence of the Internet with digital television. However, we should not underestimate the social and political problems relating to (in)equality of access and also user initiative in both distorting and reducing the impact of the technology in the political sphere (Milner, 1999).

New ICTs at the Systemic Level: Organisations, Institutions and Democracy

Although use of new ICTs at the organisational and elite levels of politics is more extensive than at the mass level, there is again little consensus on the likely impact of new ICTs for political organisations and institutions. Initial speculative literature predicted nothing short of a political revolution. More recent empirical research, however, has tended to downplay the impact of ICTs to the extent that political systems and political institutions and organisations will simply adapt the technology to their own ends. Three main scenarios of institutional and organisational impact can be detected from the diverse range of literature: revolution, reform and no change.

Revolution, Erosion and Direct Democracy

At the radical end of the spectrum some commentators consider that the unique characteristics of the technology will produce revolutionary changes within the political organisations and in the system as a whole. The representative role of political and governing organisations will be eroded and eventually removed, as citizens engage directly and individually in governing themselves. In terms of models of democracy the ideas of erosion equates most closely to notions of direct democracy and, in particular, the classic model based on unmediated popular voting. The accounts of direct democracy via digital networks in a mass society are somewhat hazy in terms of the specific mechanics of the process. However, it is clear that Athenian models of civic life form a template, whereby existing structures and institutions of representative governance are replaced by virtual meeting places through which citizens vote directly, via electronic networks, as individuals on matters of policy. Clearly some degree of devolution of power within present nation states to a more local level would take place. Citizens in a particular area presumably would decide local agendas. Nation states would wither away. Matters requiring broader geographic discussion and consent would be done on-line between communities (perhaps via a smaller executive, membership of which could be rotated and appointment made by drawing lots). While the details are sketchy, it is clear that the current mechanisms for mediation of popular opinion in the shape of politicians, parliaments and councils would disappear and other hierarchical branches of the state, such as the administrative branch, would be extensively flattened.

From this radical perspective, Negroponte envisions that the modern state will not simply wither away but even more dramatically evaporate – 'like a mothball, which goes from a solid to a gas directly... without first going into a gooey inoperative mess' (1995, p. 236). In short, the political system as we know it will dissolve as the new media become increasingly incorporated into everyday life.

Although these views may seem highly fanciful, and impossible to test at this early stage, such visions have found allies within the political sphere, particularly amongst anti-system parties or candidates. For example, the idea of a technologically driven political revolution are underscored in the document *Cyberspace and the American Dream: A Magna Carta for the Knowledge Age*, released on the WWW in 1994 by Newt Gingrich's Progress and Freedom Foundation, an organisation dedicated to the promotion of radical Republican philosophy. The authors argue that as the gap between the knowledge rich and the knowledge poor, is eliminated in this new era, the centralised power of the state will inevitably melt away. Cyberspace democracy will empower those closest to the decision.[8]

Such thinking is not limited to the American arena, similar examples can be found in the European context. Graham Allen, a UK government minister, has argued in the past that the new electronic media will lead to the removal of intermediaries such as parties and representative assemblies as direct electronic participation becomes possible.[9] According to this erosionary perspective, innovations such as e-voting and debates with our representatives are merely the tip of the iceberg in terms of the changes we might expect to witness in liberal democracies.

Reform, Reinvigoration and Lean Democracy

A less revolutionary approach envisages reform of the political system but not necessarily institutional erosion. Indeed, the emergence of new technologies provides considerable opportunities for the 19th century institutions of liberal democracy to reinvigorate themselves and ensure their continuing relevance into the 21st century. In order to survive and prosper, political organisations will need to adapt to, and harness, new ICTs. Consequently, some have suggested that a halfway house of mediated direct democracy is the possible outcome of the impact of ICTs on politics (Budge, 1996). Others have argued for the creation of a lean democracy (Mulgan and Adonis, 1994; Leadbeater and Mulgan, 1997). The basic goal is a political system with greater transparency and accountability where the administrative wing of the state, rather like the re-engineering or downsizing of business firms, becomes more efficient at product delivery. The role of government becomes more to recruit and balance citizen demands in a responsive fashion, rather than to offer any broad plans for reshaping society and the economy. Whilst this line of thought sometimes uses the language of democracy and participation it is one based on notions of consumerism and public mangerialism, and is often more interested in economic issues than governance *per se* (Bellamy and Taylor, 1998; Coleman, 1999c).

Both mediated direct democracy and lean democracy stress that parliaments and parties may have to adapt to more direct modes of participation that will erode their representative function, but there is no reason why they cannot still provide useful political leadership, mediating and aggregating roles in society (Budge, 1996; See also Chapter 4).

Generally, reformers point to three specific areas of institutional/organisational reform that could be fostered by new ICTs.

Intra-organisational democracy: Internally political organisations such as parties or pressure groups could be made more democratic. The establishment of Intranets could enhance individual members' abilities to inform the leadership's decisions and hold leaders accountable. The greater volume and speed of information flow offered via computer-mediated communication combined with its interactivity and decentralisation into people's homes, means that members can have more frequent and direct access to organisational elites to communicate their opinions on policy matters, and organisational structure. Such developments would also provide members with more information on what their leaders are doing, more quickly, and thus promote the accountability of elite-level decision-making.

Furthermore, the independent adoption of the new media in its external or more public face (i.e. the WWW) by intra-organisational groups or prominent individuals will allow them to communicate their views to a local, national, and global audience more frequently and effectively. The current lack of central control over the Internet means that central organisational elites would not be in a position to prevent the widespread dissemination of internal views, and possible dissent, if they chose to publish them in this manner. Again this could potentially empower grassroots members.

Already within the UK it is clear that many political organisations have created internal computer communication systems (ICCS) for their members and staff. All the major UK parties possess such networks, along with some of the larger trade unions, such as Unison and pressure groups such as Friends of the Earth. Currently, ICCS channels are generally used as information exchanges or discussion fora, rather than allowing decisive votes on policy issues or promoting direct accountability of leadership elites (Gibson and Ward, 1999b). This partly reflects the fact that ICCS have tended to have limited memberships and are heavily weighted in favour of central or full-time organisational officials. Nevertheless, even at this formative stage, one trade union has already experimented with holding a pay ballot via e-mail that led to an increased turnout.[10]

Inter-organisational relations: Established political organisations and institutions may have to come to terms with a more pluralist and less predictable political system where previously dominant political organisations are open to greater challenge than before. This 'equalisation' thesis rests on the basis that the Internet is a truly different medium and is likely to exact a significant degree of change on organisational behaviour. Its central tenet is that minor and fringe organisations are more likely to use the new media and more likely to gain from the net and thus be better able to challenge their major counterparts (Bonchek, 1995; Stone 1996; Rash, 1997; See also Chapter 6). This contention is based on the low costs of using the media and its lack of editorial control. To create a relatively sophisticated Web presence is comparatively cheap both in terms of finances and skills. Unlike television or radio, anybody with a small amount of resources and time can create a site that is capable of attracting a global audience and reduce communication and administration costs. Moreover, in cyberspace, the lack of editorial control means that political organisations can more easily communicate their undiluted message. This is of particular benefit to minor/fringe groups who may be locked out of the traditional media debates or lack the resources to compete. Already journalists in the UK have noted the successful use of new ICTs by small networks of environmentalists, human rights and social justice groups to get their message across. From using e-mail to mobilise anti-roads protesters at the local level by loose networks such as Reclaim the Streets, to the international grassroots cyberspace campaign to ambush the Multilateral Agreement on Investment, the WWW and e-mail are increasingly seen as essential campaign tools (See Chapter 7).[11] As a result, Doherty comments in relation to radical protest networks: 'by cutting the costs of networking and making it more difficult for governments to maintain secrecy, the net has reduced the slope of the playing field for protesters of all types' (1999, p. xviii).

Citizen relations: The third area of potential reform is institutional-citizen relations. In common with the erosion school, reformers contend that ICTs provide the opportunities for more direct citizen involvement in the political sphere. However, rather than being rendered impotent by such innovations, forward-thinking political organisations and institutions can harness the technology in a number of ways.

- To increase transparency and inform the public of government by placing large amounts of governmental information on accessible web-sites. The Internet has been seen as a useful publicity and informational tool by nearly all political actors. For instance, with complaints about decline in the serious coverage of parliamentary affairs some have heralded the Internet as the saviour, 'a new champion of parliamentary coverage, likely to transcend all that has gone before it, now racing to the rescue of under reported MPs' (McKie, 1999, p. 18).

- To increase the amount of citizen input into initial decision making and about service delivery and performance. The UK government has already experimented to a limited degree through UK Citizens On-line Democracy (UKCOD) gathering comment on the Freedom of Information White Paper (See Chapter 4). While local authorities such as Hammersmith and Fulham and Gloucester have obtained public comment on local issues particularly regarding planning and development policies (Cremin, 1999, pp. 23-24), more ambitious authorities such as Brent have engaged in electronic debates via bulletin boards around specific issues, such as council tax rates (see Chapter 3).

- To use ICTs to deliver services more efficiently and quickly at a lower cost (Freeman, 1997; Lawson, 1998; See also Chapter 2). The Labour government has been particularly keen to use ICTs to modernise the health service, recently launching NHS Direct, an on-line information service staffed by medical personnel to answer queries and offer advice. Lord Freeman a former Conservative minister for public services, neatly encapsulates this line of thinking, arguing that :

> We need, I believe, to introduce a fundamental change to the way in which government provides services to its citizens and businesses by using electronic means... . We need to ensure that government services are accessible twenty four hours a day, seven days a week, every week, convenient in access, however remote the citizen may be located, quicker and cheaper for the user of the service as well as the taxpayer (Freeman, 1997, p. 24).

In sum, reformers suggest that reforms in all three areas (intra-organisational, inter-organisational and citizen relations) could enhance the performance of Liberal democratic institutions and indirectly reinvigorate their role by increasing citizen satisfaction, thereby ensuring their survival well into the next century.

No Change - Politics as Normal

In response to the more revolutionary, speculative and theoretically driven literature, an empirically based scenario has emerged – that of no change – claiming that the Internet is not necessarily as unique as has been suggested and that it is unlikely to bring about radical changes in governing structures.

Sceptics point to historical precedent as a useful guide for interpreting the impact of the Internet. They point out that the response to new technological developments such as the telegraph, radio and television have led to grandiose claims about renewed democratic spirit, freedom and reformed political institutions most of which has not come to pass. Brown and Svennevig draw parallels with the early development of radio in the USA:

the cycle of innovation seen in previous technologies suggests that the Internet will become incorporated into existing structures and patterns.... . An observer in 1919–20 would have seen radio as an inherently interactive medium that allowed ordinary people to communicate instantaneously over long distances and pointed to the network of amateur user groups that had come into being. What might not have been mentioned is that these users had built their own radio sets and very often used Morse code to communicate. The emergence of radio broadcasting stemmed from a model where people liked to listen to what was going on but could not be bothered to build or use two-way sets, thus radio became a passive medium and the active user became a peculiar minority. While many groups rushed into radio in the US they soon found themselves asking the questions that they asked about web-sites today; what is it for, what can we put on it, How can we pay for it? (Brown and Svennevig, 1999)

Those who favour such a null hypothesis also note that governments and dominant political actors can deploy their resource and pre-existing power advantages to control and neutralise any pluralist tendencies of the new media (see Chapters 9 and 10). Resnick (1999) argues, (in direct contrast to the equalisation thesis) that increasingly the large traditional political forces will come to predominate as they do in other media. This is because established organisations have more resources to devote to creating web-sites and using the ICTs creatively. They can afford to pay professional web designers and full-time staff to maintain their sites and respond to voters, whereas, smaller volunteer-run organisations are reliant on the goodwill of members or supporters who lack the time and skills to manage web-sites on a continous basis. Furthermore, established organisations can maintain their advantage because they appear on more search engines, have more links from other web-sites and can use their dominance of the traditional media to advertise their web presence, thus they are easier for voters to locate. Not only do they have these resource advantages, but governments and established political actors can, and increasingly do, attempt to regulate the Internet. As Shapiro highlights:

From content control and privacy to intellectual property, electronic commerce, and the Y2K problem, legislators at the state, national and international levels are becoming intricately involved in setting digital policy. With more than 200 Internet related bills alone considered during the 105th US Congress, the idea that government cannot control the Internet has become pretty laughable (1999, p. 19).

Sceptics further argue that contrary to the reformers' arguments there is no inherent reason why the technology should be used by existing organisations for democratic or participatory purposes. In fact, often political actors are using the WWW to replicate or do more efficiently what they already do. Empirical surveys of national government agencies, parties and local authorities world-wide have indicated that much of the content of political web-sites is about basic information provision, political marketing or crude propaganda, rather than any new interactivity with their members or the general public (Friis et al, 1998; Horrocks and Hambley, 1998; Gibson and Ward, 1999b; see also Chapters 3, 6 and 7). Indeed, central elites who have greatest access to and resources for Internet technologies often regard it as a useful means of pushing a top-down message to their supporters and in doing so of strengthening the control of the organisational elite (Smith, 1998).

Finally, normalisers are keen to emphasise that we should not forget that politics is but a small part of the total Internet content. Moreover, because citizens actively need to search out information, then political sites are likely to appeal only to the politically committed, not the mass of non-partisan voters. As a consequence, organisational changes exacted by the new media are likely to be small (Margolis et al, 1997; 1999).

The Process of Change: Technology as the Determinist?

The accounts of significant social and political change while differing in the actual outcomes, all share an unspoken assumption that it is the new technology that is in the driving seat. All these authors posit an internal logic to the new communications technology, which once unleashed on society will wreak inexorable changes on the operation of our existing political institutions, namely their erosion or significant transformation with good or bad results. As such these arguments can be considered to be exponents of technological determinism, the philosophy that argues that it is the imperatives of technology that drive history. In the extreme, this view would argue that politics essentially does not matter to the course of human development (Smith and Marx, 1994; Bijker, 1995; Dutton, 1996; Tranvik and Selle, 1998).

An alternative scenario arises, however, if one moves to the other end of the spectrum to consider the alternate social constructivist theory of technology. From this viewpoint political actors would attempt to shape technology to fit their needs and demands (Bijker et al, 1987; Bijker and Law, 1992; Bijker, 1995). Such a perspective would clearly indicate a moderation in the level of change to be expected when democracy meets digital technology. Indeed, given the radically redistributive implications of new ICTs for established elites it seems plausible that social and political structure in a sense fight back to reduce the likelihood of their own erosion or removal.

In approaching the revolution versus reform or no change debates the perspective adopted within the chapters here is, as one might expect from social scientists, more sympathetic to social constructivist theory, than to technological determinism. While technology clearly creates opportunities for change in existing practice, no inevitable development toward one particular outcome – perfect democracy or panoptic dystopia is assumed. Essentially, the technology is seen as a new means to accomplish existing goals, and perhaps leading to the formulation of new goals. The movement towards those goals depends upon the motives and opportunities presented to the political actors within the system.

Conclusions

Even in the short lifetime of the WWW, accounts concerning its political impact have seemingly swung full circle, from predicting wholesale change on the one hand, to suggestions that the new ICTs' revolution is largely hype, which will be incorporated and controlled by the existing political order. Arguably, it is partly because the initial accounts appeared to be so radical, that the backlash has become equally trenchant. However, in attacking the more naively optimistic scenarios of democratisation through the new media, it is possible to lose sight of the fact that change is undoubtedly occurring. Equally, because the changes at this formative stage are not clear-cut, it becomes difficult to separate the hype from the reality. Mixed messages are emerging: at the mass level, significant expansion has taken place in a relatively short period. The Internet is moving towards the mainstream but there is still a very long way to go. Even if 90 per cent penetration rates are achieved, aside from the novelty factor, we can still ask how far the public will be interested in using new ICTs for political participation when they are plenty of other (more) rewarding things they can offer.

At the systemic level, the response has been patchy. So far many political actors have rushed to establish a presence in cyberspace, but having done so have little clear idea as to what to do next. Their on-line activities have so far been (small c) conservative. They have tried to use the new media in much the same way as they have the old – for staid top-down information provision and *ad hoc* uncoordinated campaigning. Consequently, part of the task of the rest of this book is to understand how and why political organisations have moved on-line, the difficulties of doing so and why some organisations and institutions have responded more successfully to the challenge than others.

Notes

1. The title of the chapter is taken from an editorial from the largest selling British tabloid newspaper *The Sun*. Even though *The Sun* is not given to understatement, the editorial is illustrative of the kind of hype that has emerged around the Internet. The full text is as follows:

    The Internet is delivering power to the people. At last, the consumer is king. Communism has collapsed – but here is a force that is truly taking power from the few and transferring it to the many. It has happened in America. It will happen here. Perfect information. Perfect democracy. Perfect competition. Choice for all. (*The Sun*, 2 August 1999).

2. *The Independent on Sunday*, 21 February 1999, p. 57.
3. See research by Inteco, a market research company, at the end of 1998.
4. Figures produced by AoL suggest that American users log on for an average of 55 minutes each time. See *The Independent*, 28 October 1999, p. 23.
5. See *The Guardian G2*, 14 January 1999, pp. 6–7 and *The Guardian Online*, 10 June 1999, pp. 2–3.
6. Research conducted by MediaMetrix for *The LA Times* showed that surfers now spend 20 per cent of their time on the Web visiting only the top 10 sites. In 1998 the figure was 16 per cent. (BBC News Online, 25 August 1999).
7. *The Guardian*, 25 October 1999, p. 3.
8. http://www.townhall.com/pff/position.html, Release 1.2, 22 September 1994.
9. *Wired*, September 1995, pp. 46–48.
10. The University lecturers' union Natfhe used e-mail to hold a pay ballot and provided additional details of the pay deal and background to the ballot on-line. (*The Independent*, 5 November 1999, p.3).
11. See for example, John Vidal's article on environmentalists and human rights groups' use of the Internet, (*The Guardian G2*, 13 January 1999, pp. 4–5); or Tim Hodlin on Kurdish independence groups' use of e-mail to spread their message across Europe (*The Independent on Sunday*, 21 February 1999, p. 17).

2 Whitehall On-line: Joined-up Government?

PAUL G. NIXON

This chapter will focus on the ways in which ICTs are being adopted to aid in the reshaping of government services to provide a 'one-stop shop' approach to the government citizen interface or what Tapscott (1996, p. 166), calls 'Internetworked government', which is also characterised as joined-up government.   It examines, in particular, the content and implications of the government's recent White Paper 'Modernising Government' (Cabinet Office,1999).[1] The chapter will outline the major proposals contained within the White Paper, particularly although not exclusively those under the heading 'Information age government' and seek to assess their implications for the ways in which government is organised. Using innovative communication and information systems implies changing the relationships between and within government departments and agencies. Such changes would suggest the need for a restructuring of bureaucratic operation in order to adapt to the potentialities provided by further ICT utilisation. The danger for a government, at least outwardly, committed to devolving power is the potential centralisation of control. This could be viewed in stark contrast to the government's moves to devolve power to National Parliaments in Scotland and Wales and it could also give rise to potential conflict from within the government organisation.

We are moving to a period of our history where the distribution of information and service delivery could be posited as being more characteristic of society than the production of goods. As Peterson and Sharp note 'a good argument can be made that the accelerating pace of technological change in the late 1990's make it a more important determinant of the way in which economies, polities and societies are organised than ever before' (1998, p. 1). The consequences of ICTs in terms of affecting the socio-economic system are exemplified by the need for new skills and knowledge; turbulence as new replaces old and by the emergence of new dominant players (Peterson and Sharp, p. 53).

This is as true of governance as it is of commerce. The level of information available and the demand for it grow daily. More and more people have access to the technologies that enable them to access information from around the globe with the push of a button. Digital democracy is emerging, albeit slowly, from the development of ICTs and the concomitant, gradual, evolution of social structures and norms (Castells, 1996, 1997a, 1997b). As Chakravarti and Krishnan (1999) note:

> IT has given rise to transition from an industrialised model of big government – centralised, hierarchical and operating in a physical economy to a new model of governance, adaptive to a virtual, global knowledge based, digital economy and fundamental social shifts.

Similarly, Coleman (1999c, p. 16) observes 'the most compelling analyses to date perceive this phenomenon as being rooted within the evolving structure of advanced capitalism'.

The objectives of implementing electronic governance mean fundamentally revolutionising how government operates and interfaces with the citizens that it serves. This implies new relationships between government, agencies, civil servants, businesses and citizens. The utilisation of ICTs offers the possibility of joined-up government being articulated via a co-ordinated service delivery interface. These one-stop shops would replace the labyrinthine organisational forms in myriad locations creating a responsive, open, organic type of government where quality can be constantly monitored and improved. In order for this to happen many changes need to occur in outlook and attitude as well as in structures and processes in order to bring the governance of the country up to date with other areas of the economy.

That the need for change exists within the UK government and Parliament can be illustrated by reference to a recent speech given to a Gorbachev Foundation meeting in Boston, USA, in March 1999 by Graham Allen MP, the Government Chief Whip. He said 'When I became a government minister less than two years ago I moved into an office under Big Ben which didn't even have a jack for a fax machine'.

The White Paper is the latest stage in a developing tapestry of initiatives that have sought to engender better government via the adoption of ICTs. Whilst the broad thrust of each of these initiatives seem to share the same aims and values it is important to recognise the kaleidoscope of differing value systems under which each of the policy initiatives were created. Some of the major influential initiatives are briefly identified below.

Governmental ICT Initiatives

The *US National Information Infrastructure* (NII) was the catalyst for initiatives to integrate existing and emergent ICTs into a coherent national, and sometimes pan national, strategy for change. It was the championing of this vision by Clinton and Gore that really gave NII the crucial impetus (Bellamy and Taylor, 1998, p. 133). The NII was the conduit by which the US government sought, via a pump priming role, to create the conditions to engender a cohesive advance of the information society. The NII was designed to keep the USA in the forefront of technological development but also to be able to exploit that technological knowledge into competitive commercial success. It sought to create a common, standardised and easily accessible information infrastructure. This was to be achieved primarily through private sector investment. Government's main role was as facilitator although it recognised its own part in extending the universal service[2] concept by providing access to

> government information and improved government procurement. The Administration will seek to ensure that Federal agencies, in concert with state and local governments, use the NII to expand the information available to the public, ensuring that the immense reservoir of government information is available to the public easily and equitably. Additionally, Federal procurement policies for telecommunications and information services and equipment will be designed to promote important technical developments for the NII and to provide attractive incentives for the private sector to contribute to NII development (NII, 1994).[3]

Similarly the *EU Information Society Initiative* (ISI)[4] sought to position the EU and individual member states in order to be able to compete in the global information market. The major driving force behind these moves was the publication of the Bangemann Report (European Council, 1994). The proposals of the Bangemann report are similar in ethos to the NII. This report reflected the rhetoric of the free market and sought to encourage the member states, via the European Council, to commit to undertake an almost evangelising role in the development of the information society. This was to be achieved by engendering what Bangemann (European Council, 1994, p. 23) termed a 'virtuous circle of supply and demand' through development programmes and funded projects in order to stimulate confidence in the creation of an information society (Raab, 1998).

The *G7 Government Online Project* is part of the G7's (now G8) attempts to seek to create a global infrastructure that shares knowledge while promoting fair competition and equality of opportunity. It seeks to achieve this via regulatory frameworks that stress individual and corporate rights while promoting the need for interconnectivity and interoperability in order to develop global markets for networks, services and applications. The *Government Online* part of the project urges governments to demonstrate the viability of the activity in the information age by shifting government actions towards on-line service delivery a 'reinvention of government' (Osborne and Gaebler, 1992, cited in Taylor 1998, p. 149).

Building upon previous parliamentary and government reports the then Conservative, UK Government's Green Paper *government.direct* was published in November 1996 (Cabinet Office, 1996). It was put together by the Cabinet Office's Central Information Technology Unit. The Green Paper attracted a variety of responses[5] (Tang, 1998). The emphasis of the Green Paper followed from a recognition that ICTs had the ability to play a part in 'enabling the restructuring and modernisation of public services in the United Kingdom' (Muid, 1992, p. 75). The Green Paper's aim was to provide better services that are efficient and open and perhaps most importantly given the prevailing climate in relation to public service, 'to secure substantial cost savings for taxpayers through the delivery of an assortment of public services' (Cabinet Office, 1996).

Modernising Government: The UK Strategy

The White Paper *Modernising Government* (Cabinet Office,1999) seeks to present its proposals as 'a vision for transforming the way government works for people' As Dr Jack Cunningham, Minister for the Cabinet Office at the time, commented in a recent press release the White Paper seeks to deliver a programme of measures that are designed

> to improve the way we provide services, we need all parts of government to work together better. We need joined-up government. We need integrated government. And we need to make sure that government services are brought forward using the best and most modern techniques, to match the best of the private sector - including one-stop shops, single contacts which link in to a range of government departments and especially electronic information-age services. These are key new initiatives. It is important that we act upon them now - and we will.[6]

The White Paper sets out the government's agenda for 'modernising policy-making, providing responsive and high quality services, the introduction and use of new technology to meet the needs of citizens and business, and harnessing public service staff as the agents of change' (Cabinet Office, 1999). Indeed, ICTs are being used to encourage a wide range of comments that are actively sought on the White Paper via e-mail contact with the Modernising Government Secretariat.[7] The nature of government or governance is changing. As Taylor notes there is a 'paradigmatic shift in thinking, towards an interpretation of the State as being concerned less with provision and more with facilitation, enablement and partnerships in the management and delivery of public services' (Taylor 1998, p. 145).

The Labour Party, as part of its manifesto commitment, promised to reform the business of government to bring it up to date and to equip it to respond to the needs of society in the 21st century. The government has perceived that whilst private sector business has responded to the challenges and opportunities presented by adapting to living in an information society the public sector has lagged behind. With an increased reliance upon ICTs and organisational restructuring, the private sector is seen as being ahead in the race to enter the information age, although this may be seen as an overgeneralisation and may only fully apply to larger organisations with the capital to invest in such re-engineering.

The proposals contained within *Modernising Government* contain a long-term programme for change and service improvements that are central to fulfilling the manifesto pledges via the Government's programme of renewal and reform. As the White Paper notes

> The Comprehensive Spending Review published last year, set new priorities for public spending with significant extra investment in key services such as education and health. It also identified key, cross-cutting issues that are best tackled across organisational boundaries. It is important that we build on this foundation to set clear priorities and a strategy for government as a whole (Cabinet Office, 1999).

There are three broad aims contained within the proposals:

- to ensure that policy making is more joined up and strategic;
- to make sure that users of public services, not providers, are the focus, by matching services more closely to people's lives;
- to deliver public services that are high quality and efficient (Cabinet Office, 1999).

Together they articulate the vision of the government outlined by Dr. Jack Cunningham, then Minister for the Cabinet Office to provide 'not government for those who work in government, but government for people

- people as consumers, people as citizens'.[8] The subsequent programme underpinning the aims of the White Paper, which it must be remembered is not yet fully developed, will be centred on five key commitments:

- policy making will be based on results that matter, not simply reacting to short-term pressures;
- public services will be shaped to meet the needs of citizens, not the convenience of service providers;
- public services will be efficient and high quality. Mediocrity will not be tolerated;
- information age technology will be used to meet the needs of citizens and business;
- public servants will be valued, not denigrated (Cabinet Office, 1999).

It is the purpose of this chapter to mainly concentrate on the fourth element - information age technology usage. It is, however, at times, quite understandably difficult to decouple the interwoven schema that underpins the logic of the five commitments. In the interests of presenting a joined-up chapter, let us first consider the first two commitments in particular, as they have vital interlocking facets that impact upon the ways in which technology can and will be used to meet the government's stated aims in this area. The proposals, in each area, will be examined and potential challenges and opportunities will be identified.

Policy-making

The government is determined to become more long-term in its view of policy-making. It seeks to develop 'policies to deliver outcomes that matter, not simply reacting to short-term pressures' (Cabinet Office, 1999). Previous governments have sought to reform government and public sector service provision in general via a series of largely incremental measures. Agencies have been created to devolve power away from the centre, privatisation, both in terms of existing organisations and compulsory competitive tendering; and greater managerial responsibility have all re-aligned the ethos of the public sector closer to that of the private sector. Critics of the government feel that those measures, while improving value for money and service delivery have failed to address the problems inherent in operating a disjointed and outmoded system of policy-making.

The scope of government has been rolled back in recent decades. The announcement, within the White Paper, of a drive to remove regulatory frameworks that are deemed to be inimical to the modernisation of the government and its policy process, provides scope for the intensification of that process by government 'avoiding imposing unnecessary burdens' (Cabinet Office, 1999). As people become more used to a consumerist society, they raise their expectations of government, where it still retains responsibilities or acts as a facilitator, thus a new focus is needed. Cross argues that 'a strong message that emerged from the consultation process was that electronic services will have to be better than existing services if customers are to be won over'.[9] One can more readily identify the advantages to the government from the proposals in the White Paper than one can identify the advantages to the citizen. Whilst they may be there they are more opaque.

There is no doubt that the government are not just seeking to alter the structures of government policy-making but also the ethos under which it takes place. Thus the government is proposing a new form or structure of policy-making based upon the following: 'Designing policy around shared goals and carefully defined results, not around organisational structures or existing functions' (Cabinet Office, 1999). The underlying change intimated in this rather bland statement is a root and branch change in the structure of the Civil Service and other government agencies flowing from the notion of joined-up government. Just as major corporations have had to restructure, and others will need to follow, to meet a new business environment so government needs to re-orient itself into the modern environment if it is to retain its relevance. The Civil Service Management Committee of Permanent Secretaries has been created to attempt to achieve change in the civil service and to provide strategic policy planning across government. Although one might expect to see a strange alliance of opponents to re-structuring with internal 'departmentalism' and the Civil Service Unions worried about potential job losses and fostering some resistance to change, the Civil Service has been broadly welcoming of the government's proposals.

'Making sure policies are inclusive' and 'Involving others in policy making' (Cabinet Office, 1999), are aims that are to be met by the instigation of a major programme of listening to, consulting and involving a wider range of citizens in the process of policy formulation. This will involve such diverse bodies as the People's Panel (comprising 5,000 people selected to be a nationally representative sample), the Home Secretary's Race Relations Forum, the Listening to Women exercise, and the Listening to Older People exercise. Building upon their experiences in the 1997 general election campaign the government are eager to involve selected groups and individuals in policy debates via the use of focus groups.

Policy making is also to be improved by 'Improving the way risk is managed' and 'Becoming more forward- and outward-looking' (Cabinet

Office, 1999). These are somewhat vague exhortations that reflect the government's preoccupation with presenting the Third Way, between 'socialist' planning and free market, as a type of social democracy driven by moral values and entrepreneurial impetus.

Responsive Public Services

The government will deliver public services to 'meet the needs of citizens, not the convenience of service providers'(Cabinet Office, 1999). They will seek to achieve this by investing in further projects over the next three years to encourage public bodies to work together to deliver services more efficiently via the utilisation of ICTs and to make those services more accessible to the user. An existing example of this can be seen in the NHS Direct phone line. Citizens can use a 24 hour a day helpline to access information on health care without the need for an appointment. This service not only provides immediate round the clock advice from health care professionals at the dial of a phone, but it is also expected to help to pay for itself by taking pressure off General Practitioners' surgeries and hospital accident and emergency departments. It is also hoped that potential problems may be able to be identified at an early stage thus allowing a greater probability of successful treatment and the possibility of reduced expenditure.

There is to be a 'major initiative to align boundaries of public bodies; more than 100 different sets of regional boundaries in England alone'(Cabinet Office, 1999). The confusion and potential duplication inherent in the present system 'complicates administration, reduces efficiency and frustrates joined-up government'(Cabinet Office, 1999). Thus, building upon this spatial re-alignment, central and local government are to be encouraged to work together to create a 'one-stop shop' where local people can access information and assistance relating to a number of services at one visit. One-stop shops can improve the responsiveness of government to the public by providing 'a co-ordinated group of information and services to support their needs... across related programs at a particular level of government, across local, and state government levels, and between public and private sector providers' (Chakravarti and Krishnan, 1999). People using public services at such 'one-stop shops' will, theoretically, be able to notify different parts of government of details such as change of address, simply and electronically in one transaction, thus saving time and the duplication of data collection.

It is also the government's stated aim to support increased service delivery and openness to ensure that by 2004 all newly-created public records will be electronically stored and retrieved.

Information Age Government

The government have recognised that ICTs are changing our lives in ways almost undreamt of 20 years ago. There has been a revolution in the ways that information utilisation has allowed organisations to reshape themselves to meet the needs of the information age. There is an acknowledgement in the White Paper that 'Government has not kept sufficient pace with these developments' (Cabinet Office, 1999). The applications of ICTs by government in the UK have been on a fragmented basis that has worked against interoperability and integrated service provision, although on occasions there are sound reasons for this, as in the criminal justice system (Bellamy and Taylor, 1996; Taylor, 1998). The White Paper sets out the need for change in the ways in which IT is used within government. It proposes a corporate IT strategy for government. This strategy would

> set key objectives for managing, authenticating and identifying data, using commercial open standards wherever possible; provide co-ordinating frameworks for specific technologies; champion electronic commerce; and use the Government Secure Intranet (GSI) to boost cross-departmental working (Cabinet Office, 1999).

The ethos behind the White Paper has been evolving for a number of years. The moves towards the notion of a joined-up system of governance based upon ICT utilisation have developed for some time. For example, Tony Blair, Prime Minister in 1997 promised that, 'by 2002, 25% of dealings with Government should be capable of being done by the public electronically' and that, 'by March 2001, 90% by value of low value purchases by central government should be carried out electronically'.[10] Of course, at first glance, this seems to be a bold promise, indeed the White Paper goes much further in promising that '100% of basic dealings with government be deliverable electronically by the year 2008'(Cabinet Office, 1999). What is not defined in the above statement and indeed what the White Paper fails to adequately explain is what exactly does 'electronically' mean?

On hearing of electronic governance many people immediately imagine new technologies to equate with computers. However, 'electronically' in the context of information handling could also imply utilisation of telephones and faxes. Before we scoff at this idea we should remember that in a global context these are new or yet to emerge technologies. Many of the world's population have never made a telephone call (Loader, 1998). Digital technologies give us the opportunity to use such media to communicate with human data operatives or even directly to voice-activated computers. In other words, electronic deliverability could be operationalised via a providing service, with which many of us are already familiar from the commercial sector, such as insurance companies, i.e. a network of multi-departmental call centres, where operatives could use a mix of technologies to provide advice to citizens as well as recording data, via a terminal, or to a central data bank. This data could then be shared across existing departments, engendering economies in time and money by reducing duplication. While small-scale pilot schemes in local government are being initially evaluated as successful, as we will see further below there are other considerations to be borne in mind before such a scenario could be operated on a wider scale.

The government set a target that by the end of 1999 all Departments should be participating in the Government Secure Intranet. It has recently appointed 30 senior officials who will act as change agents within each Department. Their role will be to champion the information age government agenda within the Department and its agencies. The use of rhetoric here is interesting and chimes with the moralistic basis for other policy interventions by this government, e.g. the appointment of a drugs 'Tsar'. 'Championing' is redolent of jousting or fighting the good fight against evil. Thus information age government becomes the new crusade. Of course the problem with this approach is that it appears to encourage a fragmented or devolved championing of policy goals. Remember that this Departmental attitude is evident right up to Cabinet level with Ministers loathe to have their own personal domain downsized. Even if one discounts the distinct possibilities of interdepartmental rivalries or the inclination to provide protection from change for one's own department, one is still left with the problem of policy co-ordination. It is difficult to effectively implement policy if there are potential differences, albeit small, surrounding the perception of policy goals and the ways in which those goals should be implemented at the government-citizen interface. The fear would be that the departments would effect change at the pace of the slowest participant unless there is an enforcer or *'primus inter pares'* who can take decisions based upon the needs of the government as a whole.

To enable this crusade to be undertaken, the government will provide the IT base to facilitate a transition towards working as a learning organisation. It will also seek to develop a range of applications on the GSI to support effective working across departmental boundaries. There is an inevitability of structural change as the information flows and relationships challenge the existing structures and procedural domains necessary for the development and implementation of policy. The business of government must adapt to its environment and as Taylor notes, 'once this point of view is taken, new arguments are brought forward to reinvent and re-engineer government organisation through bringing about alterations in these flows and domains' (Taylor, 1998, p. 150).

Assessing the proposals from outside the confines of Whitehall the government have identified ten key drivers that they see as creating the conditions necessary for the success of their policies.

- Household access to electronic services through developments such as interactive TV. But there will also be a very wide range of public access points, with advice on hand.
- Much more user-friendly, inexpensive, and multi-functional technology as TV, telephones and broadcasting converge.

These two drivers are thought to be important in order that this move to a joined-up government is not seen as being technologically and thus socially exclusive. The government needs to 'ensure that the Information Society does not lead to exclusion, adding to the divisions that still exist in society' (Micossi, 1996, p. 1). However, it is almost inevitable that access will be stratified. Indeed, the more the government choose to have their services available to access via Internet-based portals, the more likely it is to create unequal levels of access. Those with access to their own computer terminal will be able to access many government services from the comfort of their own home. Those without will have to travel to use 'public' terminals. However conveniently sited, one may well have to queue to use them in situations that are not as private as one might wish.

One could draw an analogy with transport. It is not difficult to foresee the creation of First and Second (euphemistically called standard these days) Class access. Those with private means would, in effect, be able to purchase a superior citizen to government interface. They would be able to choose, in as far as it is possible, to utilise the service to meet their own needs, they would have the means to update and customise their tools of access and to access any data in privacy. Those using the public service would be forced to use a system designed for mass use and thus demand would exceed supply at peak times, it would be located in public places thus not necessarily affording privacy and it would not necessarily be regularly updated. This argument also holds true in the event of these services being delivered by some form of combined computer/digital television. New technological developments and constant updating would mean that the less well off, providing that they could afford such items in the first place, would be able to update their equipment, and thus their access to government, at less frequent intervals.

- As part of this, less dependence on keyboard skills as remote control pads, voice command, touch screens, video-conferencing and other developments make it easier for users to operate and benefit from new technology. Other skills will be built up in schools, in the workplace, and across the community.

When this government came to power they claimed that in order to transform what they saw as a moribund economy into one fit for the 21st century, education policy would need to be given a higher priority than it was hitherto. Joined-up government depends upon the participants having sufficient skills and competencies to perform the functions required by the move to ICT utilisation. Service delivery agencies require staff with IT skills to access and maintain data banks. It is for this reason that the government propose to set up 'learning labs' which allow the staff involved to meet and 'test new ways of working, new ways of delivering services and to give them an opportunity to try out new ideas and take risks' (Cabinet Office, 1999). Although there is a dichotomy at play here, in that while creating a new form of specialist within government, the expert on new technology, there is also a move towards a de-skilling of tasks at officer level and a flattening out of organisational hierarchies (Zuurmond, 1998).

This need for training in the skills necessary for ICT utilisation will be complemented by the ability to access information on a wide range of educational resources through the National Grid for Learning. It is the focal point to facilitate learning on the Internet. It functions as content provider, with over 70,000 pages of information being accessed more than 80,000 times a day, and as a programme of access to that content. Content can be accessed in schools, libraries, colleges, universities, workplaces, homes and elsewhere. As the White Paper notes 'the National Grid for Learning initiative aims to connect all schools to the Internet by 2002. Currently, 30% of primary schools, 90% of secondary schools and 45% of special schools in England have some form of Internet access' (Cabinet Office, 1999).

There will also soon be access to a panoply of lifelong learning resources, available to individual citizens and businesses via the University for Industry. Utilising modern information and communications technologies, it will deliver high-quality open learning available via your computer terminal or for those without or for those courses that need a more collaborative mode of delivery, at learning centres set up across the country. Again there is a sense of this being more easily accessible to those who have their own terminals and thus perpetuating exclusion.

- Continuing dramatic increases in computing power, and in the power of networked computing, together enabling government services to be delivered more conveniently, accurately, quickly and securely.

It must be remembered that while on the surface this seems to be a good idea, there will be economic and social consequences that could flow from this. The above again indicated a centralisation of information, which implies a centralisation of provision if not of access to that provision. Also, adopting ever more powerful networked solutions require a constant updating of hardware, software and the skills to operate them. Such updating, as we have noted in the case of individuals, is costly. The most likely cost efficiency to fund such investment would come from the number of jobs and real estate costs that might be saved by centralising the service. This would of course have social costs.

- Widescale take-up of multi-purpose smartcards, with which citizens can identify themselves, use services, safeguard their privacy and, increasingly, make and receive payments. Cards will also evolve into still more powerful technologies.

Such cards are one of the lynchpins of an integrated approach to modernising government. They would contain digital signatures and potentially support a number of different functions on each card. As the UK has no central, standardised system of identification numbers, such as in Sweden or Denmark, the government must seek a means of standardising identification in order for the government/citizen interface to benefit from the opportunities offered via ICT adoption. To overcome the potential problems inherent in producing what would in effect be an identity card by any other name, the government are seeking to enter into discussions with banks and other organisations in order to benefit from their undoubted experience in such matters. Indeed, they are being encouraged to set up 'access paths similar to the private finance initiative'.[11] With the advent of partnership arrangements, which have been outlined above, it is feasible to predict that the government may seek to engender acceptance of such technology by making services accessible via a card issued by, and also serviced by, not 'big brother' government but by the bank of one's own choice.

However, the use of such smart cards would require the use and acceptance of a common standard of digital signatures. Digital signatures act as identification and authentication when interfacing with government. They would be needed for identification purposes for interaction either on-line, by telephone or even in person in order to guarantee security and privacy. The government intends to legislate to 'ensure legal equivalence between digital and paper and pen signatures and work with financial institutions and others so that their digital signature products can be used to enable government transactions' (Cabinet Office, 1999).

Whilst some people may have concerns around the security of digital signatures many people already operate a form of digital signature almost without realising it when they access their bank account via an Automated Telling Machine (ATM) using their Personal Identification Number (PIN). The government is cogniscent of the need to safeguard the information held on its behalf by using a firewall to prevent unauthorised access and potential contamination of the data. The White Paper promises to

> deploy privacy-enhancing technologies, so that data is disclosed, accessed or identified with an individual only to the extent necessary [and that the government will] provide a proper and lawful basis for data sharing where this is desirable, for example in the interest of improved service or fraud reduction consistent with our commitment to protect privacy (Cabinet Office, 1999).

It must be recognised, however that joined-up government as outlined in the White Paper greatly enhances the state's capability for surveillance of it's population. The threat to privacy must be considered a potential threat until a freedom of information act is enacted to enable the citizen to be aware of the information held upon them, its uses and to have the ability to challenge the validity and veracity of that information.

- Government forms and other processes that are interactive, guided by on-line help and advice, to enable collection of all the necessary information at one time.

As the White Paper outlines, the government 'intends to make information about regulations more accessible from a single source and to increase greatly the scope for businesses to respond electronically to demands for information from government'(Cabinet Office, 1999). The government will also be 'funding a study into the development of a single business register from the Invest to Save Budget to provide electronic identification of businesses for their dealings with government'(Cabinet Office, 1999).

Access to sufficient quality of information is vital to all users. 'Even universal, easy-to-use access is of little use if the information is fragmented, contradictory, out-of-date, poorly indexed, or simply not of interest or use. Considerable effort needs to be given to the task of developing and maintaining information and services that focus on what citizens really want and need' (Chakravarti and Krishnan, 1999). Thus the White Paper promises to

> make sure that government services are significantly improved - that they reflect real lives and deliver what people really want. Better provision of better services available from government at all levels is central to the approach of modernising government - in schools, in hospitals, in doctors' surgeries, in police stations, in benefit offices, in Jobcentres, in local councils (Cabinet Office, 1999).

As a consequence of this, restructuring many information services could become accessible as and when the citizen chooses to interrogate them, 24 hours a day, 7 days a week, 365 days a year.

- Smarter knowledge management across government, which increasingly enables government to harness its data and experience more effectively, and to work in new ways.

Government agencies and departments hold very large amounts of data and they hold that information for different reasons and uses on a variety of retrieval systems, many of which are outmoded. This gives problems in accessing that data effectively and efficiently. The Department of Social Security's ACCORD system[12] has begun to address these issues and the government will introduce data standards. There is certainly a move towards data sharing between departments and agencies. Although as Taylor argues, 'whilst there may be a strategic case and desire for changes in the collection and sharing of information across a system, there is also a case to be made against it in favour of constitutional separations and separate information domains' (1998, p. 149). Different organisations have differing informational requirements and it is possible that organisational effectiveness could be undermined if any centralised data bank is not flexible enough to meet the needs of its diverse users.

- Use of government web-sites and other access points as single gateways, often structured around life episodes, to a whole range of related government services or functions.

The government produced guidelines for government web-sites in late 1999 to bring about a more coherent approach to the use of web-sites for giving information and eventually delivering services. Nevertheless, a National Audit Office report entitled *Government on the Web*, painted a fairly gloomy picture of government web-sites and a general lethargy in moving on-line. The overall impression was one of Whitehall paying lip service to these type of reform proposals.[13]

- Repackaging of government services or functions, often through partnerships with the private sector, local government or the voluntary sector, so that they can be provided more effectively.
- Flexible, invest to save approaches, where the huge potential of new technology to increase efficiency is used imaginatively to fund better-designed processes.

Many of the government's proposals contained within the White Paper illustrate the questions of access as being of paramount importance in the world of electronic government. The White Paper seeks to address this by investigating new forms of service delivery. The government is seeking to widen access to its services by providing access points. The Post Office will be equipped with a modern on-line IT platform to facilitate electronic provision of government services across Post Office counters. Currently, the government are 'looking at how the public service can work in partnership with the private sector and voluntary organisations to deliver public services in innovative ways' (Cabinet Office, 1999). The government is discussing with outside agencies such as banks, the Post Office, supermarkets, accountants, interactive broadcasting companies, the information technology industry and others about how they can become partners in the delivery of public services.

Indeed, banks are one of the key partners in the form of electronic governance envisaged within the White Paper. The government's proposals are predicated upon 'access to and use of personal accounts, managed by banks and other institutions, by as broad a section of society as possible'(Cabinet Office, 1999), in order that payments such as benefits could be made into an account of the citizen's choice via the ACCORD system which is the DSS programme for the next generation of IT. It will be central to modernising social security services at the turn of the century. New technology provides an opportunity to simplify the increasingly complicated set of financial transactions between citizens and government including a closer integration of the tax and benefit systems. The government will seek to create 'as simple a set of transactions for the citizen as possible, avoiding duplication of effort by Departments and achieving best value for our investment'(Cabinet Office, 1999).

As the White Paper notes 'society is not homogeneous'. The government's task is to design services, and procedures to operationalise them, that are inclusive. They should not exclude sections of society from developments in information technology but include them alongside those who find the ICT transition less of a threat and who have had the resources to enable adoption of the new technologies. The information society provides almost unlimited potential for development and the government should attempt to increase choice of how citizens receive services.

Conclusions

The important question to be asked about the adoption of ICT use to change the way we govern is to ask why? What do we achieve? If one were to be critical of the approach adopted in the White Paper it would be that it is an insular report that seeks not so much to revolutionise government but to reform it. It is a document that places economic savings and efficient services above the opportunity to allow citizens to interact in the decision-making process.

There appears to be an over reliance upon technology as being the answer to the problems of governance. The rhetoric of technological shifts are not always translated into successful implementation. Technology is a tool that can aid us in improving society but it does not, of itself, provide solutions to questions such as inequality, power, democracy and justice. One can see the gap between rhetoric and reality exemplified in some of the past experiences with new technology projects, e.g. the Benefits Agency's National Insurance Recording System 2 (NIRS2).

The notion that government can, given the diffuse nature of modern governance, plan and control the future development of the services delivered via structures employed either directly or more likely indirectly under its nominal control remains one that is open to challenge. It offers new technology as a determinist force for change but makes little attempt to deal with the political issues that lie behind the recognition of a need for change. Democratic institutions are, by nature, highly complex. They provide spaces for the expression and debate of political differences. The integration of this democratic act is, in part, what makes government different from the private sector. It also implies that rationalistic information systems do not lend themselves to operation under constantly evolving, competing perspectives on what is to be achieved and how.

One might suggest that the decentralisation of services via a form of quasi-privatisation as noted above, must indeed re-enforce rather than deconstruct individual institutional identity. This would create a scenario of a government machine that is joined-up, perhaps, but not seamless. The

White Paper seeks to ally ICT use with existing conceptual theories around decentralisation and one-stop shops. It is important to remember that decentralisation and one-stop shops are not new concepts and that their use has not managed to break down institutional barriers to radical change within government. As noted earlier there are problems of privacy and data verification that needed to be addressed by a robust Freedom of Information Act, honouring a Labour pre-election promise. The 1999 proposals for a Freedom of Information Act, put forward by the Home Secretary, have disappointed those seeking to open up governance to a wider level of public scrutiny and who view them as 'half measures', that potentially weaken the proposals contained within the White Paper *Modernising Government.*

The White Paper fails to set out exactly how the culture of the public sector as a whole and the Civil Service in particular will be changed. The notion of combatting departmentalism is glossed over. New relationships and structures are hinted at but not defined. Traditionally the model of public service allows officers to inform, explain and interpret whilst elected representatives debate and decide. The blurring of duties involved in the logic of *Modernising Government* throws up a potential problem for the government. The way information is collected, what is collected, how it is collected and the uses to which it is put all impact upon the structures and procedures needed to enable governance to take place. Indeed it, in part, structures the government-citizen relationship. The emphasis on entrepreneurialism within government service contained in the White Paper implies an as yet undefined devolving of power in order that one would be able to take those risks in order to produce a vibrant, flexible and responsive public service delivery mechanism.

The White Paper and particularly the part on information age government is by necessity only a starting point. As technological, cultural and social changes occur at a seemingly ever increasing rate, the government is forced to plan for a tomorrow utilising today's (some might argue yesterday's) technological capabilities. As the White Paper admits:

> We know that we cannot picture now exactly what information age government will look like in 2008. The pace of technological change is fast and exhilarating. Business will be transformed by e-commerce. Before 2008, there will be further technological break-throughs which cannot be foreseen now. (In 1978, some commentators might not even have predicted the personal computer, let alone the Internet.) The Government's strategy must be flexible enough to take advantage of such developments, rather than locking citizens, business, government and our partners into rigid structures which may be overtaken (Cabinet Office, 1999).

Hence, the White Paper views the future as being one where '[the government]... will use new technology to meet the needs of citizens and business, and not trail behind technological developments'. This implies an almost entrepreneurial government seeking to lead developments in the information age and not simply to follow them. The development of information age government is only one facet of societal change that ICTs have the potential to help to engender. The potential move to a more direct style of politics/democracy will impact upon the way in which we govern ourselves but there is little scope for this within the White Paper. Government or governance still remain something done 'to', or 'on behalf of' citizens and not 'by' or 'with' them.

Despite the misgivings expressed above, the White Paper does move government forward, although not, perhaps, far enough or fast enough. The one certainty of the future is change. For modern governance change will be the only constant thus *Modernising Government* should be viewed as a further stage, just one more step, in a continual process of change in a constantly evolving environment.

Notes

1. The document is available on-line at: http://www.documents.co.uk/document/cm43/4310/4310.htm. Unless otherwise stated all references to the White Paper refer to the on-line version of Cabinet Office (1999).
2. For explanation see http://metalab.unc.edu/nii/universal-service.html. Also see Bellamy and Taylor,1998, pp. 136–40.
3. http://metalab.unc.edu/nii/NII-Executive-Summary.html.
4. Visit http://www.ispo.cec.be for a overview of activity.
5. For a comprehensive view of the responses to this paper see http://citu.gov.uk/greenpaper/comments.htm.
6. Cabinet Office press release, CAB 71/99, 30 March 1999. Available at http//:www.cabinetoffice.gov.uk/moderngov/1999/whitepaper/related/pr1.htm
7. See Moderngov@gtnet.gov.uk.
8. See Cabinet Office press release CAB 71/99, 30 March 1999.
9. Cross, M. (1999) 'What Can HMG.ORG Offer Us?', *The Guardian On-Line*, 25 March, p. 3.
10. Originally from 1997 Labour Party Conference speech. Cited at http://www.citu.gov.uk/25percent.htm.
11. Cross, M. (1999) 'What Can HMG.ORG Offer Us?', *The Guardian On-Line*, 25 March, p. 3.
12. ACCORD is short for Access to Corporate Data. It was set up to provide a route for the delivery of future IS/IT services in line with the Department's IS/IT strategy.

13.   For a general discussion see *The Guardian*, 21 January 2000, p.21.

3 Local Government and ICTs: 21st Century Governance?

JANIE PERCY-SMITH

The potential of information systems and information and communication technologies to contribute to effective local governance has been recognised for a period of some five or more years (FITLOG, 1994a; Bellamy *et al*, 1995; Percy-Smith, 1995, 1996; SOCITM, 1996; Steel, 1996; Horrocks and Hambley, 1998). From the mid 1990s onwards there have been a number of attempts to imagine a radical future for local government in which information, services and democracy are delivered electronically (Horrocks and Webster, 1995; Kable, 1995; Percy-Smith, 1995).

Further impetus has come from Europe. In 1994 The Bangemann Report on *Europe and the Global Information Society*, was published (European Council, 1994). The emphasis in this report was very much on the contribution of telematics to industrial policy and economic development. Since then there has been an increasing emphasis on the contribution of telematics to democratic processes and to widening access to public services especially at the local level. One result has been the European-wide promotion of 'digital city' initiatives - demonstration projects intended to stimulate innovation in the provision of more and better information and accessible and responsive public services, through the application of telematics. More than 50 UK local authorities are engaged in pilot projects under the EU's Telecities programme (Horrocks and Bellamy, 1997, p. 381).

There have been a number of other factors that have encouraged increasing numbers of local authorities to seek to apply ICTs to their core activities. These include: the emphasis over a number of years on the need to 'get closer to the customer' to ensure a more accessible and responsive service; the introduction of decentralised systems and one-stop shops for the delivery of services; the need to demonstrate that local authorities and their

47

partners are consulting with local communities, especially important in relation to urban regeneration initiatives; local government reorganisation and the increasingly competitive environment in which local government operates and the need for more effective 'place marketing'. However, despite these drivers of change, in terms of actual developments local government has tended to lag behind the private sector (Dutton *et al*, 1994, p. 1).

More recently there has developed an increasing preoccupation with what has been termed 'joined-up' working or *government.direct* - the more effective integration of public services - which has at its heart the idea that services can be delivered more efficiently and effectively using electronic means (Cabinet Office, 1996; See also Chapter 2).

The recently published local government White Paper (DETR, 1998) provides a context within which the contribution of ICTs to local governance might be re-examined. New roles are being envisaged for the local authority as a whole, for members, officers, citizens and the community sector. How can ICTs contribute to and support these new roles?

In the first section of this chapter an overview of the current uses of ICTs in local politics is presented; in the second section, the main elements of the White Paper are examined focusing particularly on aspects of the proposals to which ICTs could make a contribution. Finally, a number of issues are identified that need to be confronted in developing an effective ICT strategy in local government.

Current Uses of ICTs in Local Government

In reviewing the current uses of ICTs in local government it is important not to be carried away by the 'hype' surrounding a few high profile projects. Although such projects are important, not least in demonstrating in concrete form the potential of ICTs, they are for the most part small scale and experimental. The majority of local authorities are only slowly getting to grips with the implications and possible applications of ICTs.

Information Provision

The area where perhaps the greatest progress has been made is in electronic information provision. A recent survey of local authority Internet access carried out by the *Municipal Journal* suggests that almost every local authority in the UK now has Internet access and most have an Internet strategy (Burton, 1998). Around 300 local authorities have their own web-sites. A majority of these web-sites combine promotional information aimed at potential tourists and inward investors and information about the local authority, local services and local events aimed primarily at local citizens (Gill and Yates-Mercer, 1998; Horrocks and Hambley, 1998, p. 39). Many, if not most, of these web-sites are well-designed, easily accessible and user-friendly.

Information on the local authority is also being delivered through public access kiosks and terminals located, typically, in libraries and community centres, and in some areas, even in corner shops (Dawson, 1997, p.7). Typically, information is provided about a range of local authority functions including planning applications, benefit entitlements, public transport, school and nursery provision, local college courses, and the council itself. The advantages for the local authority and citizens are clear: savings can be made in terms of staff time; information is available at more locations and over a longer period of time.

However, such systems typically incorporate a number of limitations. First, most are solely funded from local authority sources (Horrocks and Hambley, 1998, p. 41) and therefore do not contain information on services provided by other local agencies which will, in many cases, have their own web-site providing details of the services they provide. Given the fragmentation of service provision between an increasing number of providers in the public, private and voluntary sectors, this is problematic for citizens. It also reflects the extent to which services are still, to a significant extent, 'producer-led' rather than being oriented to the needs of citizens. Most citizens neither know nor are interested in whose responsibility a particular local service is; they simply require information from a single source. There are, of course, some notable exceptions. For example in setting up its local web-site, Surrey Web, Surrey County Council approached over 2,000 local public, private and community organisations before the site was launched, to foster joint ownership. In addition, non-profit making organisations are offered free Web space and training.[1] In Lewisham there is a multi-agency group whose remit is to use telecommunications to support public services generally (Quirk, 1997, p. 50).

Second, most local authority web-sites and information systems only allow information to be transmitted in one direction - from the council to the citizen. Most do not, as yet, allow citizens to go one step further and either access services electronically or comment on the information they have received. In other words the interactive potential of the technology is not being exploited to the full. Again this situation is beginning to change with some local authorities considering and/or piloting systems that allow limited electronic service delivery.

Third, the development of local authority web-sites is typically not part of a broader policy or strategy. Horrocks and Hambley (1998, pp. 40-1) found that 60 per cent of local authorities have neither a policy nor a strategy covering the development of their web-site, although there is increasing awareness that this is important. This point is reinforced by the SOCITM IT Trends Survey (1997), which shows that in 40 per cent of local authorities the co-ordination of web-site content is carried out by IT departments. Bellamy *et al* (1995, p. 15) write:

> in practice, the design of most EIP [Electronic Exchange of Information with the Public] applications has been producer-driven rather than customer-defined. Thus, although some local authorities go to considerable lengths to ascertain the public's information requirements, our general conclusion is that EIP is not shaped primarily by citizens' need, but by the technological and organisational paradigms and interests of those who control it. Likewise, information is specified by the professional discourses of those who manage it.

Service Delivery

We begin to get a glimpse of what is possible if anywhere near the full potential of the technology is used when we look at the electronic delivery of services. There are two ways in which technology is currently being used to this end. First, there is the development of the one-stop shop which is underpinned by electronic systems. Typically a wide range of local authority services are delivered through a single physical location. Front-line staff access electronic information relating to a variety of council services in response to an enquiry. The benefits are clear: the citizen is not required to know which department is responsible for a particular service or the location of that department's offices. They simply need to know the location of the council one-stop shop. Individuals are not required to make use of the technology themselves; a front-line worker still does that on their behalf. In addition, networking information

> could permit much more organisational and operational intelligence to be distributed to front-line staff, allowing more decisions and transactions to occur without reference to back offices of public bureaucracy (Horrocks and Bellamy, 1997, p. 381).

Examples of local authority one-stop shops supported by electronic systems includes the London Borough of Brent's system of one-stop shops which provide services to the public through a single office that can deal with all kinds of enquiry.

The other model that is being developed is the delivery of services through interactive kiosks (Goss, 1997). The London Borough of Newham is currently improving access to local services through electronic access points in local communities. Access to information kiosks allows residents to obtain information (on MPs' surgery hours, leisure facilities, libraries, police and local benefits offices) 24 hours a day, 7 days a week. This is seen as the first step in developing a fully interactive system that will include a videoconference link from a local service centre to back-office specialist staff (Steel, 1996; Turner, 1998, p. 20). Similarly Hertfordshire County Council's Herts Connect project is aiming to use the Internet to provide front-line services (Tanburn, 1998, p. 22).

There are four main drivers behind the introduction of such systems. The first is the cost savings to be made by making citizens 'self-servicing', although there is widespread recognition of the significant start-up costs involved. The second is the recognition that services should be more responsive and more accessible to local citizens and one aspect of this is to provide services at physically more accessible locations than a central office. The third aspect is the more recent idea of the 'seamless web' of services provided from a single point. Finally, there is the need for local government to continuously improve the services it offers, both to meet the requirements of Best Value, but also to keep up with improvements in service delivery in the private sector which result in generally higher expectations (Denison, 1998). Clearly there is a long way to go not least because of the fragmentation of local services and service providers that has already been referred to.

Internal Management and Communications

Perhaps the most obvious application of ICTs in local government is to improve internal communications and information exchange. This has (at least) four different aspects to it: first lateral communications, the exchange of information across departments within the council; second, vertical communications, the exchange of information up and down the hierarchy; thirdly, the exchange of information with elected members; and finally, exchange of information with partner organisations. All of these involve applications that are now commonplace in many large organisations, the development of internal networks and the use of electronic mail. Both are important to improved efficiency and effectiveness and can contribute to greater awareness of corporate objectives. However, it is the third of these -

information exchange with elected members - that is perhaps the most interesting. Elected members, typically, fit in their council activities around their other commitments. Attendance at the council chambers can often be time consuming and may be regarded as futile. Electronic delivery of information, briefing papers, committee reports and so on may contribute to more effective use of their time. A practical example of this type of application is by Swansea City Council who have provided computers at home for elected members to give them access to e-mail and local authority information. This is a key point which I refer to later in the context of the discussion of the local government White Paper (DETR, 1998).

Political Applications

Many, if not most, local authorities are some way along the line in using ICTs in the delivery of information, the delivery of services and to improve internal management and communications. However progress in terms of applying ICTs to local political processes is rather more limited. In earlier work, (Percy-Smith, 1995, 1996), I have suggested that ICTs might contribute to local democracy in the following ways: by facilitating consultations with local people over key policy issues and the direct involvement of citizens in decision-making and the policy process; streamlining local electoral processes through electronic voting; enhancing the quality of information available to citizens on local politics and politicians; increasing local accountability through interactive debates between politicians and the public; offering the potential for direct democracy through, for example, electronic town meetings; and, finally, creating the potential for empowering local community organisations by developing electronically-linked networks of groups. At the moment only a minority of local authorities have used technology in any form as a means of enhancing democratic processes (Sweeting and Cope, 1997, p. 6). However, despite the limited progress being made in practice, a recent survey showed that 62 per cent of all local authorities in Britain recognise that ICTs could make an important contribution to democracy (Taylor, 1998, p. 153).

A few local authorities are beginning to introduce some limited interactivity and community involvement in decision-making into their web-sites. However in most cases this is little more than an e-mail link to the 'web-master' or, occasionally, some kind of electronic feedback form (Horrocks and Hambley, 1998, p. 40). Where there are local experiments that are designed to contribute in some way to local politics these are as likely to be initiated by local community groups or other organisations as by

as the standardisation of common terms including offence categorisations. It is also concerned with systems analysis, modelling, planning and implementation. However, its operation is far from exclusive. For example, the development of police data handling systems, by far the most important in the criminal justice system, has never been within its clear purview and is now the province of the distinct Police Information Technology Organisation (PITO).

Turning from ICTs mainly in court administration to ICTs in trial process, the Lord Chancellor's Department's *Consultation Paper: Resolving and Avoiding Disputes in the Information Age*, sees technology for judges as including:

> document creation, electronic communications, document management, retrieval of external information, internal information resources, case management, courtroom technologies, and promulgation (putting their decisions on the Internet and on a judicial Intranet) (Lord Chancellor's Department, 1998a, Ch. 4).

Thus, after years of neglect and underinvestment, the 'front-office' full-time judicial staff have been issued with around 420 personal computers by the Court Service from 1996 onwards under the JUDITH (Judicial IT Help) project,[6] although there seems to be no plan to assist the 30,000 lay magistrates. Access to ICTs is meant to confer a number of benefits for the judiciary. It allows the efficient accessing or inputting of data in the courtroom, including the taking of benchnotes from which directions to a jury, a judgment or a sentence (Strand, 1991, p. 1) can be compiled. A further important task identified for judges is the proactive formulation of case plans and their execution. Even the humble personal laptop computer can facilitate easy access to court documents from home or while on circuit. Litigation support technologies include document indexing, review, search, full text retrieval and document image processing to assist with discovery and trial. The expectation of the Court Service is that 'in the immediate future, ... all staff and all judges will need to have access to a computer to do their work' (Court Service Information Services Division, 1998, para. 1.1.4 and see also para. 3.1).

Yet, the results so far are mixed. Some insiders relate that the uptake of ICT has been 'an immense success', though it is driven by the personal initiative and enthusiasm of individuals from the cohort of higher judiciary and has not received the funding and training necessary to make the same outcome universal (Brooke, 1998). Others paint a less rosy picture. The Lord Chancellor's Department's *Consultation Paper* recognises two problems:

The first is that not all judges who want technology have yet been equipped, although plans are in hand to overcome this shortcoming. The second is that many judges will not want to use ICT even if it is available. There is scope here for firmer targets. It could be stipulated that, within five years, every judge in the land is expected to use IT in his or her daily work (Lord Chancellor's Department, 1998a, Ch. 4).

Whether this materialises remains to be seen. It is in any event disappointing to hear that the judiciary may be forced to take up ICT strategies on the government's terms. The channel of communication provided by the Internet could be an important safeguard for independence – allowing the judges to explain themselves to the public without the spin of government or even the self-serving interests of the media interfering with the message.

Even if not all judges are self-motivated to take up ICTs, there may be pressures from other court users that force them to keep pace. For example, there is an increasing use of ICT by solicitors and barristers (Tantum, 1991; Susskind 1996; Wall and Johnstone, 1997a, 1997b; Kelly, 1998), with the consequent need for protocols about systems and formats and the possible linkage of courts to professions as already envisaged by the Court Service:

> in due course, appropriate information on the Court Service Intranet should be opened up to the professions and the public, once data protection and security issues have been resolved. Electronic data exchange services will be developed and piloted with the intention of providing better communications with court users, the legal professions and other Government agencies. As we make it possible for documents to arrive in courts in an electronic form, we expect to move towards the 'paperless office', and this will require the development of new electronic document management and records management systems (Court Service Information Services Division, 1998, para. 8.1).

In practical terms, the links will involve electronic communications with the courts, the electronic publication of information, and support for lawyers' ICT equipment in court and in court buildings. The application of ICTs to the litigants in court could include the presentation and computer aided transcription (CAT) in real-time of evidence (Plotnikoff and Woolfson, 1993; O'Flaherty, 1996). This allows not only a clear and accurate record, but also searching, indexing, linking, annotating and analytical procedures not possible with the printed word. Technologies could also be used to facilitate the evidence-giving of litigants, for example, to screen juries or witnesses through video-conferencing or other linkages.

This form of testimony is allowed in some circumstances under section 32 of the Criminal Justice Act 1988, and the use of ICTs can bring enhanced scrutiny to the process, although it does reduce the courtroom's atmosphere of solemnity and threat, which are part of the pressure on the witness at least to take the proceedings very seriously, if not to tell the truth (Widdison, 1997).

The Court Service has expressed great interest in all of this technology which it sees as having an important role in the 'courtroom of the future' (Court Service Information Services Division, 1998, paras. 5.4.6 and 6.1). The model often cited, drawing together many of these initiatives, is the Courtroom 21 Project. This is a joint project of the William & Mary School of Law (Virginia) and the National Center for State Courts,[7] and is billed as 'The World's Most Technologically Advanced Courtroom' being used for both demonstration purposes and occasionally actual trials.

This chapter now turns specifically to the impact of the Internet. It will examine actual and potential usage by the criminal courts themselves; and actual and potential usage by 'outsiders' in relation to criminal court processes.

Actual and Potential Internet Usage by Courts

From the viewpoint of court administrators, judges and other legal professionals, the on-line court can perform a number of very valuable functions. These will mainly revolve around providing a better working system for the servants and the 'customers' of public justice through improvements in the quality of the process. There are also possible benefits to the outcomes of justice, including boosting the denunciatory function of justice. Other possible uses are directed more at the public, such as allowing active public participation in the justice system and educating the more passive wider community. Finally, the Internet may provide an alternative forum for dispute resolution.

Improvements in the Quality of the Process

This objective is not only confined to the eradication of undue delay but also seeks to bolster the knowledge base of lawyers and the ways in which experiences can be shared. Of relevance here is the JUDITH project mentioned earlier, which is to allow access to the judicial communications network known as FELIX, which comprises open and closed conference facilities, a messaging system that includes the ability to transfer files.[8] The provision of word processing, e-mail and conferencing facilities has been agreed between the Court Service and the Judicial Technology Group (JTG);[9] it is also planned that a pilot project to evaluate the benefits to the judiciary of using the Internet will be taken forward. This work will form part of the Government Secure Intranet (GSI), which will eventually replace the role of FELIX in providing e-mail and conferencing facilities for all judges. All judges are to receive computers and training is to be offered in consultation with the Judicial Studies Board. ICTs in the hands of judges could also allow access to new knowledge as well as the sharing of it. One example might be a greater reliance upon legal research through LEXIS (Bosworth, 1991, p. 59). This could eventually lead to an adjustment to the style of judgments, which become more dependent on reasoning and less on the inherent wisdom, pragmatism and authority of the judge. This approach ties in with the expectation of Lord Chancellor Irvine in human rights cases, where teleological reasoning is expected to play a greater role (Walker and Akdeniz, 1998d). It is possible that what counts as precedent could also change. Internet technology allied to other forms of ICTs could ensure that most cases from Crown Court upward could be recorded and reported. Should all cases be available for later citation? In fact, the courts have tried to delimit unreported cases by placing strict conditions on them.[10] This may be less justifiable once issues of accessibility and cost cease to be important, and the effect will be to re-empower the parties, rather than the judges, to decide relevance and authority, with perhaps a greater emphasis on the standing of the authoring judge, rather than the venue of judgment.

Another form of knowledge-based development could involve the use of local area networks to create localised guidelines and practices, for example in regard to sentencing. These might be especially relevant to magistrates' courts, although the new managerialism has often been an excuse for the stifling rather than the encouragement of local initiative (Raine, 1989, p. 176).

The ultimate achievement of ICTs would be the replacement of the judge with some kind of expert-system software that reaches smart decisions in response to the input of sets of data facts. It has indeed been suggested that the development of information technology will have profound impacts upon how legal professions deliver their services to clients and potential clients (Susskind, 1996). As legal information becomes readily accessible, it is said that the role of the lawyer will become less the demonstrator of legal texts or dispute resolver and more legal risk assessor and knowledge engineer. There may be at least two flaws to this thesis. One is that the inherent complexity and open texture of many laws mean that mere accessibility and knowledge do not, without the training of a lawyer, allow sound interpretation according to legal science. Law in the real world is not about 'rule-based, deterministic decisions' but it is an interpretative life science that requires weighting and judgement between values based on moral precepts (Anderson *et al*, 1993, pp. 1771, and 1800). Given this normative setting, it seems most unlikely that any Internet-based program could either achieve the subtlety required or avoid undue legal conservatism by always settling in conventional terms. The other doubt is whether the law is, or will ever be, electronically available to the citizen in the street. Such an objective is very difficult to achieve, given the rapidly and constant changing composition of law, especially in a common law, uncodified system.

As well as impacts on justice professionals, the Internet could be used to reach out to a wider clientele and in that way improve the provision of justice within the system. Lord Woolf certainly saw this potential of ICTs:

> technology could provide the basis for information systems, available in court building and other public places, to guide the public and court and legal matters... . Given the projected level of usage of the World Wide Web, this should be one of the preferred means of delivery of information for the public. Additionally, I am impressed by the idea of using more general community information systems for the delivery of legal guidance (Woolf, 1996, Ch. 21, para. 9).

The Court Service already has Internet pages with organisational and policy information and a scattering of court judgments.[11] Listing information for the commercial court is available on the Internet from other sources.[12] Another current source of information on the Internet is Smith Bernal, the official shorthand-writers, who are making available on their subscription web-site all the approved judgments from the two divisions of the Court of Appeal and the Crown Office List going back to May 1996.[13] From now on, all such judgments will be posted there a month after they have been approved. Following review, it is proposed that all Court Service related material will eventually be available on the Court Service site. As far as the Lord Chancellor's Department (1998b, para. 105) is concerned:

> Future plans include providing Daily Lists from other divisions of the High Court, and increasing the number and variety of judgements available on the site. It is also intended to put onto the site a large number of the most commonly used court forms and information leaflets, which would help small businesses, the professions and organisations such as Citizens Advice Bureaux.

However, these grand plans also cause concern, as the Court Service has admitted that 'there has been no clear policy for co-ordinating publication of information... and this could lead to more fragmentation and an undue drain on Court Service resources' (Court Service Information Services Division, 1998, para. 8.3).

The Court Service does envisage the eventual use of intelligent kiosks to provide members of the public with a simple interface for requesting and providing information (Court Service Information Services Division, 1998, para. 11.3.1). In this way, 'Kiosks are expected to support business strategy by improving the quality of service offered to the public and by reducing the level of routine and repetitive work being carried out [by court staff]'. Members of the public and lawyers should be able to obtain or file court documents that could be utilised for electronic data exchange through the Internet. All these possibilities are strongly endorsed by the Lord Chancellor's Department's *Consultation Paper: Resolving and Avoiding Disputes in the Information Age* (1998a). In this way, the law could become more available to the 'latent legal market' (Susskind, 1996). This will leave private lawyers to cater for the wealthier sector of the legal needs market, although the implications of opening up in this way may be both palatable and unpalatable:

> the prospect that formal law might become broadly accessible, a part of everyday existence for most people, is quite revolutionary and not without controversy. But that revolution is what information technologies will make possible... . Some observers note the increasing encroachment of law on daily life – the 'juridification' of the social sphere – with trepidation. Others, however,... either assume or applaud it. The debate turns on many things, including fundamentally conflicting visions of what 'law' is: Is it a weapon of destruction that threatens to tear the social fabric as its influence spreads, or it is an essential system of support for valued and valuable social relationships? (Anderson *et al*, 1993, p. 1799).

Certainly, such an approach would eventually have a radical impact on what constitutes 'the court', since in the future:

> The marketplace for virtually all goods and services, including justice, [will be] the network itself, cyberspace. The courts' physical forums [will be] steadily, inexorably disappearing (Johnson, 1993, p. 1751).

In this way, the technology can be used to shift radically the nature of the court's persona; it becomes not just a paper-free and networked environment but takes on a virtual existence (Hook, 1998). Other jurisdictions have already started along this path. In Arizona these include 'QuickCourt', which is an interactive multimedia computer system found in court and public library buildings that offers information and instructions to litigants and produces legal documents for use in court cases.[14] In Singapore, there is an Automated Traffic Offence Management System which comprises a network of self-operated kiosks at which accused persons may plead guilty to minor traffic offences; there is apparently still the involvement of a human magistrate to accept the plea.[15]

The Denunciatory Function of Justice – Naming and Shaming

The advent of a policy of naming and shaming, whether with felons, failing schools or ineffective hospital surgeons, can offer yet another facet for Internet use. In the case of the criminal justice system, changes of policy have so far been related to the readier identification of juveniles and young persons. In addition, police forces in a number of localities have also sought to encourage publicity for certain categories of adult offender, such as those involved with prostitution. These are often relatively low level offences, which might otherwise escape the attention of newspapers. The posting of names and photographs on the Internet, a record that certainly lasts longer than a newspaper and reaches a much wider audience may be a further disincentive to transgression. An example of this policy in action is the public notification pages of the police of St Paul, Minnesota, which even includes arrestees, and is billed as a 'direct response to the fears, anger and demands expressed by law-abiding men and women'.[16] Other conceivable offence types that might be treated in this way include, shoplifters and child sex offenders, whose photographs are already circulated amongst police forces and by police forces to vulnerable localities.

Naming and shaming can work in both directions. The low cost and accessibility of the Internet allow individuals and groups to obtain a hearing for their legal points to an extent to which they could not afford in other media outlets and in circumstances where court appearances might not be available. The defendants in the so-called 'McLibel' case have made very effective use of the Internet as part of their campaign, which includes the pressurising of McDonalds to give up their legal action and business practices (see Chapter 7).

Active Public Participation in the Justice System

The conflict between community involvement in, and professionalisation of, the criminal justice system provides the organising theme for this topic. This conflict has become particularly acute in England and Wales, where trends of specialisation, technological sophistication and managerialism have tended to marginalise the role for lay persons within the environment of criminal justice. These trends can be evidenced by diminished lay involvement in the judiciary, for example, through an increase in professional ('stipendiary') magistrates (Seago *et al*, 1995). Lay involvement in trial process, focused on the role of the jury, also seems to face official hostility in the UK. For example, there are also concerns about the viability of juries in dealing with complex frauds that arises from a tension between efficiency and technical accuracy versus community involvement and the mediation of law through social standards (Home Office, 1998).

Problems such as these could be eased by informational campaigns that could include the medium of the Internet. Thus, it would help if the public were more familiar with the local courts and their processes. Becoming a juror or a magistrate might seem less extraordinary or difficult. In regard to the magistracy, a broader knowledge in this way might also avoid the 'self perpetuation' of particular social strata, especially the middle class who 'provide the backbone of the Bench and form its dominant culture' (Raine, 1989, p. 66). Of course, Internet users are at present predominantly middle class, though there are several government initiatives afoot to ameliorate this social exclusivity (Walker and Akdeniz, 1998d). Therefore, the immediate impact of Internet recruitment might be to encourage a younger, rather than a more socially diverse, cohort.

There is a more general audience to reach. Part of the characteristic of local justice at magistrates' court level is meant to be the accessibility of the local court-house. This accessibility is diminishing as court-houses are closed. However, even if the physical entity becomes more remote, its virtual presence can become more readily accessible and to a potentially greater audience than the relatively few members of the public who have ever bothered to sit in a public gallery. The two can be linked – the Internet could be used to advertise open days in the physical court buildings. Several magistrates' courts do operate open days,[17] though very few have web-sites, and fewer have sought to advertise their activities in general, or the roles of lay persons in particular.

In summary, the Internet could become the virtual welcome mat for the public. It could provide citizens with a history of the court, details of its location, pictures of judges and personnel, audio clips of welcome and explanation and, above all, an invitation to participate (Hambleton, 1995).

Educating the Passive Wider Community

The courts may be the third and least dangerous estate,[18] but they are nevertheless part of the state and it behoves all democrats to take note of what is being transacted in their name. Therefore how far can ordinary citizens inform themselves as to the courts and their business and personnel via the Internet? Potentially, the answer is a great deal, but the reality falls far short of that point.

Consider, for example, the availability of the basic building blocks of the law – the statutes and cases. Lord Woolf complained of the 'allegedly excessive costs' levied for permission to reproduce primary legal source materials such as statutes (Woolf, 1996, Ch. 21, para. 10). Since 1996, the position has significantly improved. Some statutes are now available – from 1996 onwards – in the web-site of the Stationery Office.[19] As pre-1996 statutes are not available, the presentation of contemporary individual statutes in this segmented way is of limited value. It takes no account of important factors such as commencement dates, secondary legislation, later amendments or case interpretation. As for case reports, House of Lords judgments have become officially available,[20] plus a scattering of selected cases from other tiers of the court structure.[21] Smith Bernal allows access to others,[22] though this is a private site and is not advertised to the general public. Official concerns about copyright seem to be diminishing (Chancellor of Dutchy of Lancaster, 1998), but there is still no completion of an official comprehensive and consolidated statute book, despite the plans for its birth around 1992 (Waugh, 1991). Much more ambitious systems exist elsewhere.

The Australasian Legal Information Institute (AustLII),[23] a jointly operated 'research infrastructure facility' of the Faculties of Law at the University of New South Wales and the University of Technology, Sydney, was established using a mixture of mainly public funding. The Law Foundation of New South Wales also assists AustLII in obtaining access to primary legal materials to be included on AustLII. AustLII has a broad public policy role that is to put on the World Wide Web legal information of importance to the general public, which includes primary legal materials (legislation and decisions of courts) and secondary materials. In this way, it is building up a public law library on the Internet. In addition, the user-friendly site of the High Court of Australia[24] does not content itself with a list of judgments, but includes also a virtual tour and in future the submission of documents.

Several American states have also provided Internet-based legal educational sites. For instance, the Web pages, 'Colorado Courts at a Glance', are expressly designed to give citizens:

> a better understanding of your courts and the justice system. In a free society, it is important that citizens have an independent judiciary to protect their constitutional rights. To maintain an independent judiciary, it is important

that all citizens understand the constitutional role and function of their courts.[25]

Information available includes a description of rights in relation to criminal justice, types of courts, the appointment of judges, judicial discipline and performance.

Responding to 'an ever-rising tide of "lawyerless litigation", explosively changing information technology, and an economic landscape that increasingly makes qualified legal help too expensive for many people', the Supreme Court of Florida pioneered in 1994 the 'Access Initiative' (Waters, 1997). The technology was very much centred around the Internet on the grounds that programs using Hypertext Markup Language (HTML) can be obtained freely and cheaply and is in wide public usage – 'open standards' for an open information policy. Web-page design was handled entirely in-house, again to minimise costs, and efforts are being made to form partnerships with local libraries that can act as distribution points. It is felt that the Internet has indeed allowed the distribution of detailed information, such as 'streaming audio' of oral arguments, court forms and Supreme Court judgments, quickly and inexpensively into every community served by a court. More detailed information has been developed, such as: the 'Judge's Page', which informs court personnel about new developments in the law; a 'Press Information Page', which quickly distributes information to the news media including 'downloadable' briefs in pending cases; a 'Kids' Court', aimed at helping school-age children and their teachers to learn more about the legal system; and an Internet 'Self Help Center', offering a large number of books, brochures, and forms explaining Florida law to laypersons. Taking the last aspect further, it is a further aim that local court centres should develop community-based mediation programs, all linked together through the Internet with the Florida Supreme Court acting as the central repository of information and support material.

With these precedents in mind, it is obvious that, in England and Wales too, the Internet could 'change the distance between the Court and the public' (Katsh, 1995, p. 163). An altered stance may in any event become necessary with the passage of the Human Rights Act and the further juridification of political and social life which means that

> the judicial system will serve as a forum for civic discourse about the norms and values that underlie those disputes and will play a significant role in building or reshaping the social, economic, and political institutions involved in them. (Anderson *et al*, 1993, p. 1762).

Thus technology and modes of communication can be (re)constitutive of the nature of the institution, including by encouraging a wider range of evidence and advocacy becoming relevant at trial (Chesterman, 1997, p. 143). Admittedly, the Internet might not be the only way of achieving the goal of reaching out to a passive and ignorant public. An alternative is shown by the American-based cable channel, Court TV that commenced operations in 1991.[26] This tends to give greatest prominence to current reporting of well-publicised cases and so does not present an entirely balanced picture of life in the courts (Harris, 1993). Yet, the prospect of a United Kingdom equivalent seems to be remote. Successive senior judiciary have turned their face against televising of the court proceedings.[27] Nevertheless, the judges have recognised the value of having some channel of communication within their own grasp, and, following cases in which they felt they were misquoted or misrepresented, they have been advised by the Lord Chancellor's Department (LCD) to ensure that journalists are provided with a written summary of sentencing remarks in cases likely to attract media interest.[28] The Internet could afford access directly by the public to such information. Indeed, the Internet could provide a third way to the debate about televising or not televising. The technology offers the possibility of real time transcription that can then be published to a wide audience at low cost. This strategy has several advantages over live broadcasting (assuming that livecasting is not utilised). It avoids the perceived intrusiveness and distraction of television. The emphasis is on what is said in court rather than, say, the colour of the defendant's eyes or the shortness of the prosecutor's skirt. The text (or at least the site) could also be linked to wider legal information that could provide explanations of terms and processes in more general terms. Moreover, specialist television channels such as CourtTV would probably not be viable in the UK since there is not a sufficient volume of cases of interest to the public. It is notable that the Parliamentary Channel[29] likewise failed to survive as an independent operation.

If the courts and judiciary do not manage the public interface with the legal system, then it seems increasingly likely that the litigants and their lawyers will take that step. In fact, a recent study by the Lord Chancellor's Advisory Committee on Legal Education and Conduct, *Lawyers' Comments to the Media*, (1997, paras. 28, 50, 62), found that the police were the principal utilisers of media outlets, outstripping the instances of defence lawyer intervention by a long way. The media can be conceived as part of the criminal justice system that is meant to be both in public and publicly accountable; the media thus assist with account giving and the ability of the courts to give an account (Ericson, 1995). However, the relationship is at present restricted by the bureaucratic nature of much court work and by the distance of key figures within it, such as judge and jury. The Internet cannot alter these basic circumstances, but it could provide a way both for journalists and the public as a whole to be afforded greater insights into court work.

An Alternative Forum for Dispute Resolution

There is great interest in alternative dispute resolution on the civil side. Almost as strongly in the criminal process, the victim support movement has prompted the questioning of traditional adversarial justice which is seen as often exclusionary from the point of view of the victim. In any event, boundaries between civil and criminal are breaking down. Here again, the Internet may provide a possible model that can transcend the simple replication of traditional paper-based processes in a computerised environment (Anderson *et al*, 1993, p. 1767). In this way, 'the courtroom [becomes] only one component of a much greater dispute resolution system', all served by the same technology (Lederer and Soloman, 1997).

Perhaps the best known example is the Virtual Magistrate.[30] This is a pilot project based in Villanova University for resolving disputes that arise on computer networks about on-line messages, postings, and files. The Virtual Magistrate Project offers arbitration for rapid, interim resolution of disputes involving, for example, copyright or trademark infringement, misappropriation of trade secrets, defamation, fraud, deceptive trade practices, offensive materials, invasion of privacy, and other wrongful content. The Virtual Magistrate makes a judgment as to whether it would be reasonable for a system operator to delete, mask or otherwise restrict access to a challenged message, file or posting, or even to deny access to the speaker. The filing of complaints and communications between the parties and the Virtual Magistrate Project will normally take place by e-mail.

Such initiatives, which admittedly more often substitute a Sysop's decision for formal litigation, have had limited impact. The Virtual Magistrate scheme was unable to find ISPs who would include resorting to binding arbitration in their customer contracts, and parties would not agree to be bound in this way after a dispute had arisen.[31] Similarly, CyberTribunal found it difficult to bring respondents into an ADR procedure, but there is some hope that the concept will be taken up by 'CyberMerchants', as commerce on the Internet and disputes arising from it becomes more common.[32] One must assume that, until then, complainants can more often than not obtain satisfaction in terms of their private interests from either commercial Sysops (in terms of disputes about libel and other forms of offence) or can act through normal consumer channels in regard to purchases.

Breaking down the public-private divide along similar but more authoritative lines, the Court Service or the police could offer standard forms and advice for private mediation. Hence, the Court Service becomes multi-layered with different doors for different purposes (and possibly as importantly, at different prices). The Lord Chancellor's Department is sympathetic to these ideas on the civil side (1998a, Ch. 4). However, the avoidance of formal courts brings dangers. If courts, especially local courts, are to appreciate and reflect local concerns and outlooks, this almost certainly requires some public expression of the perceived culture of the locality (McInnes, 1998).

Overall Analysis

In common with its application in other 'political' settings, (Walker and Akdeniz, 1998d), the Internet has been both under-utilised overall and mainly confined to one-way information transfer rather than two-way communication (see Chapters 3, 4, and 6). There is, of course, some benefit in information transfer in this way. Internet technology allows the disembedding of time and space, (Giddens, 1990), so that, for example, knowledge that was once the preserve of an exclusivist gatekeeping profession, such as lawyers, can be made more widely available even to those who do not attend courts or law libraries and made available instantaneously. The virtual legal community is far less bounded than its physical counterpart and could provide a forum for taking soundings on judicial policies and performance as well as providing more committed and informed lay participants within the process. As was stated by the European Court of Human Rights in *Worm v Austria*:[33]

> There is general recognition of the fact that the courts cannot operate in a vacuum. Whilst the courts are the forum for the determination of a person's guilt or innocence on a criminal charge..., this does not mean that there can be no prior or contemporaneous discussion of the subject matter of criminal trials elsewhere, be it in specialised journals, in the general press or amongst the public at large.

Yet this wider perspective tends to be lost in the New Public Management approach largely taken to date. Although the criminal courts have not yet been audited in respect of the application of the Internet, this task has been undertaken in regard to the civil courts. The aims of the Lord Chancellor's Department's *Consultation Paper: Resolving and Avoiding*

Disputes in the Information Age (1998a) appear wide and balanced. So, alongside the usual concerns for economy, efficiency and effectiveness there is an apparent concern with justice and access to justice, placing the emphasis on substance rather than process and even reorienting the nature of justice: 'We ask is the court a service or a place?' (Lord Chancellor's Department, 1998a, Preface). However, there is ultimately an overwhelming customer-service orientation, which means that: 'In the future, however, there is the possibility that IT will eventually enable legal service to change from being a form of advisory service to a type of information product', (Lord Chancellor's Department, 1998a, Ch. 2). This runs the danger that the customer is king and will lead to even less public involvement in the court process and less public knowledge about court transactions. The more the courts are conceived in terms of being a service at the behest of the private litigant, the more the consumer litigant will question the public aspects of the service. It also leads to the concern that the quality of justice must suffer, as is admitted in the following comment:

> Even if a virtual hearing is less satisfactory than the conventional method, is it not preferable that many more cases could be disposed of, even if at a lesser standard (a Rolls Royce for a few or a Mondeo for many)? (Lord Chancellor's Department, 1998a, Ch. 4)

Conversely, the *Consultation Paper* expresses very little concern for the non-consuming but onlooking public. They are hardly recognised in the document and are problematic when they do fleetingly make an appearance:

> Future use of digital audio recording in courts opens up the prospect of the live, digitised sound from a hearing being transmitted back to a solicitor's office for study and research. In high profile cases an audio feed might eventually be made available over the Internet, or via a private service running over the Internet. This may also prove possible with video in the longer term, but this would raise even more issues than audio transmissions (Lord Chancellor's Department, 1998a, Ch. 5).

Too often these wider matters are seen as merely 'ancillary effects' or issues (Anderson *et al*, 1993, p. 1765).

Actual and Potential Internet Usage by 'Outsiders'

The production of a more informed citizenry is as much the responsibility of that citizenry as it is of the state. So, how have non-state institutions taken up this challenge?

In the USA, the populist 'LECTRIC LAW LIBRARY'[34] has the goal of allowing easy access to law-related information and products all free of charge. It includes a substantial 'reference Room' and extensive sections on business law, data for legal professionals and a 'Lay Person's Lounge', which includes descriptions of the legal system in general, legal aid and assistance, wills and estate planning, consumer rights and protection, employment matters, information for investors, and some other family and contractual matters. Overall, the pages are often informative, lively and engaging, although at the same time, the humour can be distracting and the coverage patchy, as the site often relies on Web materials obtained from other sources rather than generated internally and systematically.

As for the UK, the British Council have produced a very short overview of the British legal system,[35] but the only substantial attempt to use the Internet to engage with the public in regard exclusively to legal matters is a site entitled UK Law Online, operated through the CyberLaw Research Unit of the Faculty of Law at the University of Leeds.[36] This project, which commenced in 1997, took up as its main object the raising of public awareness, appreciation and understanding of the English, Scottish and Northern Ireland legal systems by use of the medium of the Internet. The project has involved the creation of a web-site in order to educate the public as to the nature and impact of their legal system by providing complex legal information – including explanations and not just primary materials – in a comprehensible way.

The Internet is the chosen medium since it is a new interactive medium that involves direct and continuous access to a mass audience. The users have direct access to the team by electronic mail, but the project is not intended for individual legal advice. Rather it is intended to offer generalised education and the improvement of comprehension of important legal issues. The main target audience comprises non-lawyers, especially school students, but the web-pages also include some detailed information that would be of value to more professional users such as lawyers, law students, academics, researchers and journalists.

Some of the limitations of this private enterprise path to public legal education must be admitted. One pressing concern is lack of finance. The initial year was sponsored by the Hamlyn Trust, but that income has now ceased, consequently the rate of progress must relent.

One would expect that major sponsors of legal education would be the legal professions. One would suppose that to inform the public of the rights and entitlements would be good for business if not the civic soul. However, the performance records of the professions are very disappointing in the UK. Contrary to popular image, it is not the case that lawyers are wholly averse to new technology (Wall and Johnstone, 1997a, 1997b). Therefore, the problem relates more to the perceptions of their professional bodies in regard to their missions in life – that they exist to advance the interests, and to regulate the activities, of their members, rather to pursue any wider public policy agendas. The General Council of the Bar makes no mention of any interface with the public,[37] while the Law Society of England and Wales confines its education to a 500-word description of the English legal system, although it does perform a more civic role of law reform (whether this is on behalf of its members or the public may be debated).[38] The American Bar Association (ABA), perhaps reflecting the more political role which law plays in the USA, makes a much more impressive attempt, although not really via the Internet.[39] Its web-site has a section of ABA materials for consumers, educators and schools. These arise through the work of its Division for Public Education which has the objective of increasing public understanding of law and its role in society. However, most of the site simply advertises the extensive range of printed and video materials on sale from the ABA, and there is relatively little web-based instruction yet available.

Conclusions

Before complaining about the lack of progress by the courts in taking to the new modes of communication, it is worth entering some caveats. One is to challenge the assumption that ICTs are bound to deliver the expected benefits. Their use in organisational change is unpredictable, as the social contexts into which they are inserted can profoundly impact on the directions of exploitation (Davenport, 1993; Bellamy and Taylor, 1998).

Conversely, their potential to achieve a powerful impact, bringing about the 'dematerialisation' of court process, may not be as desirable as the advocates of change may pretend (Katsh, 1995). The saving of the rain-forest by the advent of the paperless court file is one thing, but the abolition of 'old style, face-to-face hearings', even on appeal or rehearing, is quite another (Widdison, 1997). The point is not simply about how well testimony and real evidence can be effectively tested in a virtual setting, a point raised earlier, rather, participation and observance are important rights that signify the autonomy of the defendant and the legitimacy of public oversight, as has been recognised under Articles 6 and 10 of the European Convention. Equally, the idea that witnesses and the jury could operate more efficiently if dispersed (presumably to the costless site of their own abodes), not only raises vulnerabilities in terms of contamination by attention to extraneous evidence, intimidation and the insecurity of communications, but ignores the way in which personal interaction may assist in the verdict-making process. This is reflected by concerns that arise when jurors are separated when considering the verdict.[40]

> One of the strengths of the jury system is that they do act as a body, and if there is disagreement then individual jurors can look to others of the same view for support. If they continue their discussions outside the jury room, then those of a weaker disposition may be open to persuasion without having the support of others of the same mind.

The issue also arose in *The People of Colorado v Kriho*,[41] in which there were complaints that a juror sought information from the Internet about possible sentences. So, orality remains not just a 'ritual' (Anderson *et al*, 1993, p. 1777),[42] but a central feature of the adversarial process, both in court and in the jury room, and the distanciation or dissolution of the court-house can be seen to result in the diminution of justice as well as a silencing of civic expression. In addition, the complexities and costs of the new technologies may threaten the equality of arms between prosecution and defence with the result that the latter may be unable to explore and expose the defects in the former's construction of events.[43]   Furthermore, the uncoordinated use of technology may confuse the jury and increase costs and delay.   Conversely, linkages between different databases held by criminal justice agencies, as propounded by the inter-agency Committee for the Co-ordination of Computerisation in the Criminal Justice System, may threaten rights to privacy.

One of the reasons for the hesitation is that there is no body with overall charge of ICT policy. The Information Technology and the Courts (ITAC) Committee, formed in 1988 from seven constituent bodies – the Bar Council, the Law Society, the Society for Computers and the Law, the Crown Prosecution Service, the Lord Chancellor's Department, the Metropolitan Police and the Serious Fraud Office,[44] recommended in 1990 that a single policy body be established to direct and co-ordinate the introduction of court technology.   However, the policy and its implementation remain split even within the courts system, with no court-based equivalent to the Police Information Technology Organisation. One might compare the more directed approach in the USA Federal Courts, where the Judicial Conference of the United States represents all Federal judges and controls the Administrative Office of the United States Courts and the Federal Judicial Centre (Greenleaf and Mowbray, 1993).   It is responsible for the Long Range Plan for Automation in the US Courts of 1992 and for administration of the Judiciary Automation Fund, approving the expenditure of $71.4 million on computerisation of the Federal Courts, to be spent in accordance with the annual revisions to the Long Range Plan through the Office of Automation and Technology (OAT) of the Administrative Office of the United States Courts. The Judicial Conference has a Committee on Automation and Technology consisting of 14 judges. Likewise, the Technical Information Service of the National Center for State Courts (NCSC) is the principal co-ordinating body for the use of information technology in State Courts. The National Center for State Courts[45] was founded in 1971 on the advice of Chief Justice Warren E. Burger in order to provide leadership and service to the state courts. Its Court Technology Programs include a Technology Information Service which provides details of software and equipment suppliers.

In terms of substantive goals to be achieved in England and Wales, what at first sight appears to be radically empowering policy developments turn out, like many other parts of the New Labour reform agenda, to be more about modernisation than democratisation. This may be true of development of ICT policy in general (Walker and Akdeniz, 1998d), and it certainly seems to be true of ICT strategy in the courts, as is reflected by the following, narrowly conceived principles on which the Court Service's overall strategy is based:

- the IT strategy will be determined by the business strategy, which will take full advantage of IT opportunities;
- all new information systems (IS) services should be provided under a Private Finance Initiative (PFI) contract;
- where possible existing PFI contracts will be used for the provision of such IS services;
- no IS development or technical support work will be undertaken by Court Service staff. (Court Service Information Services Division, 1998, para. 2.1).

The more specific objectives with respect to the criminal justice system are:

> to modernise administrative procedures in the Crown Court and to improve links with all the other agencies involved in the criminal justice system. Improving procedures will result in much-enhanced efficiency and higher quality of service (Court Service Information Services Division, 1998, para. 5.1).

Without a single reference to accessibility, democracy, participation or even justice, this is the language of Arthur Anderson, not Thomas Paine. At a time when pressures are often for greater seclusion of the criminal process and certainly for greater technocratisation and managerialism, the Internet could counterbalance some of the exclusivity of the process. It could provide concrete foundations for public debate and perhaps change that is even more radical and participatory than Lord Woolf and other commentators have predicted (Katsh, 1995, p. 196).[46]

Notes

1. The positions in Northern Ireland (see Lord Chancellor's Department, 1998a, Annex B, para.31 and the Criminal Justice Review Group, (see 1998, Annex B, p. 34 http://www.nio.gov.uk/review.pdf) and Scotland (Scottish Office, 1998, para. 10.13) are not covered in this paper. In terms of Internet development, those jurisdictions are well behind England and Wales.

2. The source of the dangers is primarily the (private) media outlets, but it is assumed that there is least state responsibility to react to their actions which threaten the rights of others, and it is arguable that fundamental rights such as in the European Convention are in any event directly applicable to relations between individuals (Clapham, 1993).

3. This is a Next Steps agency that administers the higher criminal and civil courts see http://www.courtservice.gov.uk/cs_home.htm.

4. The Local County Court System (LOCCS) Agreement, now called the Courts Computer Systems (CCS) Agreement, has since been the subject of a procurement contract with Electronic Data Systems Ltd (EDS) (see *The Times* 18 September 1996, p. 2; Court Service Information Services Division 1998, para. 1.1.3, Annex D). This provides intranet operational IT support to the Court Service. A second PFI contract – the ARAMIS (A Resource And Management Information Service) Agreement – provides corporate management information, accounting and financial systems throughout the Court Service and was signed in December 1997: Annex E.

5. http://www.courtservice.gov.uk/itstrat.htm.

6. See Mander, 1993; Woolf, 1996, chap. 21 para. 5; Gibb, F., 'Judges surf into court' *The Times,* 13 August 1996, p. 37; Court Service Information Services Division, 1998, para. 3.2.

7. http://www.courtroom21.net/.

8. There are around 490 judges with access to FELIX: (Court Service Information Services Division, 1998, para. 3.2).

9. This is a liaison forum consisting of judges and Court Service (and sometimes representatives of EDS), which follows on from the Judges' Standing Committee on IT (JSCIT) founded in 1990.

10. See *Roberts Petroleum Ltd v Bernard Kenny Ltd* [1983] AC 192; *Practice Statement* [1998] 1 WLR 825 para. 8.

11. http://www.courtservice.gov.uk/.

12. See http://www.smlawpub.co.uk. The Court Alerting Service is accessible free of charge at this site.
13. See Smith Bernal court transcripts at http://www.casetrack.com/. House of Lords' judgments are at http://www.parliament.the-stationery-office.co.uk/pa/ld199697/ldjudgmt/ldjudgmt.htm; Acts of Parliament at http://www.hmso.gov.uk/acts.htm.
14. http://www.supreme.state.az.us/qkcourtd.htm. Colorado has also taken up similar ideas: http://www.courts.state.co.us/ct-index.htm.
15. For computerisation in the Singapore Supreme Court see: http://www.gov.sg/judiciary/supremect/computerisation/index.html.
16. http://www.stpaul.gov/police/prostitution.htm.
17. For example, the Leeds District Magistrates' Court held an open day on 26 September 1998. According to the Clerk to the Justices, Richard Holland, 'Today we wish to demonstrate to the people of Leeds the important role within our community, and the invaluable support given by other agencies, which make it possible for the highest quality of local justice to be administered'.
18. See Hamilton *et al*, (1987).
19. http://www.hmso.gov.uk/acts.htm.
20. http://www.parliament.the-stationery-office.co.uk/pa/ld/ldjudinf.htm.
21. http://www.courtservice.gov.uk/cs_home.htm.
22. http://www.casetrack.com/.
23. http://www.austlii.edu.au/.
24. http://www.hcourt.gov.au/.
25. http://www.rmll.com/slv/courts/cctsam.htm.
26. See http://www.courttv.com/.
27. For the views of Lord Chief Justice Bingham, see *The Times,* 9 October 1997, p.7. The rejection of televising by Lord Chancellor Irvine does emphasise the dangers of a 'live media event' and 'live coverage' (LCD Press Release 244/97).
28. 'Judges advised to brief media' 94/13 *Law Society's Gazette,* 1997, vol. 5.
29. http://www.parlchan.co.uk/.
30. http://vmag.vcilp.org/.
31. The author thanks Professor David Johnson for this information (e-mail, 30 August 1998).
32. The author thanks Aubert Landry for this information (e-mail, 10 September 1998).
33. Appl.no. 22714/93, 1997-V, [1998] 25 EHRR 454 para. 50.
34. http://www.lectlaw.com/.
35. http://www.britcoun.org/governance/uklaw/system/index.htm.
36. http://www.leeds.ac.uk/law/hamlyn/.
37. http://www.barcouncil.org.uk/.
38. http://www.lawsoc.org.uk/home.asp.
39. http://www.abanet.org/.
40. An example is *R V Goodson* (1975, 60 Cr App R 368) in which a juror, in the presence of a court bailiff, made a telephone call from a payphone within the

court hallway. Not only was the juror discharged, but also the defendant's appeal against conviction was allowed as the jury was incomplete 'in the jury room'. Similarly, in *R v Tharakan* (1995, 2 Cr App R 368), jury deliberation in the hotel to which they retired overnight resulted in the overturning of the conviction.

41. D.C. Colorado (1997), http:www.fija.org/.

42. It is arguable that with Crime and Disorder Act 1998, we are moving into a 'third way' – the family or perhaps communitarian model (Griffiths, 1970).

43. An example might be the analysis of 'heli-tele' pictures in the Casement Park cases: Committee on the Administration of Justice, *Pamphlet no.19, The Casement Trials* (Belfast, 1992). The European Commission on Human Rights concluded that the screening of media witnesses from the defendants did not violate Article 6(1): *X v UK*, 20657/92, 15 EHRR CD 113.

44. The membership has since grown by the inclusion of the Home Office (apparently replacing the Lord Chancellor's Department), the Central Computer and Telecommunications Agency (CCTA), the Council of Circuit Judges, the Association of District Judges, the Legal Aid Board, and the Justices Clerks Society Information Technology Policy Committee.

45. See http://www.ncsc.dni.us/.

46. Since the paper was originally written, the Lord Chancellor's Department (1998c) has confirmed its policies in regard to ICTs in its wide ranging White Paper *Modernising Justice*, Cm 4155.

6 British Party Activity in Cyberspace: New Media, Same Impact?

RACHEL GIBSON AND STEPHEN WARD

In 1994, if a political party or interest group had even a rudimentary Web site, it was a pioneer of the Information Age. In 1995, if a party or organisation had a flashy series of Web pages that included graphics, audio, video and text it was hip. In 1996, if a candidate for president had a web site, he would likely give out the address for it during televised appearances.... . By 1997, if a party or interest group did not have a Web site it was run by a bunch of idiots (Hill and Hughes, commentating on the American party context, 1998, p. 133).

This chapter provides a broad context for understanding parties in cyberspace by establishing some basic facts about parties' presence on the web. It focuses on three interrelated areas: why and when parties go online; what they are actually doing on-line; and what implications their activities have for parties and the party system. In doing so we will revisit the continuing debate about party competition on-line and bring it up to date by assessing parties' current activities on the WWW. Through these questions we not only want to classify party web-sites and analyse evolving on-line strategies, but also shed some additional light on the broader debates about the continuation and future form of political parties.

There has been much recent speculation about the role and health of political parties from both journalists and academics. The importance of parties as primary link between citizens and the state and as a vehicle of participation and organisation in the political arena has increasingly come under question (Seyd and Whiteley, 1992; Katz and Mair, 1994, 1995; Richardson, 1994; Whiteley *et al*, 1994). The emergence of new technologies and their potential impact on politics has further heightened this interest in the future of political parties. Some radical commentators have seen the rise of the new media leading to further weakening and erosion of traditional political institutions (see Chapter 1; Mulgan and Adonis 1994; Lipow and Seyd, 1996). Others have argued that the new media present opportunities for political movements, and more minor parties to break through into established political debates (Stone, 1996). Existing empirical work, however, has indicated that although the Internet may alter the style of politics, it is unlikely to exact radical change upon the party systems (Margolis *et al*, 1996; Gibson and Ward, 1998a, 1998b).

In carrying out this study, it is acknowledged that the Internet, as yet, is not a mass based medium of communication, and thus, the various propositions derived about its impact are only testable on a provisional basis. Such a proviso should not act as a limitation on the utility of any such studies, for two reasons. First, Internet usage is clearly growing at a fast pace, doubling in the space of less than a year (see Chapter 1). Second, and perhaps more importantly, by 1998 many political parties had web-sites for three to four years and were becoming more aware of the Internet's unique qualities.

Why Parties Go On-line: Strategies and Opportunities

Given the relatively small Internet audience of the 1990s it is useful to ask why parties go on-line. Based on our existing studies of UK parties web-sites (Gibson and Ward, 1998a; Ward and Gibson, 1998) we identify six primary goals of party web-sites:

Information dissemination – The Web's lack of editorial control and the ability to store large volumes of information at minimal cost, means that party web-sites can be used primarily as libraries, on-line archives, or as educational resources, providing up-to-date information such as press releases and policy documents. This function may be particularly attractive to parties that are continually dealing with requests for information from researchers, journalists, schools and individual voters. The site can therefore promote the party through information provision and dissemination but additionally act as an organisational labour/resource saving device for the party management.

Campaigning and electioneering – One of the major functions of parties is to campaign for support, gather votes and win elections. Whilst the Web audience may currently be limited, small numbers of votes can still swing constituencies and elections. Therefore parties, may adopt the technology in order simply to exploit every media opportunity available and gain advantages over their rivals. Eye-catching and dynamic web-sites can be used to attract voters by providing policy material, manifestos, details of candidates/representatives and electoral statistics. Moreover, the narrowcasting features of the web allow parties to target their message to particular sections of the voting public. For example, parties can provide pages for marginal constituencies, business professionals, women or environmentalists. Through 'cookies' parties can even personalise the pages for individual visitors.

Resource generation and recruitment – As with advertising in the traditional media, party web-sites provide opportunities to raise funds and recruit supporters. Parties can sell their merchandise (books, clothes, posters, household items emblazoned with party logos or slogans), solicit on-line donations via credit cards, and recruit new members through membership forms which can be returned via the click of a button. Although such activities can be achieved without new technologies, they open up new channels for such transactions such as extending a party's reach to an international as well as a domestic audience. One minor party in the UK claimed that their web-site had allowed them to raise enough funds to stand three or four candidates at the 1997 general election (interview with party webmaster 1 July 1997).

Networking and organisational linkage – One of the major features of the WWW is the ability to link together pages and sites. For parties this presents opportunities to network both internally and externally. Internally, the WWW promotes linkage between the national party with its constituent parts. Parties can offer hypertext links to local or regional parties, internal pressure groups and their government representatives. This can aid the internal flow of information around the party and offer cheap publicity for constituencies and MPs. Links to external organisations are useful for the purposes of cementing a party's image or culture. Hence, parties can offer links to pressure groups or issue concerns with which they want to be identified. Left of centre and Green parties often provide connections to human rights groups or environmental campaigns on the web. Overall, such links may be a useful means of enticing visitors to web-sites. The small Northern Ireland Alliance Party originally created a web-site with a large range of links about Irish politics in general. The party's strategy was that voters would be attracted initially by the access to the links, but then drop into the party's own pages as well (interview with party webmaster, 14 August 1997).[1]

Participation and interactivity – The interactive features of web-pages, such as, email, bulletin boards and on-line chat rooms clearly open up the possibility of greater direct dialogue with voters. In an age where voters are increasingly viewed as consumers, the Web allows parties to seek the opinions of voters/members on policies, create on-line opinion polls and gather instant feedback. Some parties, such as Plaid Cymru, have already offered on-line referenda and a number of parties in the UK (notably, Labour, Scottish National Party and Sinn Fein), have already operated direct on-line discussions with leading politicians. Indeed, leading modernisers within the Labour Party have specifically recognised the Internet's potential as a communications and participation tool in its drive to widen membership (Labour Coordinating Committee, 1997, p. 9).

Party competition – Although parties may develop on-line strategies over time, these are sometimes *post hoc* justifications. Interviews with British parties indicated that peer pressure is a key factor in the uptake of new technologies. While a few parties may pioneer the technology, most are adapters responding to their competitors. Hence, once a number of parties create web-sites on-line, others follow, partly through a fear that their opponents are gaining an advantage (Ward and Gibson, 1998).

The Potential Impact of the New Media on Political Parties: Hypotheses and Current Evidence

Mapping and explaining parties' web-site functions and strategies are important, but perhaps an even more pertinent question is what difference parties' on-line activities could make, especially in terms of campaigning and party competition. According to much of the literature on party change, inter-party competition in Western democracies is in decline. Both the catch-all and cartel models of party change have pointed to the traditional electronic media as an important factor restricting levels of competition between parties (Katz and Mair, 1994, 1995; Kircheimer 1966; Moar, 1996). As television and radio have begun to dominate the modes of party communication with the public, minor parties have been placed at a considerable disadvantage. Coverage has tended to focus disproportionately on the major parties, whilst at the same time many smaller parties have been unable to compete since they lack the resources and expertise to mount sophisticated and increasingly costly media strategies. Thus many minor parties have found it difficult to publicise their agendas and mobilise support through the electronic media and consequently they have been unable to mount significant electoral challenges.

Given the new capabilities of the Internet as a medium of communication, particularly its lack of editorial control and comparatively limited cost (see Chapter 1), it is worth considering how far the new media might open up the political arena. Specifically, can it provide voters with greater access to new and smaller political parties? Two potentially differing scenarios for inter-party competition can be envisaged:

- *Increase in the level of inter-party competition*: the decentralisation of information control on the Internet will allow the increasingly aggrieved excluded minor parties to mount a serious challenge to the established parties control of the communications media. Smaller parties will be able to compete on an equal footing with the major parties to communicate their message to the wider electorate. Certainly small parties have not been slow in proclaiming the democratic benefits of the Internet (Stone, 1996). As one minor party leader has stated:

  > Without the benefit of size, or the media advantage of support for newsworthy violence, it is difficult enough for us to get a reasonable share of coverage from local journalists, but almost impossible in the national or international media. The Internet has brought a certain welcome equality to all of us (Alderdice, 1996).

- *No-change or decreasing levels of inter-party competition*: the resources (financial, labour and skills) necessary to compete effectively on the Internet increase, squeezing out competition from minor parties. The study by Margolis *et al* (1997) of party campaigning in the USA, for instance, argues that the growing sophistication of web-sites meant that the Republican and Democratic parties retained their dominant position in this new media (see also Calbrese and Borchert, 1996 for a more general discussion of the impact of commercialisation of the WWW). Taken to an extreme, mobilisation of resources in this manner could lead to a diminution of party competition as the quality threshold for proper representation on the Net is raised beyond the financial reach of all but the most IT-skilled and well-resourced parties.

Existing Evidence: Studies of Parties' Activities in Cyberspace

Evidence collated from a number of existing studies in the USA, Europe and New Zealand has all indicated that while there is considerable party activity on the Internet, the impact of the media on party behaviour has thus far been minimal (Margolis *et al*, 1997, 1998; Smith, 1998; Gibson and Ward, 1998; Lofgren, 1998; Voerman, 1998; Ward and Gibson, 1998; Roper, 1999). Of course, the Internet is still in its formative era, but parties are clearly not exploiting the full range of its capabilities most notably its participative and interactive elements (see particularly Hoff and Lofgren, 1997, on Danish parties). Criticism of parties' on-line efforts has fallen into two categories: either that the sites are dull, text-laden and lacking any unique features, or that sites are superficial electronic advertising brochures, full of gimmicks and flashy graphics, but lacking any real substance. One critic described the main British party sites as

> inadequate. The Labour Party's site is a shambles, the Tory one deeply boring and the LibDems' effort, while much the best, hardly justifies the 'we're so wired' posturing they have indulged in.... Politicians have made much of the importance of the Internet. They are right but it would be nice if they put their home pages in order before lecturing the rest of us.[2]

Furthermore, and possibly more significantly, early trends from most of these studies suggest that there is unlikely to be much benefit to minor parties, despite their advocacy of the Internet as a campaign tool.

Whilst some commentators (Rash, 1997) have suggested that minor parties generally lead the way with innovation on the WWW, surveys appear to indicate that they are outstripped by their major rivals particularly in electoral periods, as Margolis *et al* (1997, 1999) have indicated. Indeed, our earlier studies of British party Internet activity seem to confirm the pattern of an initial levelling of the playing field followed by a normalisation of competition where the large parties replicate their traditional dominance of the media on the WWW. For example, the results of our initial survey in 1996 appeared to offer some support for equalisation of party competition in cyberspace:

> The Internet is allowing minor parties in the United Kingdom to mount a more significant challenge to their major counterparts than in the other media. The Internet equalises voters' ability to access party information, and the quality of minor parties' web-sites rivals that of their major counterparts (Gibson and Ward, 1998, p. 32).

However, by the time of the 1997 General Election campaign, divisions between parties were more apparent and our conclusions were more sanguine:

> Evidence regarding the quality of web-sites' design suggested that a gap was developing between major and minor parties' sites. These findings would suggest that if visual appeal is a chief criterion for voters' perusing a party's site then the WWW will simply reinforce the dominance of the larger, better resourced parties (Ward and Gibson, 1998, p. 110).

Such findings were supported by a comparative study by Margolis *et al* (1999), which indicated that the two main British parties (Labour and Conservative) did indeed predominate in cyberspace, although not to the same degree as their large American counterparts. The question remains, therefore, to what extent is this an ongoing process? If Margolis *et al's* (1997) normalisation thesis holds true, then we should expect to see the major parties continuing to strengthen their advantage, initially built up during the 1997 general election. Consequently, the empirical evidence presented below aims to revisit some of these debates, by offering further up-to-date data on web-site activity and seeking to draw out trends based on annual studies from before, during and after the 1997 election.

Data and Methods

Presence and Access – The presence of parties on the Web was established using three different major link sites: Yahoo's UK political parties page; Richard Kimber's political parties page at Keele University; and Julian White's political parties page.[3] The date of parties' entry into cyberspace was determined using a variety of methods: postal questionnaire, e-mail questionnaire and information provided on the parties' web-site.[4]

Function of party Web-sites – The data for assessing the functions of parties' web-sites and their campaign effectiveness was drawn from a survey of 15 party web-sites conducted during October and November 1998. The parties were selected to include all those parties that had representation in Parliament and others were chosen on the basis of the ideological diversity that they introduce to the analysis (for a full listing of parties see Tables 6.1 and 6.2).

The five functions of the web-sites: information provision, campaigning, resource generation, participation and networking were assessed using a variety of indicators to form an additive or ordered index for each function. All the functions, except information provision were measured using more than one index as these functions were considered to be more complex and multi-dimensional.

Operationalisation of Functions

The appendix at the end of this chapter gives a complete scoring for complete scheme for party web-site performance. The higher the score attained the more the function was emphasised by the party in its Web-pages.

- Information provision was operationalised with an additive index ranging from 0 to 8. This assigned one point to each 'information' feature present on the web-site including such features as party history, biographies, and press releases.
- Campaigning was the most complex of the functions being broken into four sub-functions: design sophistication (the overall visual and dynamic appearance of the site); accessibility (how easy it was to access the entire site and navigate around it); freshness (how frequently the party updated its site); and targeting (to what extent the party used the narrow-casting capabilities of the Internet to target certain groups of voters). While design sophistication, accessibility, and targeting were all measured with simple additive indices indicating whether parties had such features as graphics, text only options and special pages for certain sections of the electorate, freshness was measured with a two-dimensional index. The first component scored a party on how frequently news/press releases were placed on the site, this score was then adjusted according to whether the home page was clearly up to date, or out of date.
- Resource generation was broken down into two dimensions – financial and physical or human resources. It was measured on two ordered indices ranging from 0 to 3. The first index measured parties efforts to mobilise physical support (i.e. seeking volunteers and members via post or on-line). The second index measured parties' efforts to solicit financial support (selling merchandise, soliciting postal and on-line donations).
- Networking was measured on an ordered scale from 0 to 4 based on how many links they made to other organisations both internally and externally. A point was assigned if the parties provided links to: local/regional party organisations; internal pressure groups;

MPs/MEPs or prominent figures; external (national or international) organisations.

- Participation was broken down into three dimensions: openness, feedback and debate. Openness refers to the extent of opportunities for visitor input via direct email contact and was measured by an additive index ranging from 0 to 6. Feedback refers to the actual nature of input sought by the party and was measured by an additive scale ranging from 0 to 3. The index focused on how far the party structured the input and whether it was substantive in nature. Debate refers to how far the site offered its visitors 'space' to interact in real time with other visitors and party elites. This was measured on an ordered index ranging from 0 to 3 and focused on whether parties incorporated bulletin boards and/or on-line discussion.

British Parties On-line: The Evidence Revisited

Presence

Since the Labour Party moved on-line in 1994 there has been a rapid expansion of party activity in cyberspace. Our first survey at the end of 1996 identified 28 parties on-line. By May 1997 this had risen to 33. The current survey located 46 parties with a web-site. Table 6.1 indicates that the main period of growth was in 1996 in preparation for the general election and Figure 6.1 provides a graphic illustration of a domino effect in the growth of web-sites. Parties do indeed seem to have been stimulated into action through peer pressure and the coming election campaign.

While parties of all sizes, ideological persuasion and geographical location have taken to the Web, in terms of the speed of adaptation, there is little in the UK that would support the notion that marginalised parties have been the innovators. The Labour Party's reported start date for their web-site is the earliest (October, 1994) and within 18 months (April 1996), virtually all the parliamentary parties possessed their own web-site. The sole exception being the small UK Unionist Party. By contrast, of the fringe parties, only the extreme right wing National Democratic Party and National Front could be counted as pioneers, creating their sites as early as 1995. In short, the non-parliamentary parties have been relatively slow to move into cyberspace.

Table 6.1 UK Party Web-site Launch Dates

Order	Date Established	Party Name (s)
1	October 1994	Labour
2	April 1995	Plaid Cymru, Sinn Fein
3	July 1995	BNP
4	August 1995	N.I. Alliance
5	September 1995	NDP, Greens
6	October 1995	Conservative
7	November 1995	UUP
8	January 1996	SDLP
9	February 1996	SNP
10	March 1996	SLD, Worker's Party
11	April 1996	DUP, UDP, PUP, Scot Greens
12	May 1996	Scottish Conservatives
13	June 1996	Liberal Party
14	July 1996	New Communist Party
15	September 1996	UKIP, Referendum, Islamic
16	October 1996	SEP, N.I. Greens
17	March 1997	SPGB
18	April 1997	Prolife Alliance
19	May 1997	CPGB
20	October 1997	National Front
21	January 1998	Mebyon Kernow
22	November 1998	UK Unionist Party
23	February 1999	Scot Labour, Pro-Euro Cons

Evidence gathered from party questionnaires, interviews and email questions. This list represents 76 per cent of total number of parties on-line in February 1999 (46).

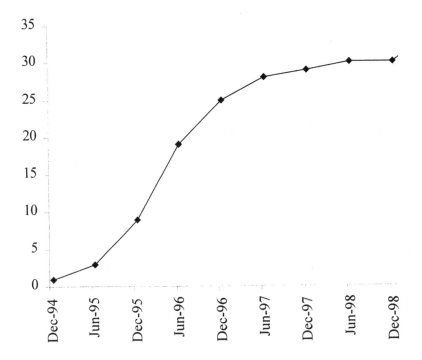

Figure 6.1 Number of UK Parties On-line

Source: Based on figures from Table 6.1

Access

Although web-site presence provides a measure of activity in cyberspace, in determining the impact of such sites, access is clearly of key importance. Fringe parties may have a presence on the WWW, but if their sites were difficult to locate then any potential benefits were lost. The survey used two main methods of gauging access: first, via three indices providing entry to British party sites (a general Yahoo search, and the more specialised sites of Keele University and Julian White's political pages). Second, through the use of Alexa statistics on the number of links into party pages (backpointers).[5]

The Yahoo page provided access to around 33 parties in an alphabetical list format, although some parties, for example, the British

National Party were not directly recognisable from the list since they were covered by a multi-purpose heading of white nationalist. The specialist pages provided additional links to more of the fringe parties: 39 on the Keele site and 34 on Julian White's index. In all of the indices, some of the smaller (non-parliamentary) parties such as the Socialist Labour Party were the most difficult to locate. Yet, in the main, the indices presented a fairly extensive coverage of party life in the UK.

The additional figures on links into party sites showed no clear message. Although many of the parliamentary parties had the greatest number of backpointers, particularly the main three parties, the pattern was somewhat distorted by the Northern Ireland parties. The Social and Democratic Labour Party and the Democratic Unionist Party were in the top three in terms of links into their web-sites, and in the case of the former, it had nearly three times as many links as its nearest rival the Conservative Party. One possible explanation for this distortion is the large international audience interested in Irish politics, notably in the USA, where there are many nationalist organisations and a large expatriate Irish community.

Web-site Function

Table 6.2 reports the parties' scores for each function, the range of the index, and the mean score of the parties for this function. This table indicates that parties' overall emphasis was on information provision and also resource generation via their web-sites, rather than networking, participation or campaigning. Only on the two former indices was the mean score beyond the mid-point of the index range. This broad conclusion hides important differences in terms of the emphasis placed by the parties on each function. Interestingly, both the Conservatives and the Labour Party fell below mean in terms of information offered by the site. Equally, while most parties were making some financial hay out of the Net, some have clearly developed more of a taste for it than others. Mainstream parties such as Labour and the Liberal Democrats engaged in on-line revenue raising, selling party goods and services. The Referendum Movement and the Ulster Unionist Party also scored quite well on this measure. Most of the smaller parties did not exploit its potential, however. While this reticence could reflect an aversion to using the technology for these purposes, it is more likely to indicate a lack of financial resources to produce merchandise, and also staff resources to deal with sales.

Table 6.2 Party Web-site Performance Scores

Function	Con	Lab	Lib Dem	PC	SNP	SDLP	UUP	DUP	SF	Green	SEP	Ref	NDP	NF	Lib	Range	Mean
Campaign																	
Design	5	3	1	2	5	1	2	1	2	2	0	2	4	5	1	0-6	2.4
Access	2	4	3	2	2	1	2	4	2	3	1	3	1	2	1	0-6	2.2
Freshness	5	-2	10	4	8	9	4	4	4	8	-4	0	0	4	3	-5-10	3.8
Targeting	3	0	2	1	4	2	2	2	0	0	0	0	0	1	0	0-6	1.1
Cumulative	15	5	16	9	19	13	10	11	8	13	-3	5	5	11	5	0-28	9.5
Info. Diss.	5	3	6	8	7	7	7	6	8	7	2	7	3	4	8	0-8	5.7
Network	2	3	2	2	4	0	0	0	0	3	0	0	0	2	1	0-4a	1.2b
Particip.																	
Openness	4	4	4	2	5	1	4	1	3	3	1	1	2	1	2	0-6c	3.1e
Feedback	2	0	1	1	0	0	0	0	2	1	0	0	0	0	0	0-3	0.5
Debate	0	0	0	1	0	0	0	0	1	1	0	0	0	0	0	0-3	0.2
Cumulative	6	4	5	4	5	1	4	1	6	5	1	1	2	1	2	0-12d	4.0f
Res. Gen.																	
Recruit	2	3	0	2	3	2	2	2	2	2	0	3	2	0	2	0-3	1.7
Finance	0	3	3	0	1	1	2	1	2	1	0	3	2	1	0	0-3	1.5
Cumulative	2	6	3	2	4	3	4	3	4	3	0	6	4	1	2	0-6	3.3

a. 0-3 for parties without MPs/MEPs.

b. Figure is the mean for parties with MP/MEPs. For parties without MP/MEPs mean = 1.

c. 0-5 for parties without MPs/MEPs.

d. 0-11 for parties without MPs/MEPs.

e. Score is mean for parties with MP/MEPs; for parties without MPs/MEPs, mean = 1.7.

f. Score is mean for parties with MP/MEPs; for parties without MPs/MEPs, mean = 2.

Parties performed poorly on the campaign measures with a mean score of only 9.5 out of 28. Only the Conservatives, the Liberal Democrats, and the Scottish National Party placed significant weight on campaigning. The Liberal Democrats were particularly active in maintaining site freshness, whereas the Conservatives scored more highly for design appeal and targeting. The Scottish National Party were perhaps the best 'all-rounders' in campaign terms, falling down only on accessibility to their site. Labour surprisingly fell far behind the competition, scoring poorly on design and suffering from a failure to keep the site fresh. They still invited the reader to visit their 1998 virtual conference site, three months after the conference had been held. Other parties scoring above average on the campaign dimension included the National Front, the Greens, the Democratic Unionist Party and the Social and Democratic Labour Party. While the National Front gained most of their points from the design of their site, the Democratic Unionists had made their sites among the most simple to access and navigate, while the Social and Democratic Labour Party had made a clear effort to keep their site up to date for visitors. On the whole, those parties that failed to perform well on this dimension were those lacking parliamentary representation, most notably the Liberal Party, the National Democrats, the Socialist Equality Party, and the Referendum Movement.

In terms of participation, the two major parties, the Liberal Democrats, the Scottish Nationalists, the Ulster Unionists, Plaid Cymru, Sinn Fein, and the Greens, all scored well. Breaking down the scores into their sub dimensions, however, it is clear that the latter three parties offered most scope for substantive feedback and member debate. Most parties were content to offer basic e-mail contacts on their sites. Thus, while some of these sites appeared to be open to input, in most cases the participatory emphasis was superficial. Essentially, parties were not engaged in two way dialogues with voters via their web-sites.

In terms of networking, Labour, the Scottish National Party and the Greens all made higher than average use of this facility, although in the main, a significant number of smaller parties did not provide many networking links from their sites. One third of parties (5) had no links whatsoever.

Discussion

Based on this evidence it is argued that the WWW does allow minor parties a wider platform to reach voters than they are provided with in the traditional media. Some of the fringe parties, such as the Progressive Party or the Socialist Equality Party that barely register outside of cyberspace share equal billing with Labour and Conservative on major party link sites. Further, through their network of WWW links they secure an even wider degree of exposure. Such findings are tempered, however, by the fact that Internet does not exist in a vacuum but is related to other forms of the media. The major parties can, and do, advertise their web presence through the traditional media. Web-site addresses are now commonly shown on party political broadcasts and in newspaper advertisements. Consequently, it seems reasonable to suggest that the dominance of the traditional media by the major parties gives them an additional bonus in directing voters to their web-sites.

Overall, the parties approached the Web in rather utilitarian terms, using it as a tool for information provision and resource generation, rather than a new 'space' for promoting interaction and inter-organisational links. It was interesting to note that the major parties were not as generous with the information they supplied as the minor parties, suggesting a certain complacency on the former's part. In addition, the findings from this analysis showed that the major parties had not cornered the Web market in terms of campaigning capability. A divide did appear to exist, however, between parties within and outside Parliament in terms of the effectiveness of the site for attracting voters, according to the dimensions measured here. Further, the major parties seem to have grasped the potential of the Web for generating resources more than their minor counterparts.

Conclusions and Prospects

These results are not presented as a definitive account of parties' performance on the Web. What is clear, however, is that the initial phase of party web-site development is over. Most parties have had a Web presence since at least 1996. More notably, parties have failed to seize the new communication opportunities offered to them by the Internet. Sites are used for top-down information dissemination for interested members of the party, the wider public, and journalists. Resource generation is engaged in a limited way, and largely by the bigger players. Only a few of the smaller parties have experimented with participatory devices.

When placed in the context of earlier studies, the results of the 1998/99 survey take on more significance in terms of trends in party on-line behaviour. The gap between major and minor parties that appeared during the general election seems to have ameliorated. The data from this survey suggest that any divide developing between parties is not between Labour, Conservative, and the rest, but between parliamentary and non-parliamentary parties. Even here the divide is not clear-cut since parties such as the Greens or far right parties produce competitive sites. Thus, there does not seem to be an inexorable move toward domination of the Web by the large parties, but rather an ebb and flow in levels of competition. This is partly due to the minor parties improving their sites, but it also the result of lack of major party interest during the periods of 'peacetime' that follow an election.

The idea that elections serve as the primary driver to party web-site development is clearly endorsed by evidence from the US experience. American political web-sites are the subjects of more rapid innovation and change than those of any other country. With its candidate-centred politics and permanent electoral cycle the urge to exploit all media opportunities is intense. Given this broad conclusion, therefore, one would not predict British parties to become engines of experimentation in the web wars at any point soon.

Notes

1. The Northern Ireland Alliance Party's original webmaster left and the site subsequently went into abeyance. When a new site was designed in 1999 the large-scale Irish politics links had been reduced. This is perhaps indicative of the precarious nature of small party web-sites, which are often reliant on one or two individuals for their management and updating.
2. Bowen, M., *The Financial Times*, 25 September 1998.
3. The web addresses were as follows:
   http://dir.yahoo.com/Regional/Countries/United Kingdom/Government/Politics/Parties_and_Groups;
   http://www.psr.keele.ac.uk/parties.htm and http://www.ukpol.co.uk/index.htm.
4. Note that all methods run the risk of bias since these dates are only established through parties' self-reporting their Internet debut.
5. Alexa is a freely available software program that counts the number of links into a site, based on frequent trawls through the Internet. For further information see http://www.alexa.com.

Appendix: Scoring For Party Web-Site Performance

1. **Information Provision** 0–8 (additive index, 1 point each item)

- values and ideology – statement regarding overall goals and philosophy of party

- policies – presentation of party position on issues (not manifesto)

- documents – i.e. manifesto, White Papers, statements on internal party matters

- press releases and speeches

- who's who – biographies of leading party figures and/or election candidates

- party structure

- party history

- election statistics

2. **Campaigning**

a. Index 1: Design Sophistication 0–6 (additive index, 1 point each item)

- graphics

- frames

- moving/flashing icons

- sound

- video

- games

b.   *Index 2: Accessibility* 0–6 (additive index, 1 point each) text only option

- general site search engine

- constituency/MP search engine

- no extra software necessary

- home page icon link on lower level pages

- foreign language translation

c. *Index 3: Freshness* -5 – +10 (composite index adding scores from (1) and (2) below):

(1) Press releases/news items (ordinal index)

- 5   daily updating

- 4   2-3 day updates

- 3   weekly updates

- 2   monthly updates

- 1   less than 6 month updates

- 0   more than 6 month updates

(2) Home page updates

- 5   fresh – clearly current

- 0   neutral – neither up to date nor out of date

- -5   stale – clearly out of date

d. *Index 4: Targeting* 0–6 (additive index, 1 point for each category targeted)

- marginal constituency

- economic/professional

- identity-based (i.e. women, homosexual, racial)

- young people

- issue-based (e.g. environment)

- cookie (additional point)

3. Resource Generation

a. *Index 1: Physical resources* 0–3 (ordinal index)

- 3 joining party directly online

- 2 offering joining forms to download & post or explicit email contact to join

- 1 soliciting help short of joining

b. *Index 2: Financial resources* 0–3 (ordinal index)

- 3 donating/purchasing merchandise directly online

- 2 offering forms to download for donation/purchase or explicit email to contact

- 1 promotion of donation / purchasing merchandise

4. Networking

a. *Index 1: External Networking* 0–4 (ordinal index)

- 4   50+ links to outside sites

- 3   21-50 links

- 2   11-20 links

- 1   1-10 links

b. *Index 2: Internal Networking* 0–3 (additive index, 1 point per type of link*), 0–2 Parties without MPs

- MP/MEPs sites

- Local/regional office sites

- Internal pressure group sites
  (* sites must be independent of main party site)

5. Participation

a. *Index 1: Openness* 0–6 (additive index, 1 point per type of email contact) 0–5 Parties without MPs

- MP/MEPs

- Local/regional office

- International office

- Leader

- Party organisation/HQ

- Webmaster

b. *Index 2: Feedback* 0–3 (ordinal index)

- 3   on-line questionnaire or opinion poll on substantive issue relating to party and/or policy

- 2   invitation to submit specific party/policy-based comments via e-mail

- 1   general invitation to submit comments via e-mail

c. *Index 3: Debate* 0–3

- 3   opportunities for online debate with leaders

- 2   chat rooms or interactive discussion

- 1   bulletin or message board facility

7 Environmentalists and the Net: Pressure Groups, New Social Movements and New ICTs

JENNY PICKERILL

Environmental organisations have been widely recognised for their innovative use of the media, often deploying it to raise public awareness and pressurise reluctant politicians and policy-makers (Hansen, 1993). Recently environmental organisations, informal groups, and individual direct action protesters have begun utilising new ICTs, to aid their campaigns (Young, 1993; Brass and Poklewski Koziell, 1997). 'Far from being the bunch of technophobic Luddites portrayed in the popular press, Green activists have been switched on to the power of the Net for years' (Lawson, 1995, p. 42).

This usage has involved the whole spectrum of the British environmental movement; the more institutionalised non-government organisations (NGOs) such as Friends of the Earth and Greenpeace, and also the informal, looser networks of individuals involved in groups such as Earth First!, RoadAlert!, McSpotlight and Reclaim the Streets. Web addresses, advice on use, e-mail etiquette and suggested service providers are included in a vast array of magazines, leaflets and campaign guides associated with aspects of environmentalism (Encyclopaedia of Direct Action, 1995; RoadAlert!, 1997; Burton, 1997).

Each of these organisations, groups, networks or individuals are motivated by one or a range of environmental issues to which they want to draw public and/or political attention in order to alter public policy and social practice. In this way they are all trying to achieve something politically, whether it be a state legislation change or altering the progress of a local development. The purpose of this chapter is thus to consider how the use of new ICTs by such groups affects their ability to achieve their goals either for a specific campaign or as an organisation as a whole.

The use of ICTs by environmentalists has not been subject to much critical analysis and certainly not in terms of its political implications. There is also a distinct need for empirical evidence about its use. The main tenet of this chapter is that the use of new ICTs has enhanced some of the environmental movement's cohesion and ability to co-ordinate campaigns, but it has not created a new space for political representation. The Internet and e-mail has been used as a supplement to the many media already employed by environmentalists. They have transferred much of their information onto the new media and use e-mail networks in much the same manner as they utilised word of mouth and networks of telephone trees.[1] Thus many environmentalists have not been blinded by the optimism surrounding the capabilities of the new ICTs and are realistic about their limitations. This focus on practicalities is significant in this era of utopian hyperbole surrounding new ICTs. However, despite innovative use of the Internet and e-mail environmentalists have yet to fully utilise the possibilities of ICTs being more than simply a communication tool. They have not challenged their techniques of protest or practically explored the potential of electronic civil disobedience, such as on-line protests, or used it as a tool for organising simultaneous global demonstrations.

This chapter will begin with a consideration of how environmental politics are played out within Britain and then it will briefly consider the possibilities new ICTs offer. Based on recent empirical research in Britain the use of ICTs in the environmental scene will be overviewed and then the Save Westwood Lyminge Forest campaign in Kent will be examined in detail in order to illustrate this wider picture.

Environmental Movements, and Environmental Politics

New, transforming, creative or radical ideas are often nurtured in non-institutional politics, the 'politics of the people', grassroots, dynamic groups unconstrained by formal laws or constitutions. 'Social movements' emerge as combinations of individuals join and project their opinions into the political arena. New Social Movements (NSMs) tend towards informal participatory democratic modes of organisation, with a lack of hierarchy, and aim to change societal values in a paradigmatic battle with the dominant model of society and concentrations of power.

Doyle and Kellow (1995) identify five structural forms that dominate NSM activity: the individual, network, group, organisation and movement.

The environmental movement is the sum of these structures. The individuals link into a network connected by a common ideology. Examples include the Genetic Engineering Network (GEN) and the Student Environment Network (SEN). The informal groups are more permanent and stable than the network, and tend to have a clearer definition of the identity and symbol of their politics, for example, Reclaim the Streets, RoadAlert! and Justice? They are often very specific in their objectives and tend to disband once the issue has faded. An organisation is permanent, rigid, well-defined and frequently hierarchical, for example non-governmental organisations (NGOs), such as Friends of the Earth, Greenpeace and Transport 2000 (Lowe and Goyder, 1983). Finally, the movement is constituted by the boundaries chosen by the individual who is part of the network and/or organisation, these boundaries are fluid. Overall, 'Environmental movements are overarching political forms that include actors advocating all of the diverse eco-philosophies and positions' that surround environmentalism (Doyle and McEachern, 1998, p. 65).

Many of the individuals involved in networks or informal groups, or groups such as Earth First! do not believe in taking part in formal traditional politics (Rüdig, 1995; Dobson, 1997). They consciously abstain from electoral politics and instead promote do-it-yourself (DiY) politics. Rather than attempting to influence politics by lobbying MPs, or joining a mainstream pressure group, individuals choose direct action, for example against the Newbury Bypass or a Reclaim the Streets event (Doherty, 1997). This kind of DiY politics is seen as informal, participatory, all-inclusive, non-hierarchical and challenging to the dominant political order. Hence, they are both trying to change the government's policy and mobilise the mass public against the threats of environmental degradation. This is a mixture of short- and long-term aims, preventing a local development and proposing an alternative value system to the current political order which is seen as being unable to resolve the existing ecological problems (Dalton, 1994). Political parties are perceived as unwilling to challenge the status quo because of their desire to be re-elected and thus involvement in electoral politics is seen as a distraction from the potential of the attempts at public mobilisation for direct action (Martin, 1984).

Organisations also have a fundamental role within environmental movements. They can incorporate parts of the networks and groups discussed above and also form separate collections of individuals. These more 'moderate' organisations are often defined as NGOs[2] – permanent, and well defined, with a constitution. They are principally autonomous from government control and operate at local, regional, national and transnational levels (Charlton *et al*, 1995; Willetts, 1996). This independence enables them to introduce new, often transformative ideas into the political arena. They are involved in both the politics of non-institutional social movements and the institutional politics of government.

> Most institutional political arrangements... mitigate against the direct involvement of the public. One important strength of NGOs is their potential to provide a mechanism for some form of popular participation in political processes (Rodgers, 1998, p. 9).

Although some environmental NGOs have a close alliance to the nation state,[3] organisations such as Greenpeace and Friends of the Earth like to maintain their autonomy and are often involved in direct action and DiY politics to mobilise the mass public. Overall, however, environmental NGOs in the West are seen as political lobbyists who are becoming increasingly institutionalised[4] (Rüdig, 1995).

The British environmental scene is vigorous and vibrant and yet diverse and deeply fractionalised (Bosso, 1991; Merchant, 1992).[5] It is composed of many diverse elements who have a variety of ways of being politically active. The conventional organisations and NGOs tend to use traditional lobbying methods and encourage public participation in the political system, while the more informal groups employ direct action techniques. The purpose of this chapter is to consider how the use of new ICTs is stimulating or altering these approaches to politics.

New ICTs and Their Implications for Social Movements

> it is in the realm of symbolic politics, and in the development of issue-oriented mobilisations by groups and individuals outside the mainstream political system that new electronic communication may have the most dramatic effects (Castells, 1997a, p. 352).

Increased information exchange and communication resulting in new social networks and new space for communication could have profound implications for all components of a NSM (Rheingold, 1995; Friis, 1996). In particular, Webber (1968) suggested that new ICTs would increase individual freedoms and liberty enabling more diverse associations than those in place based communities. These democratic properties could also facilitate public participation in political processes and aid the development of social cohesion (Tsagarousianou *et al*, 1998). Much of this discourse however, is often seen as optimistic with little empirical basis.

Environmentalists take on board both the hyperbole surrounding new ICTs and simultaneously define their own representations of it as a tool for creating social networks, enabling political influence and as an arena for free speech and non-hierarchical systems of power (Young, 1993; Schwartz, 1996). Within the NSM there are also those who question its use and query the resources engulfed in its utilisation (Glendinning, 1990; Roszak, 1994). They see new ICTs as capitalist constructs which divert resources away from other more productive methods of protest (Mander, 1994).

The potential for increased political participation through the use of ICTs has been promoted by many advocates (Lee, 1995; Raab *et al*, 1996; Barbrook, 1997). 'Digital democracy' is portrayed as being able to dispel the alienation from traditional politics; 'electronic democracy can reverse the trend to direct action and rejuvenate political life'.[6] This is possible through the creation of social networks and communication networks on-line that are able to express their views to the appropriate government official, ignoring some traditional government hierarchies (Frederick, 1997). Environmentalists can also surpass the oligarchy of traditional media by using the Internet to distribute their news and thus raise their political profile (Adams, 1996; Brass and Poklewski Koziell, 1997; Warf and Grimes, 1997). This cohesion of individual groups also increases the possibilities of other NSMs emerging. Bonchek (1995) argues that the formation of collective political action is facilitated by ICTs because the use of computer networks reduces transaction costs associated with organising collective action. He also notes that current dynamics lead to unequal network access across social strata, which result in a domination of young, male, educated and affluent individuals using the Internet. The use of ICTs can also cause an increase in marginalisation of sectors of society through the creation of intolerant 'purified communities' in on-line culture (Belt, 1998). Users of the Internet bring with them their existing intolerances, such as racism or homophobia. Thus the Internet remains a social space and cultural product which is as prone to as many antagonisms as any other (Froehling, 1997; Warf and Grimes, 1997; Cleaver, 1998).

Despite an increasing awareness of ICT use by politically disenfranchised or 'counterhegemonic' groups (Warf and Grimes, 1997, p. 260), there is a distinct lack of research about the implications of new ICTs on the political achievements of the components of environmental movements.[7] Notably, O'Lear (1996, 1997) conducted a study of e-mail communication amongst environmentalists in Russia and Estonia. Through an empirical case study of the Peipsi Lake Project (PLP), O'Lear demonstrates that although e-mail access is limited, it has proved vital and effective for the transboundary ecological organisation. E-mail has facilitated internal communication between staff separated by large distances and external communication by increasing their contacts in Northern Europe. The PLP operates on a local and transborder scale and e-mail is used in conjunction with traditional forms of communication, 'e-mail helps to support the PLP on a macroscale so that it can work more effectively on a microscale' (O'Lear, 1997, p. 287). In 1996 the PLP secured a policy agreement between Russia and Estonia for improved environmental management of the Peipsi-Chudskoye lake, a success which O'Lear partly attributes to their use of e-mail.

The plight of the Zapatistas[8] and their extensive and innovative use of the Internet has generated significant academic comment (Cleaver, 1998). Although essentially a labour rights based struggle (as opposed to an environmental one), the analysis of the role of ICTs in the political struggle serves as one of only a few empirical case studies examined in detail. Use of the Internet added a new transnational dimension to the localised Zapatista struggle, and helped them to overcome the efforts of the Mexican government to isolate the protest (Warf and Grimes, 1997; Cleaver, 1998). Details of their situation were rapidly disseminated across e-mail discussion lists, newsgroups and web-sites to an international audience.[9] However, Froehling (1997) argues that the potential of the Internet as a tool for liberation can only be realised where actions on the Internet articulate into effects outside cyberspace, otherwise it remains a virtual revolution:

> In Chiapas, people are daily hurt by the conflict, through lack of resources and mistreatment, resulting in injury and death. Displace war into cyberspace, and these details retreat. Left by itself, cyberspace connects people in only a limited way and provides only an illusion of participation (Froehling, 1997, p. 304).

Rodgers (1998) has considered whether the use of new ICTs has enabled international NGOs, including Friends of the Earth, to create new spaces of political representation. ICTs are illustrated to have had a significant effect in facilitating the functions of NGOs such as cross-border organisation with a variety of social actors, informational flow, crisis response and gaining wide audience membership (Hurrell, 1995). New ICTs also help to challenge the traditional elite-defined distinctions between political actors:

> NGOs are using CMC [Computer Mediated Communication] as a means of further eroding distinctions between high/low, public/private political distinctions... e-mail provides a facility for NGOs to transcend some

traditional institutional barriers through its use as a medium to contact agencies (Rodgers, 1998, p. 8).

Rodgers (1998) identifies how new ICTs aid NGOs' existing functions of encouraging public participation and incorporating marginalised groups into political processes. Annis (1992) and Stefanik (1993) also consider the possibilities of 'informational empowerment' and how new ICTs can enable individuals 'to become activists at any level of public life' (Stefanik, 1993, p. 271). These aspects of new ICTs enhance and compliment the existing role of NGOs and grass-roots informal groups, but in this context facilitate existing channels of communication rather than creating new spaces of political representation:

> they democratize information flow, break down hierarchies of power, and make communication from the top and bottom just as easy as from horizon to horizon (Frederick, 1997, p. 256).

This information flow will only have the effect of 'empowerment' if it invokes communication, discussion and interchange with as many social and political actors as possible (Bessette, 1997). Wood (1999) has noted how a loose coalition of NGOs from across the political spectrum effectively opposed the Multilateral Agreement on Investment (MAI). Their 'decisive weapon' was the Internet.[10] This MAI opposition and the Zapatistas effective use of the Internet arguably invoked such communication across a variety of actors. Further empirical investigations are now required to assess whether such instances are occurring elsewhere with the use of new ICTs.

Challenging Boundaries? The Net, Networks and Greens

Given the size and scale of the implications of ICT usage there is a requirement for empirically based, contextual, time-specific research that examines particular components of NSMs and their relationships with new ICTs. Based on 60 interviews conducted between mid-1997 and the final months of 1998 with a range of individuals including those associated with Friends of the Earth, Greenpeace, Centre for Alternative Technology, Save Westwood Lyminge Forest Campaign, McSpotlight, SchNEWS, Green Student Network and Reclaim the Streets, it is possible to attempt such an examination. A brief overview of ICT use by environmentalists in Britain will attempt to draw out some general trends that will then be supported by a more in-depth analysis of the Lyminge Forest campaign. Some names of interviewees have been changed in order to protect their identity.

ICT Use by Environmentalists

The diversity of the British environmental scene precludes any simple generalisations about how its components utilise ICTs. There are some cases where the use of ICTs has clearly been fundamental to the campaign and others where participants feel that ICTs did not particularly alter the course of the protest. These participants often highlight how they managed in previous campaigns without it.

Environmental activists have been innovative in their use of ICTs but essentially transferred their existing methods onto the new technology. In this way they have yet to utilise its full potential and employ new techniques such as electronic civil disobedience or fully gain from the benefit of cheap, fast global networks. It is currently treated as simply another media tool to be put to use in publicising their cause and therefore not viewed in terms of providing new approaches to protest.

The use of ICTs by environmental campaigning groups and individuals appears to be prevalent and seems to be rapidly expanding since its first adoption in the early 1990s (Warf and Grimes, 1997):

> Thousands of environmental activists and organisations around the world are using commercial and non-profit computer networks to co-ordinate campaigns, exchange news, and get details on the proposals of governments and international organisations (Young, 1993, p. 21).

ICTs have been adopted by almost all sectors of the movement, spanning the established well-funded NGOs to the informal networks and groups of direct action activists. They range from Friends of the Earth and Greenpeace International to comparatively small-scale on-site protests at Lyminge Forest, Ashton Court and Teigngrace.[11] Many have only just come to terms with the technology and it is early days within which to examine any implications. As Wray suggests, 'we have only just begun to realise the full potential of how computers will change political activism' (Wray, 1998a, p. 1).

It is expected that ICT use will primarily influence the nature of communication between environmentalists and their interaction with the public and media. Such changes in communication methods could thus affect campaign organisation and mobilisation. In this sense ICTs may become the facilitator that enables components of the environmental movement to gain support, influence and possibly add political weight.

Internet web-pages are currently used by many groups to advertise their cause. It is a medium comparatively free of regulation or corporate control: 'The Internet is the first time that grassroots activists have had a media where there is a level playing field with the multi-nationals and all their millions of dollars' (Devin, McSpotlight[12] volunteer, quoted in *Undercurrents* 6, 1996).

They are able to directly control the content, image and message that they wish to portray. In the recent Birmingham North Relief Road evictions (December 1998), press releases and personal accounts of incidences were freely available and regularly updated directly from those on-site through web-pages[13] and over e-mail networks such as ALLSORTS.[14] Similarly during the Newbury Bypass protest, Friends of the Earth[15] used their web-page to keep the public up to date about the situation on site (Lamb, 1996). This information thus reached the public unfiltered by the traditional media: 'Every time you are involved in any action, campaign or idea, not just a component part, but a major part is how can we distribute it through the World Wide Web' (Paula, interview, 9 April 1998).

On 4 January 1999 a group of environmentalists occupied the Shell UK headquarters in London.[16] Using a digital camera, a laptop and a mobile phone they were able to broadcast live pictures and text on the Internet from inside the building, communicating directly with the public and the media:[17]

> Thus direct action becomes direct information, a perfect way to get around the tired reliance on the drips of misinformed publicity provided by the mainstream media (on ALLSORTS e-mail distribution list, 8 January 1999).[18]

Groups are also using ICTs in order to get information out to the press. Greenpeace used their web-site during their occupation of Brent Spar in 1995 to distribute information about the protest and argue that the press used it as a source for their articles. Others are using web-sites as a fundraising tool. Friends of the Earth encourage the public to join via credit card donations over their secure server through the web-page. The Centre for Alternative Technology[19] has an on-line shopping section and uses the site as a advertisement to attract visitors to the centre in Wales.

E-mail networks are perhaps more useful for the exchange of information between environmentalists. The Green Student Network is an e-mail discussion list that exists primarily for debate between students at British Universities:

> The purpose of GSN is to co-ordinate actions and exchange information... the network often serves as a way of exchanging ideas about original forms of action (as well as alerting about what actions are going on)... contact via the e-mail list occurs on a daily basis (Ben, Green Student Network, interview 4 April 1998).

Other groups use e-mail networks to communicate about pending issues and imminent actions, although use of Pretty Good Privacy (PGP) is advocated by some in order to protect information from surveillance:

> RoadAlert!, Reclaim the Streets, Critical Mass etc... have been largely reliant on use of e-mail, newsgroups and the web to spread the message, keep in contact and alert people quickly to what is happening (James, Green Student Network, interview, 11 April 1998).

In addition to all the discussions, Simon Festing, from Friends of the Earth, proposed that the Internet enables collaborative projects between groups such as Friends of the Earth and direct action groups to operate more easily. Michael, an environmentalist from Finland, also exemplified how the e-mail networks can encourage action:

> The reason why I am here now is because I got a contact through e-mail to Andy [Green Student Network] and read his web-site and after one year of exchanging e-mail... . I just decided to come here to help him (Interview, 17 December 1997).

E-mail, however, is not replacing traditional communication methods, it is often just employed as an additional tool. Much information is still only distributed by word of mouth for security reasons. In cases of evictions all methods of distributing the news are used, however telephone trees are deemed to be quicker and more reliable than e-mail lists. A notable distinction between the majority of ICTs and the use of word of mouth is that ICTs such as e-mail rely upon the written rather than the spoken word. It is probable that this is a significant factor in their adoption or rejection. Many interviewees have suggested that it is the combination of using the Internet and word of mouth which was aiding support for actions and campaigns, 'Information gets lost when you just use word of mouth' (Jane, interview, 10 April 1997).

The majority of interviewees have only been using e-mail networks to communicate ideas and perhaps organise actions. Reclaim the Streets have used e-mail networks to help to co-ordinate global street parties, such as the one in May 1998, but the idea, date and action plan had essentially already been organised face to face. It was used more as a global noticeboard:

almost the entire process of setting up at least nineteen street parties around the world took place in e-mail... a list of contacts had been amassed and a group of people had proposed a date after much discussion, face to face discussion... and that proposal was sent out to dozens of people that had e-mail contacts... and there was a discussion list... though from what I'm aware basically once the date had been proposed and had enthused people wherever it did there wasn't an awful lot of actual co-ordination to do because each of the events was largely autonomous (Laptop Mike, Reclaim the Streets, interview 17 June 1998).

So far, however, there has been little evidence of the use of electronic civil disobedience in Britain by environmental activists. Electronic civil disobedience is a 'form of mass decentered electronic direct action, utilizes virtual blockades and virtual sit-ins' (Wray, 1998b, p. 5). It is just beginning to be used in the USA by a group calling themselves the Electronic Disturbance Theater against the Mexican government in support of the Zapatistas. However, in Britain many such actions are still just ideas:

if we got 50,000 people e-mailing a company objecting to their practices we might crash the system. I think that if we crashed Shells' server it would be generally acceptable, though of course they could do it back to us (Tim, interview, 12 April 1998).

Several expressed a fear of breaking Internet etiquette or the trust that enables the Internet to function, though there are rumours about the spread of eco-hacking through the Internet networks of companies:

Contractors are investing heavily to protect sensitive and confidential information from militant environmentalists hacking into company IT systems. Balfour Beatty, Costain, Mowlem and Alfred McAlpine all recognise the threat from a small group of hardline anti-roads activists, some of whom possess advanced computer skills (Do or Die! 1997, p. 33).

Certainly the Metropolitan Police are well aware of environmentalists' activities:

the WWW is being used by radical groups and those intent on causing obstruction and disruption for the purpose of organising and publicising their activities (Detective Constable Steve Edwards, Open Intelligence Unit, Metropolitan Police, Personal Communication, 20 January 1998).

Overall, web-pages and e-mail networks are being used by environmentalists in Britain to effectively distribute information and for the planning or notification of actions. Whether use of ICTs is actually increasing attendances at protests is difficult to establish, although some suggest that it has. 'I know of quite a lot of people who visited the forest because they had heard about it over the Internet' (Merlin, Lyminge Forest, interview, 29 December 1998).

ICT use has certainly facilitated the ease with which information is passing within the environmental movement and to the public and media. In many cases it had aided the passing out of information from situations that the public are unable to get close to. This includes on-site protest evictions, although many participants in such actions have difficulty getting access to computers with modem connections while they are living on site. At present there is only one fully equipped mobile 'office' in a van that is able to travel to different sites around Britain. Access to equipment is one of the main problems for on-site protesters, but not such a problem for the better-resourced NGOs such as Friends of the Earth and Greenpeace. Significantly, many groups are using ICTs to build up international links with campaigns world-wide. This has occurred with both well-publicised issues such as McSpotlight and the smaller campaign at Lyminge Forest where through their Internet publicity they had visitors from Canada, Poland and Germany.

The reasons why particular environmental groups and individuals are using ICTs and the way in which they do so varies. However, many have commented that as the technology is available and it is often free, it is better to use all the opportunities that are available to them. The majority of groups have access to free space for their web-sites. There are several Internet Service Providers (ISPs) who offer free space to environmental groups for example, GeoCities, and many organisations allow the use of space such as OneWorld, Association for Progressive Communications (APC) and many Universities. Others use relatively low-cost services by Green Net or Demon. This access to relatively cheap space effectively gives them a free media with advertising space world-wide. This can significantly expand their support base. Their use of modern technology also helps to crack the image of them as primitive hippies living in a past age, 'These people are media-friendly, technology-literate and unencumbered by outdated ideological baggage' (Conor Foley quoted by Brass and Poklewski Koziell, 1997, p. 98). In this way they can be seen to be educated, intelligent citizens whose views should be listened to. Paula (Interview, 9 April 1998) also argued that environmentalists need to be part of the Internet in order to determine how it is used and to help to maintain the freedom of the medium from corporate control. In most cases a particular individual has tended to lead the use of the Web for a campaign or organisation and then encouraged and trained others. In some cases the removal of the key player results in a temporary pause in using the Internet or in updating the web-pages.

Not all environmentalists support the use of ICTs however. Within the environmental movement the use of alternative technologies has significant support. Alternative technology can be defined as including small-scale constructions within a local environment that can be produced largely by recyclable, recycled or cheaply and easily accessible parts. In contrast, high, hard, or advanced technology can refer to complex technology which requires expertise in construction and use. Environmentalists tend to disapprove of such technology, and thus the use of the Internet and e-mail fits uneasily. Computers have significant environmental consequences in their manufacture and use and are closer to the ideals of high technology than alternative technology. To overcome these contradictions environmentalists mitigate the environmental effects of computers by adapting the technology by using solar or wind power. Greenpeace and Friends of the Earth have used solar energy sources and computer hardware with low chlorofluorocarbon (CFC) and electromotive force (emf) emissions. Many also list ICTs as enabling free speech, public access and participation, an aid for democracy, being cheap and relatively easy to use. These are all attributes that would align the technology into the definition of alternative technology. Therefore in many respects some environmentalists see the Internet as a form of alternative technology, despite the fact that it has to be accessed through high technology.

At present, use of ICTs is gaining in significance for many components of the British environmental scene, but many aspects survive without it and it is unlikely to replace the more traditional forms of direct action:

> there is no doubt that this new form of campaigning can be effective. It's not supposed to be an alternative to the more direct forms of action like, for example, at Newbury, but it's an excellent complement (Devin, McSpotlight volunteer, quoted in *Undercurrents* 6, 1996).

> I wouldn't say its absolutely essential but its another tool. Word of mouth and phone calls are still there, basically. But it's creating a stronger network, both in this country and internationally (Jo Makepeace, *SchNEWS*, interview, 22 April 1998).

Use of ICTs has enabled components of the British environmental scene to become more networked and better organised. They have been able to gain access to the technology relatively cheaply and pioneering individuals have developed sophisticated sites and popular e-mail distribution lists. They are highly skilled and innovative in their use of the technology. The result is an improved effectiveness in publicising their causes and in gaining support for particular issues. They use it as an additional tool to an already large network of media that they employ. The technology has not challenged them to change the way they do things, but created an opportunity for them to extend the way in which they already operate to a wider audience (both domestic and international). Thus they have appropriated ICTs to how they wish to use them, rather than in the way others have done before. This in itself is innovative and contrasts with corporate use of ICTs, but they have simply transferred their existing methods onto the Internet and not challenged their approaches to protest. Thus the gatekeepers to many groups' web-sites remain white, middle class and often male, and few have campaigned on the damaging environmental effects of the computers that they now use daily. Despite significant emphasis on developing innovative direct action techniques they are still in the early stages of ICT use and have not begun to fully utilise its possibilities such as the use of electronic civil disobedience. Only a few are beginning to see its potential as a tool for organising simultaneous global protests and virtual sit-ins.

Save Westwood, Lyminge Forest Campaign

Expanding upon the general overview above, the Lyminge Forest campaign can be seen to illustrate many of the assertions made in more depth. The Westwood campaign was chosen as it provides a useful, clearly delineated example to examine. It is not taken to be representative in any way of the environmental movement as a whole, but as an organic local direct action protest occurring in Britain. It is not the byproduct of a particular organisation or pre-existing group. In this way its perception and use of new ICTs is not predetermined by organisational structures, but born of the ambiguous and amorphous combination of the individuals involved.

Lyminge Forest is situated in west Kent between Canterbury and Folkestone. Between August 1997 and December 1998 I visited the site nine times,[20] interviewed 12 individuals and had more informal conversations with another 10, the majority of whom lived on-site in the forest. A questionnaire was also placed on the campaign web-site from January until December 1998 to which there were 28 replies.

Westwood, part of Lyminge Forest, was occupied by protesters in March 1997 in an attempt to stop the Forestry Commission plans to sell it to Rank to be developed into a private holiday complex.[21] Their occupation was in support of the local community action group who had fought the sale of the wood for several years previously but who had lost at the Public Inquiry and a High Court appeal. In August 1997 the Forestry Commission gave Rank a two-year option to buy the site. Opponents to the development objected to the proposed scale of environmental damage, loss of important wildlife, noise and light disturbance and increase air pollution in the area (Do or Die! 1997b; Greensword, 1997).

Between ten and 100 protesters lived on site from March 1997.[22] They built tunnels, towers, tree houses and hanging lock-ons in a number of camps spread across the wood in preparation for the arrival of the bailiffs.[23] In April 1997 they were served with a court order, but the bailiffs failed to arrive.[24]

This conduct as part of the Save Westwood campaign was a clear example of non-violent direct action (NVDA) by a group of individuals, some of whom knew each other previously, who now formed an ill-defined network or group temporarily clustered around a specific issue. Their main political aim was to prevent the sale and consequent development of the forest and to ensure that it remained open and accessible for public use in the future. They intended to achieve this by making it expensive for them to be evicted and thus deter the Forestry Commission's plans to sell the wood.[25]

In order to prevent this development they (as in the loose networks of individuals associated with the campaign) employed a number of tactics.[26] Primarily their occupation of the site was an act of resistance to any attempts at clearing the wood to build the development.[27] Through this act and associated media attention they also sought to raise the public profile of the proposals in order to gain mass support to pressurise the local council and Forestry Commission. They also undertook other incidences of direct action in attempts to persuade Rank to change their mind. Notably a group of 40 protesters occupied the boardroom of Rank HQ in August 1997.[28] Finally, on some of their publicity flyers they encouraged writing to MPs to support the on-site protesters' action.

The use of these methods illustrates both a feeling of disenfranchisement with the political system and an engagement with it. They were pressuring local and national government and bypassing it beyond and below. Below they were appealing to the mass public and beyond they were tackling the corporation Rank itself. The protesters were supported by the local people who had exhausted the legal system to try and protect the wood. They saw the protesters as their last resort. David Plumstead, a local campaigner, said 'people are driven to this kind of protest, not because there is not a democratic process, but because the authorities take no notice of it'.[29]

There were many references to the campaign's web-site both in the national and local media and within environmental literature.[30] There were several requests for support and eviction alerts sent out over e-mail networks. Notably there was a call for help on the ALLSORTS list (28 July 1997), an 'eviction imminent' notice on the RoadAlert list (13 August 1997) and an eviction alert sent out through the Green Student Network (11 February 1998). Of the many different web-sites, one site maintained by Warwick Earth First! in 1997 held information about why Westwood should be saved, provided copies of articles from SchNEWS[31] and Do or Die! and an e-mail contact for those interested.[32] Similar information was also posted on the Pagan Federation web-page in 1998.[33]

The web-page under the control of the on-site protesters was started by Merlin and Sef in early 1997. This had information about why the development needed to be prevented, how the reader could help, a wish list, map, Ranks plans, a links page and a contacts page.[34] The site was aimed at encouraging visitors and at obtaining supplies from the wish list. It was updated throughout 1997 and there was a note attached, 'Sorry its taken so long to update this page but I've been living on site for six months and I don't often have access to a computer' (Web-site, 3 November 1997). It was set up by Merlin before he moved on to the site and was initially only accessible by returning to his home some miles away. In December 1997 the page was radically restructured to include colourful graphics and photographs with added information about the development, the local environment, Rank and its financial situation, and a form to fill in and send to the Rank Chairman in protest. In the summer of 1998 the web-site address changed as the Globalnet servers' subscription had expired, so it moved to a free space on Envirolink,[35] but the structure remained the same. It was updated and now included a discussion of sustainability, the use of alternative energy sources and the practice of permaculture. Overall, the web-site was extensive, detailed and designed to appeal to a wide variety of audiences (Ferst and Lineham, 1998).

The importance of computers on-site has also been highlighted by media attention concerning their use of wind turbines and solar panels to recharge car batteries. These can then be used to power lighting, CB communications, computers, radio and tunnel ventilation systems.[36]

Examination of ICT use by those at Lyminge Forest illustrates a number of assertions already identified in the general overview. First, the tactics employed to prevent the development are achieved by using a number of different tactics. The use of new ICTs facilitates this but is just one of a number of methods available to the protesters. In order to generate support for the protest in terms of extra bodies to live on-site, media coverage and raising public concern, the protesters' existence and activities need to be exposed to as wide an audience as possible. Traditionally this would have occurred through word of mouth or through underground literature such as SchNEWS. Press attention would be sought through press releases and telephone contact. Internet and e-mail are now aiding this process:

> It lets us have our say and allows us to be published without having to go through organised interest groups and power structures who may not like what we want to say or what we do (John, interview, 8 January 1998).

> I would have thought it's probably just helped to reinforce... its just another way of communicating ideas back and forth... . I think its parallel with other forms of communication and ways of passing information that we use (Wizard, interview 19 December 1997).

In terms of the information distributed via the Internet and e-mail, much of it had previously appeared on leaflets and in articles, although the pictures were new additions. Only a small amount of additional information was put onto the web-page. Even then, in terms of attracting new settlers only a few had heard of the web-site before they had arrived on site at the protest.

Second, despite the web-page providing an opportunity to include a large number of those on site, few on-site protesters had seen it or contributed to it. Of those interviewed the majority were aware of its existence, but did not particularly want to become involved and were happy to leave the responsibility of it to someone else:

> JP: Are people asked if they want to contribute to the web-site?
> Ben: No, not really. You could if you wanted to, but really Mike and Merlin do it all. When we write leaflets people tend to go round the site asking if anyone wants to help or put stuff on it, but not for the Internet (interview, 20 June 1998).

This lack of desire to be involved in the actual process of creating the web-page may highlight the necessity of technical skills to participate in it, or be seen as a distraction from the task at hand: 'We managed fine at the last protest without it' (Bob, interview 8th January 1998). The result is that there are effectively 'gatekeepers' to the web-site and despite their attempts to encourage others participation it has become the preserve of a select set of enthusiasts.

Third, this failure to involve more people in ICT use and the limited extra information placed on the web-site reflects the environmentalists' view of the medium as an additional tool and not a new technique of protest. It also reflects the many constraints that hinder political action; commitment, time, money and expertise (Warf and Grimes, 1997). Despite attempts to update it regularly, there were significant access problems to a computer with an Internet link. During the early months of 1998 an individual's flat was available for computer access in Canterbury and it was during this time that the web-site was more frequently updated. This opportunity faded in the spring, however, and despite attempts at a laptop link from on-site, access was restricted to another individual's house, this time in Folkestone:

> I think we made a minor change about a month and a half ago, something like that... it's very difficult to get us all in one place... me, Merlin, laptop, Dreamweaver [web design program] and a phone line to plug into... it's been slow (Mike, interview, 20 June 1998).

These problems, however, were put in the context of the perceived value of the web-site to the protest. With limited resources, time and money, the point has been raised, even by those who write the web-pages, that concentrating on the Internet is a difficult thing to do: 'with so few of us here all the time... so few constants... and so many different places to point ourselves' (Mike, interview 20 June 1998). The protesters feel that they have to validate their efforts with the Internet, for at the end of the day if the defences are not built, eviction will be all that easier for the Forestry Commission. A questionnaire respondent suggested that the use of new ICTs:

> disconnects us from our immediate surroundings – the earth, face to face community interaction and focuses on the abstract (on-line/virtual) reality; intellectualises the campaign which could alienate/reduce the involvement of those who do not have access to/knowledge of/interest in technology; sanitises the concept of direct action as a committed 'hands on' experience (anonymous respondent, 30 June 1998).

This does not appear to have occurred in the Lyminge campaign. The Internet is used as an added media tool by a select set of enthusiasts who remained influential and included in on-site politics, while others continued with their chosen activities. The power and influence of word of mouth and underground publications prevents the Internet from becoming the sole means of communication and in turn decreases the possibility of exclusion. Despite a variety of individuals being involved during the protest and a distinct lack of structure to its design and maintenance, there are still only a couple of core individuals participating in the web-site at any one time.

Other individuals add their enthusiasm and are trained by one another, but then move away.

Any perceived discernible effects of the web-site are hard to identify and the majority response is that it is a good thing, something that the protest might as well have as it can do no harm . Worzel suggests that it is 'like a notice board in the sky... it just speeded everything up' (interview 28 April 1998). Messages about eviction alerts or requests for help can snowball their way around the various e-mail networks. The lack of perceived impact may also be related to the non-dynamic nature of the web-site; as they were unable to update it regularly it did not form a focus for camp information.

Finally, there is evidence that use of the Internet and e-mail lists have resulted in the protest being well networked and publicised, both nationally and globally. Interest from abroad resulted in visits from Canada, Germany and Poland.[37] Notably, the TV crew from Canada first found out about the campaign through the Internet. People on site also believed that many visitors had initially heard about the protest through e-mail lists and the web-site.

Conclusions

Although environmental activists have only been using new ICTs for a few years the significant recent growth in its utilisation merits examination. Through a general overview of the British environmental scene as a whole and the more in-depth analysis of the Lyminge Forest case study it is possible to identify some broad trends in ICT use.

Primarily, new ICTs have been adopted by almost all sectors of the environmental scene, ranging from NGOs to the informal networks and groups of direct action activists. Second, the use of the Internet and e-mail has facilitated network cohesion and aided campaign organisation in terms of an improved effectiveness in publicising issues to environmentalists and the public. Third, environmentalists tend to use new ICTs as additional tools to the large array of media that they have traditionally employed. In many ways they use it simply as an extension of their use of telephone trees, leaflets and word of mouth and tend to include much of the same information on web-pages and e-mails as by using these other communication tools. It is thus being used within the current concept of tactics that the traditional methods enabled. The environmentalists have not begun to fully utilise new ICTs to enable new forms of protest to be developed. There is arguably significant potential in the use of electronic civil disobedience, virtual sit-ins and the organisation of simultaneous global protests over the electronic networks.

It will be especially interesting as new ICT use continues to increase and more environmentalists move 'on-line' to see how their use and development of new ICTs progresses; in particular, whether there is a move towards new forms of electronic protest. If such a move occurs, the importance of the Internet and e-mail may grow to the point where it becomes more than simply an additional tool but an essential facet to any environmental campaign.

Notes

1.   A telephone tree constitutes a list of individuals' telephone numbers arranged in a branch-like manner. It has a hierarchical structure so that a trigger telephone call from the 'bottom' contacts a few individuals who in turn each contact a few further individuals. In this way the original message is relayed down the branches of the telephone tree.

2.   Princen and Finger (1994) quantify NGOs as separate from social movements. It could be argued, however, that they are significantly connected in Britain, as many of the networks and groups co-ordinate with NGOs such as Friends of the Earth (Doherty, 1996). Their radical political ideology also enables them to have some similar goals to the more informal groups, arguably being part of the same national environmental movement but also reaching beyond these national boundaries to a transnational level (Rodgers, 1998).

3.   For example, the Australian Conservation Foundation had a very close relationship with the Labour government of Australia between 1983 and 1996 (Doyle and McEachern, 1998).

4.   There is a strong tendency within organisations to formalise, which Friends of the Earth tries to resist as it can result in a loss of long-term vision and encourage oligarchy.

5.   Within Britain there is unlikely to be just one environmental movement, but several co-existing with differing emphasis and political aims.

6.   See Gray, J. 'Virtual Democracy', *The Guardian*, 15 September, 1995, p. 17.

7.   Notably Lubbers (1998) considers how multinationals are beginning to develop their own counterstrategies against on-line activism.   Shell International now employ an Internet manager whose remit includes 'monitoring and reacting to what is being written and said about Shell in cyberspace' (p. 2).   Such actions are part of a strategy to counter the increasing presence of environmental activists on the Internet.

8.   In 1994 the Ejército Zapatista Liberación National (EZLN) formed an uprising against the Mexican Government in the state of Chiapas to raise their

concerns about poverty, land rights, justice and exploitation (Warf and Grimes, 1997).

9. The Zapatistas themselves did not have direct access to the Internet but had to rely upon others to publicise their message (Cleaver, 1998).

10. de Jonquieres, G. 'Network Guerrillas', *Financial Times*, 30 April 1998.

11. The protest at Lyminge Forest (1997-99) is attempting to prevent development of the forest into a Rank holiday complex (http://www.enviroweb.org/orgs/westwood/). At Ashton Court (1997-99) protesters are trying to prevent the expansion of a quarry by Pioneer into a Bristol park (http://www.gn.apc.org/cycling/ashtoncourt/briefing.html), and at Teigngrace (1997) oppose the extension of a ball clay quarry by Watts Blake Bearne. (http://www.geocities.com/RainForest/3081/newton.html).

12. http://www.mcspotlight.org/.

13. http://www.geocities.com/RainForest/3081/bnrr.html, http://www.newwave.co.uk/vivid/web/blag/bnrr/rdptest.htm, http://www.otterview.freeserve.co.uk/bnrr, http://ds.dial.pipex.com/beep/bnrr/index.htm.

14. ALLSORTS is an e-mail list related to Reclaim the Streets, which posts information from a number of sources about environmental, human rights and animal rights issues (rts@gn.apc.org).

15. http://www.foe.co.uk/.

16. As an act of solidarity with the indigenous resistance by the Ijaw ethnic group to Shell on the Niger Delta, Nigeria.

17. See Environment News Service (ENS) 'Shell Head Office Occupied' at http://ens.lycos.com/ens/jan99/1999L-01-04-01.html. See also the web-site http://www.kemptown.org/shell/.

18. E-mail: 'Direct Action on the Delta Hits Shell UK Head Office', 8 January 1999, ALLSORTS (rts@gn.apc.org).

19. http://www.cat.org.uk/.

20. Visits were distributed over the seasons in order to see the protest changing through winter and summer conditions.

21. See the following press reports for details; Garner, C., 'Back to the Bronze Age for Swampy's Friends', *The Independent*, 26 July 1997, p. 8; Krinks, P., 'Finding out what it means to live as an eco-warrior amid the trees', *Folkestone Herald*, July 3 1997, pp. 28–9; Krinks, P., 'Getting to grips with tunnel and treehouse', *Folkestone Herald*, 21 August 1997, p. 1; Newsome, R., 'If you go down to the woods today...', *The Big Issue*, November 3-9 1997, pp. 10–11; Parsons, L. 'Digging in', *Folkestone Herald*, 17 April 1997, p. 1 and p. 3; SchNEWS, 'Rank Stink!', *SchNews*, no. 114, 4 April 1997.

22. See Daly, M. 'We're going to win this one', *The Big Issue*, August 11-17 1997; Newsome, R. 'If you go down to the woods today...', *The Big Issue*, November 3-9 1997.

23. See Bellos, A. 'Green protest reaches for the sky', *The Guardian*, 3 July 1997; Goodwin, S., 'Blue Jon and Whinger dig deep to keep their wild wood free from a holiday village', *The Independent*, 3 July 1997, p. 6.

24. See Packham, D., 'Forest protest takes to the trees', *Kentish Express*, 24 April 1997, p. 15.
25. Reported in BBC1 *Countryfile*, 11 January 1998.
26. Here I am referring only to the methods used by the protesters, not by the locals who had fought the development through political lobbying of MPs and through the legal system.
27. This is an act of political resistance not merely a media stunt as they were physically and over a period of time preventing development (Rüdig, 1995; Doyle and McEachern, 1998).
28. See Daly, M., 'Eco-protesters hit Rank in new wave of direct action', *The Big Issue*, August 11-17 1997, pp. 4–5; and Krinks, P., 'Eco-warriors Storm Rank: Westwood protesters occupy leisure giant's London HQ', *Folkestone Herald*, 21 August, 1997, p. 1.
29. Quoted in *Folkestone Herald*, 17 April 1997, p. 3.
30. For details see articles listed in notes 22 and 23 above.
31. SchNEWS is a weekly free newsletter published by Justice? from Brighton. It includes information about environmental, protest and human rights issues.
32. http://www.warwick.ac.uk/~suuad/lyminge/.
33. http://www.paganfed.demon.co.uk.
34. http://www.users.globalnet.co.uk/~weaver/.
35. http://www.envirolink.org/orgs/westwood/.
36. See the following media reports: Krinks, P., 'Getting to grips with tunnel and treehouse', *Folkestone Herald*, 21 August 1997, p. 1; Newsome, R. 'If you go down to the woods today...', *The Big Issue*, November 3-9 1997, pp. 10–11; Nuthall, K., 'Eco-warriors go soft and opt for the telly', *Independent on Sunday*, 16 November 1997, p. 12; ITV *Meridan Tonight* report, 18 December 1997.
37. This observation correlates with the assertion by Warf and Grimes (1997, p. 268) that using the Internet to establish links between struggles internationally may boost the morale of the protest and 'reduce activists' feelings of isolation' fostering 'the sharing of useful ideas and strategies'.

8 The Web Wars: The European Commission and British Governments' Policy Responses to the Internet

MARK WHEELER

This chapter will focus on the issues that are shaping the European Commission and British governments' policies concerning the Internet. Information Communication Technologies (ICTs) have been seen as the centrepiece for future production, services and investment. It has been argued that new forms of electronic commerce may promote competitiveness, efficiency and growth (DTI, 1998a, p. 3).

Currently, a debate exists concerning the role of government as a policy initiator for the expansion of the information marketplace. From a libertarian perspective, ICTs are held to be a form of communication that function independently of state or societal interference. Information technology has been defined by a range of political agents as the sphere in which competitive advantage will be attained through the retraction of state intervention. Alternatively, ICTs have been seen to be representative of socio-political forms of capital. Therefore, states have a significant role in developing initiatives for the public's maximum benefit. The European Commission has commented that the Internet provides opportunities for citizen empowerment (European Commission, 1996, p. 1). The medium lowers the entry costs for the creation and distribution of content, and offers the public universal access to an ever-richer source of information. However, this dissemination of information should not be determined by income to allow for equitability.

This chapter will consider how the debate concerning state intervention/retraction has impacted upon the cryptographic policy initiatives (Raab et al, 1996; Raab, 1997; Bellamy and Taylor, 1998). As new forms of trading become available to service providers, the Internet has been seen to be a medium in which products can be sold directly to consumers. In turn, electronic forms of commerce (e-commerce) require reliable security mechanisms to preserve concepts of trust, authenticity, integrity, confidentiality and privacy. To attain the potentially vast revenues that can be extracted from the Internet, it has been deemed vital that e-commerce should be securely encrypted (OECD, 1997, p. 2).

However, political, social and economic agencies are reluctant to allow for the encryption of material, which can be seen as destructive, illicit or illegal. The unrestricted flow of data may affect public safety, national security, law enforcement, business interests, consumer needs and privacy rights. To offset these developments, the European Union (EU) has recommended that international co-operation between member states is required for e-commerce security, alongside the state's lawful access to dangerous material.

The European Commission and the Organisation for Economic Co-operation and Development (OECD) have administered an international legal framework. Both organisations have recommended that national governments should develop policies to encourage net commerce, whilst protecting citizen and consumer rights. Thus, at a national level, it has become necessary to pursue legislation that can reconcile the contradictions between the freedom of electronic commerce and the legitimate need of the state to sanction damaging material.

During the mid-1990s, the British Conservative government and the Department of Trade and Industry were influenced by the American government's response to this dilemma. Within the US, there has been the establishment of Trusted Third Parties (TTPs), who can decipher and authenticate information distributed across the Internet. There were, however, significant criticisms as this storage of information was seen to create policing agencies who could undermine the free flow of communication. While the Internet has been promoted as a medium through which economic prosperity and freedom of information can be secured, governments have been seen to be developing policy strategies that will erode these goals.

Consequently, this chapter will outline the principal issues which are facing governments as they attempt to reconcile their desire to establish a free electronic economy, while stemming the flow of potentially illicit, illegal or dangerous material. In particular, cryptography raises significant concerns about the state's access to private information. Moreover, this form of intervention stands at the centre of the debate concerning the role of the state as a key actor in creating a framework for investment and innovation within the knowledge-driven economies.

Electronic Commerce

Digital computer processing and network technologies are replacing the conventional methods through which information has been produced, stored, transmitted and distributed. These developments provide access to greater numbers of communications links, permit the distribution of commercial and entertainment material, and advance telephony along the same highways. Digital technologies allow for the easy combination of different types of information representation, such as text, audio, images and video, thereby blurring the distinctions between different types of information production and distribution. As the emerging communication networks allow for a virtually unlimited access to information, education and entertainment resources, they are reforming the means through which people communicate to one another.

The *convergence* of the discreet information and communications systems (telecommunications, broadcasting, information technology) has led to new opportunities for investment and innovation as the take up of information services has grown correspondingly. Thus, the production, distribution and use of information has become an increasingly important economic activity as information's value as a commodity becomes greater (OECD, 1997, p. 5). The catalyst for this spectacular development has been the phenomenal growth of the Internet.

These communication reforms have enabled companies to attain major savings through their existing business strategies and to achieve spectacular gains once they have changed their approaches. In 1997, three companies (Cisco, Dell and General Electric) generated e-commerce revenues of $3 billion. They expect to increase their revenues to $17 billion within three to five years. Moreover, as the net has reduced entry costs to the global communications markets, small businesses can cheaply and easily register for a World Wide Web site (OECD, 1997, p. 5). Increasingly, the Internet has delivered new products and services to consumers:

- home banking and home-shopping over the Internet;
- voice over the Internet;
- e-mail, data and WWW access over mobile phone networks, and the use of wireless links to homes and businesses to connect them to the fixed telecommunications networks;
- data services over digital broadcasting platforms;
- on-line services combined with television via systems such as Web-TV, as well as delivery via digital satellites and cable modems;

- webcasting of news, sports, concerts and of other audio-visual services (OECD,1997, p. 5).

Over the next ten years, it is predicted that the knowledge-driven economy may produce even more significant changes for commerce and society.

Problems Associated with the Converging Digital Economy

ICTs create problematic intellectual property issues. As electronic networks quickly and cheaply transmit all types of digital data, they allow for the perfect copying and distribution of such data throughout cyberspace. Therefore, significant risks exist alongside the anticipated opportunities:

> The explosive world-wide growth of open networks has raised a legitimate concern with respect to the adequacy of security and privacy measures for information and communication systems and the data which is transmitted and stored on those systems. The developing information infrastructure is a fertile environment for all kinds of computer-related crime, including fraud and privacy infringement, and electronic business will not advance until effective data security measures are adopted and trusted by users and consumers (DTI, 1998b, p. 3).

Whilst the proliferating sources of information have enhanced the services to be found, there has been an increase in the systems' vulnerability. Digital data has become subject to threats including unauthorised access and use, misappropriation, alteration and destruction. These dangers were cited by 69 per cent of British companies as inhibiting their involvement within e-commerce and trade (DTI, 1998b, p. 3).

Moreover, privacy rights are being placed at a greater risk as the information infrastructures were not designed to protect the storage or confidentiality of data. As the privacy of personal information is a fundamental democratic right, the need to secure data across the Internet has increased. In turn, this necessitates the establishment of appropriate cryptography to secure and protect digital material. As a consequence, it has been suggested that the individual's commercial activities and non-commercial rights may be enhanced.

The Security of Information Systems and Methods of Cryptography

There are several properties connected to the encryption of digital material. First, cryptography should allow for information to be made *available*, accessible and useable. Second, encrypted systems need to secure transmitted data by ensuring that information remains *authenticated*. Thus, the data retains its integrity as it cannot be modified or changed in any unauthenticated way. This means that the concept of *trust*, which is required for the transaction of goods, services or capital, may be retained for existing services and be extended for the delivery of new products. Finally, encryption must ensure that data remains *confidential* and can not be disclosed to any unauthorised users. To this end, Internet users can be certain that their *privacy* rights are being preserved (DTI, 1998b, p. 2).

Traditionally, cryptographic mechanisms were employed by governments to secure classified material. To this end, one form of encryption emerged in which algorithms were used to render information unintelligible to any person who did not possess certain secret information, or a 'key', through which to access data. Currently, *secret key* cryptography can be further advanced as digital computing allows for complex mathematical algorithms to be calculated for the encryption of data.

As costs have declined, cryptography has become more affordable and accessible for business and individual use. Moreover, there has been the growing realisation that unencrypted data may be abused. The *public key* cryptography systems have been developed for such practical use. These enable ICT users to exchange encrypted material without necessitating the need to communicate a secret shared key in advance. Instead, two mathematically related keys are employed for each communicating party – a 'public key' which is publicly disclosed, and a coterminous 'private key' that remains secret. In this manner, a public key encrypted message can only be deciphered by the user's corresponding private key. Therefore, confidential data which has been encrypted by the recipient's public key and decrypted by his or her private key may only be seen by the recipient of the message. Public key cryptography has been seen to have 'pushed' e-commerce within open networks such as the Internet. It offers a technological solution for both the problems of authenticating the identity of the user and for restricting the denial or non-repudiations of actions performed by an individual or entity with regard to the data.

An important application of public key cryptography is the 'digital signature'. This verifies or authenticates the integrity of the encrypted data. To this end, a private key will be used to 'sign' a message, while a public key will verify a 'signed' message. An essential part of this system is the 'time stamp' service. To employ a time stamp service, the user may send a cryptographic hash of the document to the stamper who will return a signed document which contains the hash, the last ten hash values and the e-mail addresses they were stamped for.

Digital signatures allow for confidential data to be exchanged between parties who do not know each other in advance. This means that it becomes more difficult to impersonate a user or sender of digital data. Most especially, the potential for fraud is reduced as a 'signed' document provides proof that it originated from the sender, who can neither easily deny having sent the document nor claim that information has been altered during transmission. Further, as anyone can publish a public key, recipients may require more dependable information concerning the identity of the key owner. Thus, informal 'web of trust' and formal 'certification authorities' (CA) third party arrangements have allowed for public keys that are not only freely accessible, but may be understood to be truly reliable and secure.

Issues and Concerns

Cryptography should ensure that ICT users have secure access to reliable and trustworthy data. Yet, the encryption of digital data raises significant questions about how cryptography can be employed for maximum public benefit. One perspective would maintain that a market-driven response would be most appropriate in the creation and implementation of an information infrastructure. Hence, the communications market should establish the products and standards for future investment and technical innovation. Alternatively, others have suggested that supranational and nation state based initiatives, developed through legislative guidelines and transparent regulatory procedures, may suit the cryptographic needs of the information market (DTI, 1998b, p. 1). To consider this debate, it will be necessary to discuss the issues that have accompanied cryptographic practices.

First, technical *standardisation* remains a necessary ingredient for current and future forms of data security. It is important that cryptographic methods are interoperable, mobile and portable at local, international and global levels (1998b, pp. 7-8). Second, although key management systems follow strict procedures so that they will not be compromised, no one cryptographic system can claim to be totally fail-safe. A number of technical, organisational and human errors effect the reliable encryption of digital data. For example, data can be deleted and passwords may be revealed. In this context, systems failure or human error can prove to be disastrous as once cryptographic keys are compromised users can no longer assume the security of the encrypted data. If cryptographic procedures fail, it becomes essential to determine who is responsible for any failure and how such parties can be deemed *liable* so that sanctions may be set in place.

Finally, there has been a growing concern about the mechanisms used to ensure *lawful access* of businesses and the state to encrypted material. For business, the need for third party access occurs if a key holder dies and leaves encrypted information with no key to decrypt it. This has led to copies of cryptographic keys being held at secure data repositories. For the state, the conflict between confidentiality and public safety has become the most debated aspect of cryptography.

A number of contradictions are apparent. For example, law enforcement agencies can legally access stored financial data or intercept communications under specific conditions referring to data protection acts. However, new forms of encryption may curtail these legal enforcements as they will prevent access to either plaintext or the cryptographic keys used to protect the encrypted material. Therefore, although there are advantages to cryptographic systems which allow for untraceable and anonymous electronic transactions, legitimate governmental concerns have been raised with regard to tax collection and money laundering.

The most contentious issues surrounding cryptographic systems have concerned their effect over the dissemination of illicit, harmful or illegal content. In particular, states have feared that private keys, whose decryption codes are kept by individuals, may be subject to criminal or terrorist abuse. As cryptographic mechanisms ensure confidentiality, it is argued that they can act as a means through which improper and dangerous material is concealed. In turn, due to the ability of cryptographic systems to ensure anonymity, national or international legal controls may be circumvented, and data could be used to incite racial hatred, to traffic human beings or to distribute child pornography (European Commission, 1996, p. 1).

The balance between the protection of privacy and the confidentiality of business or private information with the needs of the law enforcement and national security communities has proved to be politically awkward. On the one hand, libertarians have argued for the free flow of information. From this position, the democratic principle that individuals are free to express their beliefs remains sacrosanct. Alternatively, other voices have demanded greater degrees of individual and user accountability. Currently, supranational organisations and national governments are considering the appropriate policies which allow for encrypted material to retain its authentic and confidential nature, whilst protecting the public from the perceived dangers of encrypted data.

Trusted Third Parties

Therefore, as some consensus has been reached concerning the state's lawful access to encrypted data, a number of governments, most especially in the USA, have employed licensed Trusted Third Parties (TTP) as a mechanism through which to achieve lawful access whilst preserving encryption. The purposes of these organisations are two-fold: (1) to provide a range of information security services to users; and (2) to provide key recovery and key escrow for legitimate authorities and individuals to access digital material (DTI, 1997, p. 13).

Thus, a TTP is a licensed organisation that provides encryption services to a wide range of users. To work effectively, a TTP has to be trusted by the bodies it serves, so that they are confident that appropriate security measures are in place. TTPs can also assure users of the trustworthiness of other forms of data by authenticating the veracity of the material that is to be exchanged. In practice, TTPs can exist in the public and private domains, and at a local, national and international level. Moreover, trust agreements may be arranged between different TTPs to form intra-company networks.

However, the TTPs are also repositories for storing public and private security keys. This means that they can be used for key recovery, in which keys can be recovered or backed-up so that they can be recreated if the hardware crashes. More crucially, as master keys are deposited with TTPs, they can be employed for key escrow. This refers to the central storage of private keys to enable the TTP to recover the keys that have been derived from a master key. Thus, state or governmental authorities may access encrypted material that may be deemed to be of criminal or terrorist intent.

Critiques of TTPs

Internet companies and user groups have questioned whether key escrow systems will prove to be workable. To effect the highly complex and secure systems necessary for key escrow, a considerable amount of fixed capital is required. The consequent drag on resources may undermine the development of e-commerce, whilst failing to provide any benefits to law enforcers. Criminals or terrorists could encrypt their communications as a Closed Users Group and therefore would not have to escrow their keys.[1]

Demon Internet has argued that key escrow mechanisms can damage users' confidence in encryption. It is suggested that users will not submit their sensitive private keys to a licensed TTP as this will compromise their anonymity and identity. Further, secret material will become subject to abuse due to the potential for corruption amongst TTP employees or security agencies. Hackers who want to access private keys could target such a centralised storage of sensitive information. Even if user confidence was established, fears have been expressed concerning the security of private information once it is in the hands of the authorities. In particular, it is unclear when a key leaks whether authorities will accept liability and whether records concerning encrypted data will be destroyed once a warrant has expired.

Further, as a TTP, or any authority with a validated warrant, can decrypt any communication between two parties whereby either party has deposited the master key without the knowledge of the other party, user groups fear that their civil liberties will be compromised. TTPs could allow for the Orwellian use of information technology in which state surveillance subsumes the individual's liberty. In effect, TTPs could create an electronic version of Jeremy Bentham's 18th century vision of panopticon – a social control mechanism that suggested a mental state of being watched without seeing your watcher. Civil Liberty organisations contend that governments may enforce, through compulsory licensing, users to deposit their private keys within TTPs thereby invading their privacy:

> the plan involves an unprecedented level of government intrusion into daily life, because the government would potentially have access to all digital communications by all people living within the borders of the country, as well as anyone outside the country exchanging information in digital form with people within (Oram, 1998, p. 2).

Supranational Governmental and Legal Responses to Cryptographic Management Mechanisms

Therefore, the cryptography of digital data raises a series of problematic democratic issues for international and national policy-makers. From the early 1990s onwards, several supranational governmental and legal organisations have sought to establish appropriate initiatives and common guidelines for the cryptography of digital data. These include, the Council of Europe, which has developed guidelines concerning the adverse effects of cryptography for establishing appropriate legal measures to stem computer crime, and the United Nations (UN) and the American Bar Association (ABA) who are considering the guidelines to be adopted for digital signatures.

Within Europe, the OECD and the European Commission have proved to be the most important policy actors. In 1995, the OECD hosted a landmark conference in which the close international co-operation between governments, as well as co-operation between governments and industry, was advocated for encryption. The OECD created an Expert Group, which provided eight recommendations to direct member states' national policies.

- Cryptographic methods should be trustworthy in order to generate confidence in the use of information and communications systems.
- Users should have a right to choose any cryptographic method, subject to applicable law.
- Cryptographic methods should be developed in response to needs, demands and responsibilities of individuals, businesses and governments.
- Technical standards, criteria and protocols for cryptographic methods should be developed and promulgated at the national and the international level.
- The fundamental rights of the individual to privacy, including secrecy of communications and protection of personal data, should be respected in national cryptography policies and in the implementation and use of cryptographic methods.
- National cryptography policies may allow lawful access to plaintext, cryptographic keys and encrypted data. These policies must respect the other principles contained in the guidelines to the greatest extent possible.
- Whether established by contract or legislation, the liability of individuals and entities that offer cryptographic services or hold or access cryptographic keys should be clearly stated.
- Governments should co-operate to co-ordinate cryptographic policies. As part of this effort, governments should remove, or avoid creating in the name of cryptography policy, unjustifiable obstacles to trade (OECD, 1997, p. 2).

Concurrently, a committee of EU Member States on information security issues, entitled SOG-IS, was created to advise on cryptography. This led to pilot projects using TTPs for the provision of cryptographic key management services. In August 1994, the Commission Services evolved a further programme that concentrated on a Europe-wide network of TTPs (ETS). The Commission's proposals were subject to lengthy discussions between representatives of the member states with regard to the role of the member states and the Commission in introducing pan-EU services and legal enforcements concerning confidential services. From 1994 to 1997 the Commission sponsored an ETS Preparatory Programme that included eight TTP pilot projects. Member states backed an EU-wide framework for TTPs that would allow for complementary standards throughout Europe.

More recently, at an EU level, there has been a downgrading of the TTP mechanism in favour of the removal of the restrictions to e-commerce. In October 1997, the Commission adopted a policy framework for more security of Internet services. It made a clear distinction between the encryption of data that may preserve its *confidentiality* and digital (or now re-titled electronic) signatures that ensure the *integrity* of the data. The Commission suggested that the regulation of encryption could restrict the expansion of the information and communications marketplace. Instead, it proposed the following recommendations.

- A community framework for digital signatures.
- A common European certification of Certified Authorities.
- The adaptation of national legal systems to ensure that they offer the same recognition and treatment to digital as well as conventional signatures.
- An international framework for electronic communication outside the European Union.
- National restrictions over encryption must be compatible with Community law and the Commission will examine their justification and whether they respect the principle of proportionality.
- The adaptation of Dual-Use regulation for the requirements of the cryptographic products markets and its improvement through the progressive dismantling of intra-community controls on commercial encryption products.
- Instead of inefficient or cumbersome restrictions, the Commission invites and supports member states to enhance co-operation between national police forces on a European and international level.
- International agreements between the European Community and other states once a harmonised system has been established.
- The absolute necessity for interoperability between different encryption and digital signature applications to be reached through technical, infrastructure, industry and international standardisation.

- A Commission-led cryptographic services programme to develop overall strategies for the security of electronic communication.
- New projects aimed at interoperability, the enhancement of privacy and stimulating best practice and encouraging widescale deployment within the fifth research and development Framework Programme (1998–2002).
- The creation of a European Internet-Forum as a means to inform and exchange information.
- The organisation of a policy consultation period from the beginning of 1998 with governments, industry and consumers concerning 'digital signature and encryption' (European Commission, 1997, pp. 2–3).

Therefore, throughout the responses of the OECD and the European Commission there has been a clear concern to set out international standards that would ensure consistency and interoperability within national services. Both bodies responded to the issues surrounding lawful access and key escrow. For instance in March 1997 the OECD issued cryptographic recommendations which rejected the US proposal to enforce key escrow through legislation. The OECD was critical of legislation that would limit user choice and warned against any unjustified obstacles to international trade and the creation of new information networks.

The European Commission originally sought to employ licensed TTP mechanisms to ensure lawful access alongside cryptography schemes. More recently, in its proposals for a common framework for electronic signatures, it has preferred to use a voluntary system of Certified Authorities to preserve security, trust and authentication. In particular, the Commission has set out essential requirements for signature certificates and certification services, as well as placing a ban on the storage of private signature keys. Therefore, at an EU level, there has ultimately been a rejection of the TTP mechanism as the Commission has deemed that its principle role as a policy initiator should be to facilitate the development of e-commerce.

The British Government and the DTI Policy Responses

In Britain, the DTI has produced policy responses that have attempted to be compatible with the international legislative and regulatory frameworks. In March 1997, in one of its last actions under the Conservatives, the DTI published a policy document *Licensing of Trusted Third Parties for the Provision of Encryption Services* (DTI, 1997). Within this document, the

British government determined that TTPs were necessary in order for policing authorities to gain lawful access to encrypted material. Moreover, the report proposed legislation which would ensure that digital signatures were recognised by the law courts.

The main concern was the compulsory licensing of TTPs. The Department recommended that British cryptographic legislation should prohibit any organisation or TTP from providing encryption services to the public without a licence. Such compulsory licensing was required irrespective of whether a charge had or had not been made for cryptographic management services. Further, cryptographic management services offered by unlicensed foreign TTPs, for instance via the Internet, were prohibited. The proposals also placed restrictions on the advertising and marketing of unlicensed TTP services (DTI, 1997, p. 72).

During the subsequent consultation process, these recommendations were subjected to extensive criticism. First, it was argued that there should be, as in the EC response, a clear differentiation between digital signature services that were designed to preserve the integrity of data and encryption services that were employed to ensure confidentiality. Second, it was felt that the DTI had confused the methods of key recovery with key escrow or storage. Third, the communications industry believed that users would avoid TTPs because they would contravene the free flow of information. Further, other criticisms contended that TTPs would not necessarily provide an effective mechanism to stem either the encryption of criminal or terrorist material on the Internet (DTI, 1998c, p. 4). Conversely, a number of commentators suggested that while TTPs should be welcomed, that compulsory forms of licensing could prove to be problematic. Some service providers maintained that these licensing procedures were too costly and restrictive. It was felt that the DTI was trying to establish a system in which users were being told that they could use encryption, but only if all these services, such as key certification, storage, digital signatures and time stamping, were accomplished by the TTP. This strategy would undermine consumer choice and might prove to be anti-competitive as the TTPs could enjoy gatekeeping powers as the repositories of sensitive information.

Therefore, several responses advocated a tiered approach, in which varying licensing conditions would be applied to TTPs in regard to their range of encryption functions. Alternatively, another set of commentaries suggested that voluntary forms of licensing, even though they had not been discussed, could be employed. It was argued that voluntary licensing would encourage: (1) unlicensed TTPs where the market required them; and (2) a definition or clarification of those services, which would be excluded from the licensing regime.

With the ascendancy of the Labour government, the DTI's most recent cryptographic policies have advocated voluntary forms of TTP licensing. As a consequence, the DTI has recommended new proposals which will neither oblige service providers to obtain licences nor enforce them to employ any specific encryption technology or product (DTI, 1998b, p. 5). However, the Labour government still maintains that cryptographic management services should be licensed.

Further, the lawful access of communication services remains at the forefront of DTI thinking. The Department claims that, between 1996 and 1997, the lawful interception of ICT communications led to 1,200 arrests. Moreover, in the course of their communications operations, the police and HM Customs seized three tonnes worth of Class A drugs and 112 tonnes of other drugs; over £700 million pounds worth of cash and property; and 450 firearms. Thus, the government has stated that it intends to:

> enable law enforcement agencies to obtain a warrant for lawful access to information necessary to decrypt the content of communications or stored data (in effect, the encryption key). This does not include cryptographic keys used solely for digital signature purposes. The new powers will apply to those holding such information (whether licensed or not) and to users of encryption products. They will be exercisable only when the appropriate authority has been obtained (DTI, 1998b, p. 5).

In the 1998 Queen's Speech, the UK government announced a Secure Electronic Commerce Bill that would respond to the calls for regulating encrypted software, thereby reducing electronic crime. Principally, the Bill will grant the equivalent legal status for electronic signatures as already exists for written (on paper) material; establish a licensing regime, Trusted Third Party and a voluntary licensing code of practice to govern data encryption; and determine equivalent legal status between electronic and manual processes so that law enforcement agencies can access encrypted information. At the time of writing, the Parliamentary Trade and Industry Committee is inquiring into all aspects of e-commerce. It will also have to conform to the European Commission's Directive on Digital Signatures (the means through which encrypted data can be authenticated).

These developments exist, hand in hand, with the publication of the 1998 White Paper entitled *Our Competitive Future: Building the Knowledge Driven Economy*, (DTI, 1998e) in which the DTI proposed to establish a voluntary licensing scheme for organisations providing secure electronic message services. Throughout its policy statements, such as *Net Benefit: the Electronic Commerce Agenda for the UK*, the DTI has re-iterated its commitment to employ TTP mechanisms to resolve the dilemma between e-commerce, privacy rights and lawful access. It suggests that legislation will be required for the licensing of TTPs to encourage user confidence in professional key management and storage facilities. The DTI has further argued that new solutions may be realised through public and private sector partnerships. As a consequence, the DTI's response to the encryption of communication services foresees new forms of collaboration with different interested parties or stakeholders to encourage economic growth, the protection of privacy rights and the state's legal access to encrypted communication services. To this end, the Labour government's approaches to the information sector are reflective of the general principles that have underpinned its economic and industrial policies.

Conclusion

Internet service providers and users are seeking to exploit the opportunities that have accompanied the growth of e-commerce. As they expand their services, they need to remain secure and confident in their belief that communications data and financial transactions on the Web are protected by cryptographic systems. Encryption through secret keys, public and private keys, digital signatures and Certified Authorities must ensure the integrity, veracity and truthful nature of the data. Thus, governments, at a national and international level, have actively pursued policies that have been designed to encourage the development of encryption services. In particular, there have been policy recommendations concerning the international standardisation of cryptographic systems, removals to market barriers and the development of cryptographic management schemes such as the Trusted Third Parties.

However, the advocacy of TTPs, which are central repositories for sensitive material enabling policing authorities with legitimate warrants to gain lawful access to data, makes conspicuous governmental concerns over the encryption of illicit, illegal or dangerous material. States fear that cryptographic systems, by ensuring the privacy and anonymity of digital data can provide opportunities for criminal or terrorist activities. Therefore, international and national governments have been faced with a dilemma. On the one hand, they see the enormous benefits that can be drawn from the future developments within e-commerce. On the other, they want to retain control over the content which is flowing across the Internet. These policy responses raise a variety of issues that will have to be resolved in the near future.

First, if states insist on central management schemes, there are several licensing concerns. Most especially, in Britain, a debate has arisen between mandatory and voluntary forms of licensing. Internet service providers argue that compulsory forms of licensing will prove to be a drain on resources and undermine their expansion or growth. This would seem to directly contravene the current Labour Party's stated aim of establishing Britain as 'digital pathfinder' for the rest of Europe. Therefore, the current British government has determined to pursue a voluntary form of TTP licensing.

Second, such a form of centralisation would appear to go against the widely held belief that the Internet is a medium which will decentralise communication services so that they will directly respond to the individual's need. As Noam Chomsky ironically commented several years ago:

> Things are going in both directions. Institutionally the major tendency is centralisation. The other tendency in the opposite direction... is much more diffuse and nothing much in the way of organised institutional forms (Chomsky, 1994, p. 148).

In the midst of these two opposing tendencies, the employment of TTPs, which allow for the state's lawful access to the user's private digital data or communications whilst encrypting services, brings into question privacy rights in the digital future. Civil liberty organisations suggest that there are significant dangers in allowing the state or policing authorities to gain access to private forms of communication. There is a particular irony in a future situation in which services may be encrypted to preserve the integrity of data, only for that data to be accessed by an unseen third party. It is feared that the surveillance forces could abuse their powers and individual liberties will be subsumed. Further, as the civil liberty organisations have commented, state or policing authorities have hardly had an outstanding track-record in placing private rights above their own surveillance requirements.

Yet, on the other side of the debate, it is difficult to ignore the legitimate calls for greater degrees of accountability in Internet usage and the need to establish legal mechanisms to counter criminality. In particular, it is feared that encrypted services will allow criminals to traffic drugs, people or illegal pornography across the Web. Over the last ten years, the dangers have grown as the Internet has become a forum for extremist political groups. Web-sites advocating racial hatred, anti-Semitism, the murder of doctors practicing abortions and neo-Fascist beliefs have proliferated. Moreover, the example of the Oklahoma bombing demonstrated how the Internet could provide the means for 'patriotic groups' to develop associations that defied any legal circumscriptions.

Clearly the issue is one of balance. Governments will have to find ways in which the rights of users can be complimented by limited degrees of surveillance. Currently, as consultations between the legislators and the information industries are taking place, governments need to popularise these debates and raise public awareness about the crucial nature of the issues surrounding cryptography. Moreover, the concerns raised about state licensing for encryption services and the dilemma between individual liberty and lawful access draw our attention back to the role of the state as a policy initiator for the information superhighway. Presently, the development of ICTs provides national and international governments with significant challenges. It remains to be said that to maximise public benefit within the digital age, the state has an important role in facilitating the communications market so that it will be open and equitable to all sectors of society. In many respects, the future contours of the information superhighway are being set at this moment. Therefore, for the good of present and future generations, such initiatives must be thoroughly debated so that policy responses will enhance, rather than undermine, societal rights.

Note

1. Demon Internet 'Responses to the DTI's TTP Proposals', http:www.demon.net/news/features/crypt/responses/html, 10 June 1998, p. 4.

9 Policing the Internet: Concerns for Cyber-Rights

YAMAN AKDENIZ

> Information is the key to the modern age. The new age of information offers possibilities for the future limited only by the boundaries of our imaginations. The potential of the new electronic networks is breathtaking – the prospect of change as widespread and fundamental as the agricultural and industrial revolutions of earlier eras. (Tony Blair, 16 April 1998)[1]

Until the 1990s there were no restrictions on Internet usage or content. Governments did not concern themselves because Internet access was available mainly to a relatively small community of academics and engineers at universities, government research institutions and commercial research institutions. Despite the largely serious and academic nature of most material, a sub-culture also flourished of bizarre sexually-oriented, politically-oriented, and other materials often considered to be 'wacko'. The presence of such materials was tolerated by all users and even considered to be a sign of the health of the medium.

The 1990s witnessed the Internet boom in Western countries and access to this global medium became possible through not only academic and military institutions but also from workplaces and homes. The UK government is committed to the development of the Internet and electronic commerce and also committed to providing wider access to the Internet within the UK. Ongoing initiatives include the provision of Internet access from schools and the UK government is trying to build an Information Society starting with the younger generation (Chapter 2; House of Lords, Select Committee on Science and Technology, 1996, Ch. 2; European Commission, 1997, 1998).

UK NetYear, part of what Tony Blair, the Prime Minster, referred to as 'the biggest public-private partnership in any education system anywhere in the world', was launched in January 1998.[2]

In relation to the development of electronic commerce the government has produced several papers even though the Electronic Commerce Bill (which was announced in the October 1998 Queen's Speech) has yet to be finalised at the time of writing.[3]   In April 1998, the DTI published the *Secure Electronic Commerce Statement*[4] which was followed by yet another consultation paper in March 1999.[5]   In between, the government through the DTI launched the Net Benefit: The Electronic Commerce Agenda for the UK[6] in October 1998 and even though the government policy has been consistent, it has been widely criticised by the Internet industry, civil liberties organisations, and Internet users (see Chapter 8).

The DTI through its Future Unit also published *Converging Technologies: Consequences for the New Knowledge-Driven Economy* in September 1998 (DTI, 1998d). This follows the July 1998 publication of *Regulating Communications: Approaching Convergence in the Information Age* (DTI and Department for Culture, Media and Sport, 1998).

These positive developments were followed by the Prime Minister launching Britain's National Grid for Learning, which will give schools access to on-line information and teaching materials in November 1998. The four year target is to connect every school to the Internet and to train all teachers how to use it. The Prime Minister also announced new funding of £450 million for the years 2000–2002, on top of the £102 million available for 1998 and £105 million for 1999.[7] The Prime Minister also unveiled the biggest IT training and investment programme ever undertaken by a British government in April 1998.[8] The eight-point strategy for the Information Age hopes to boost IT training and deliver greater access to computers in schools, libraries and hospitals.

The Prime Minister when launching the Information Age stated that:

> We are in the throes of an information revolution. It is vital that Britain leads the way, so that we can be Europe's pioneer in what is now known as the Information Age. I have set out today an ambitious programme of how the Government can help meet the challenges of the Information Age.[9]

Most of these initiatives by the UK government are positive and 'the rise of the network society', (Castells, 1996) is encouraging for the future of the Internet at least within Britain. But at the same time there are negative developments related to the above positive initiatives.

Following the Internet boom in the early 1990s, the government, quasi regulators and the law enforcement bodies started to worry about the emergence of cyber-crimes and forms of Internet content that may be illegal and/or harmful.   While the summer of 1995 marked the start of the cyberporn debate within the USA (Wallace and Mangan, 1996), since 1996 this moral panic about Internet content concentrated on child pornography within the UK and elsewhere in Europe. Britain witnessed pressures on Internet Service Providers and calls for regulation of the Internet in the summer of 1996 that led to self-regulatory actions being taken (Akdeniz, 1997a).

Therefore, there are two major political concerns for the government. These are the regulation of Internet content, and the emergence of cyber-crimes. Further sections of this chapter will analyse the policing of the Internet within the UK in the light of developments within the European Union.[10] The emphasis will be on content regulation issues and privacy concerns in relation to policing of the Internet. The main concern for the law enforcement bodies and regulators remains the availability and distribution of illegal content such as child pornography and the publication of official secrets[11] over the Internet, the incidental use of the Internet for existing crimes such as fraud (Davis, 1998, pp. 48–61), and the emergence of specific cyber-crimes (Sieber, 1998; Wall, 1998, pp. 79–90) such as unauthorised access (hacking) to computer networks (Akdeniz, 1996a).

However, the current regulatory and self-regulatory initiatives of the UK government go further than the concerns raised for the above issues by the law enforcement bodies. Some of the policies pursued by the government may have a direct effect on basic human rights such as freedom of expression and privacy and reactions to these legitimate concerns may result in overregulation and censorship of the Internet.

Consequently, the regulation of the above politically important issues may have serious affects on the rights of individual Internet users. Specifically, restrictions on the availability of Internet content considered to be harmful but which remains legal (Internet Watch Foundation)[12] may result as an act of censorship and as an assault on cyber-speech. Equally, the government's insistence on access to encryption keys (DTI, 1998a; Chapter 8), with the introduction of a trusted third party system, (DTI, 1996, 1997), would undermine the security, integrity and privacy of communications over the Internet (Akdeniz, 1997a, 1997b, 1998a; Bowden and Akdeniz, 1998; Walker and Akdeniz, 1998a). In addition to these issues, the uncontrolled ways in which the law enforcement bodies can obtain personal information through the UK Internet Service Providers in relation to their users may again undermine personal privacy, data protection principles, and privacy of communications. The following sections of this chapter will explore these issues.

The UK Government 's Approach to Internet Content Regulation

The UK government favours self-regulatory solutions[13] for Internet content regulation rather than the introduction of any specific legislation (unlike the US government)[14] in relation to Internet content. The UK government policy is consistent with the European Union policy and with the European Commission's Action Plan on Safer Use of the Internet (Akdeniz, 1998b).

The EU Action Plan encourages the creation of a European network of hotlines to report illegal content such as child pornography by on-line users, the development of self-regulatory and content-monitoring schemes by access and content providers, the development of internationally compatible and interoperable rating and filtering schemes to protect users, and measures to increase awareness of the possibilities available among parents, teachers, children and other consumers to help these groups to use the networks while choosing the appropriate content and exercising a reasonable amount of parental control.

So far, within the UK, much of the debate revolved around the availability of sexually explicit content over the Internet (Akdeniz, 1999). However, the preferred solutions for the availability of such content have not been carefully assessed or examined by the UK government. Therefore, some of these initiatives favoured by the government (and by the European Commission) but enforced or developed by quasi-governmental bodies would almost amount to censorship of legal Internet content apart from being ineffective (Walker and Akdeniz, 1998b).

The possible drawbacks of the above proposals include: (1) the effectiveness of Internet hotlines for reporting illegal content at a national level; and (2) the serious implications for freedom of expression by the use of the current technologies such as rating systems to be applied to a certain type of Internet content deemed to be harmful. In other words, most of these systems are currently defective as they can be used for the exclusion of socially useful information on the Internet. At the same time, these defective systems give only a false sense of security for the concerned Internet users.

Illegal Content

The regulation of illegal content would be dealt with by the enforcement of national criminal laws such as the Protection of Children Act 1978, and the Obscene Publications Act 1959,[15] and the law enforcement bodies may be assisted by national hotlines to report illegal content in their investigations as suggested by the European Commission.

So far there have been many police operations in relation to the availability of child pornography on the Internet[16] and these operations resulted with many successful prosecutions involving possession and distribution of child pornography.

However, the availability of child pornography on the Internet (mainly through the Usenet discussion groups) and its provision by the Internet Service Providers (ISPs) resulted in police pressure on the ISPs. Many within the law enforcement service believe that ISPs should be doing something about the availability of such content through their servers without taking into account the technical limitations of monitoring Internet content by the ISPs. Such pressures on the ISPs resulted in the successful prosecution of CompuServe in Germany in May 1998 mainly for the distribution of child pornography.[17] Similar pressures on the UK ISPs resulted in the creation of an industry-based self-regulatory body in September 1996.

Internet Watch Foundation

Internet Watch Foundation (IWF), a self-regulatory body supported by the UK government, was announced in September 1996 initially as a hotline to deal with the existence of illegal material on the Internet. The IWF also deals with the development of rating systems at a UK level, and in February 1998 they recommended these systems as the best way to deal with the availability of harmful Internet content especially for minors.

The Department of Trade and Industry and the Home Office played key roles in the establishment of the IWF. According to a Minister at the DTI,

> as part of its remit to help ensure that the Internet can be a safe place to work, learn and play, the IWF has convened an advisory board comprising representatives of content providers, children's charities, regulators from other media, ISPs and civil liberties groups, to propose a UK-focused system for rating Internet content.[18]

In fact, no civil liberties organisations were involved or consulted as was pointed by the Cyber-Rights and Cyber-Liberties (UK) November 1997 report, leaving the IWF a predominantly industry-based private organisation with important public duties (Cyber-Rights and Cyber-Liberties UK, 1997).

IWF as a Hotline to Report Illegal Internet Content

The activities of the IWF mainly concentrate on the Usenet discussion groups and mainly in relation to child pornography. Once the IWF locate the 'undesirable content', mainly child pornography through reports made by Internet users,[19] IWF informs all British ISPs and the police.

According to the first IWF annual report that was published in March 1998 (which covers the period between December 1996 and November 1997), there were 781 reports to the Foundation from on-line users and in 248 of them action was taken. These reports resulted in the review of 4,324 items, and the Foundation took action in 2,215 of them. 1,394 of these originated from the USA while only 125 of the items originated from the UK.[20]

In the IWF's 1998 statistics, the number of reports reached 2,407 and in 447 action was taken (430 of the action reports contained child pornography).[21] These involved 14,580 items in which the IWF took action on 10,548. Of these, 9,176 of these were referred to the National Criminal Intelligence Service (NCIS), 541 to the UK police, and also 9,498 to the UK ISPs as well. A total of 12 per cent of this content originated from the UK, while 49 per cent originated from the USA.

The figures alone tell us little as the actual amount of child pornography on the Internet is unknown. It is, therefore, difficult to judge how successful the UK hotline has been. While around 9,498 items were removed from the servers of UK ISPs, it is not known how many new images are posted to various newsgroups (replacing those removed images) within the time framework of the above activities, and it is not known how much child pornography is out there in the Wild West Web while the activities of the hotline is concentrated on the Usenet discussion groups.

Another downside is that the efforts of the organisation are concentrated on the newsgroups carried by the UK ISPs. This means that while illegal material is removed from the UK ISPs' servers, the same material will continue to be available on the Internet carried by the foreign ISPs in their own servers.

The expensive monitoring of the Internet at a national level is of limited value as the few problems created by the Internet remain global ones and thus require global solutions. While the UK government should be involved with finding solutions to global problems with its international partners, the global problems do not justify expensive monitoring of the Internet at a national level by industry based organisations.

Undoubtedly, the availability and distribution of child pornography should be regulated, whether on the Internet or elsewhere. The main concern of law enforcement and regulatory bodies should, however, remain the prevention of child abuse – the involvement of children in the making of pornography, or its use to groom them to become involved in abusive acts, rather than the cleansing of the Internet of such images (Akdeniz, 1997a).

Harmful Content – The UK Perspective on Rating and Filtering Technologies

In February 1998, the Internet Watch Foundation announced its consultation paper for the development of rating systems at a national level.[22] According to an IWF press release, rating systems would 'meet parents' concerns about Internet content that is unsuitable for children'. According to John Battle, then Minister for Science, Energy and Industry, 'such ratings and filtering tools can be extremely useful in helping parents and other adults who care for children to decide on the types of legal material they wish their children to access'.[23]

The consultation document by the IWF did not discuss whether these systems were suitable for Britain or, more significantly, whether they were needed at all. A decision had already been taken by the UK organisation to develop these systems, and the consultation paper addressed how to develop the systems and had a set of recommendations which suggested that the decision in principle was already taken – rating systems are good and should be developed for use in Britain.

The arbitrary decision taken by the IWF consultation document was supported by the UK government and by the members of the Parliament. For example, Alun Michael then of the Home Office stated that:

We also encourage other non-statutory schemes which are designed to protect young people from unsuitable material such as the working group of representatives from the Internet Watch Foundation and Internet Service Providers which is devising a common ratings system for United Kingdom Internet Users... .[24]

Similarly, Mr Michael also stated that:

Filtering software packages, such as Net Nanny, are available which enable parents to deny access to material containing sexually explicit words. Building on this, a working group of representatives from the IWF and Internet Service Providers has been devising a common ratings system suitable for United Kingdom Internet users on which there is growing international co-operation. This system is expected to address legal, but potentially offensive, material without curtailing freedom of expression. The

Foundation aims to work on this system over the next 18 months and, once it is available, expects it to extend to newsgroups as well as web sites.[25]

In April 1998, Paragraph (iv) of the DTI's *Secure Electronic Commerce Statement* (entitled 'Internet content'), which was mainly concerned about the regulation of the use of encryption technology and the development of electronic commerce stated that:

> As the Internet becomes a mass medium it is only right to ensure that the most vulnerable users are protected. This has meant supporting, and encouraging, such initiatives as the Internet Watch Foundation (IWF) to ensure that the law is applied on-line in the same way as it is off-line (DTI, 1998a).

Most recently, support to the IWF was given by the Prime Minister, Tony Blair:

> The Government supports the work of the Internet Watch Foundation which was established in September 1996 by Internet Service Providers primarily in response to growing concern about child pornography on the Internet. The Foundation passes all child pornography reports to the National Criminal Intelligence Service who route these to the relevant enforcement agency of the country concerned when the material appears to have originated outside the UK.[26]

Despite the establishment consensus, it would be more appropriate to establish a Working Group, with both representatives from the public and private sector, to assess the real problem of illegal and harmful content at a UK level rather than trying to find temporary or ineffective solutions to activities that do not necessarily take place within the British jurisdiction. Such a Working Group was established by the Irish Department of Justice, Equality and Law Reform to deal with these issues in 1997. The Irish Working Group published its first 100-page report entitled *Illegal and Harmful Use of the Internet*, and considered these issues from an Irish perspective (Department of Justice, Equality, and Law Reform, [Ireland], 1998).

In the UK a substantial study together with public consultation in this field is needed before moving forward. It is, therefore, the duty of the UK government to set up such an 'independent' working group that would assess the real amount of problems and seek the best solutions. However, the creation of such an independent body or wide public consultation is not expected in the near future.[27] At the same time, the IWF continues with its policy-making process and the development of rating and filtering systems within the UK, the European Union,[28] and elsewhere[29] despite the potential problems associated with such systems.

Rating and Filtering Systems and Cyber-speech

Although the use and development of rating systems are welcome by various governments including the UK government, their capacity is limited to certain parts of the Internet.

These systems are designed for World Wide Web sites while leaving out other Internet-related communications systems such as the chat environments,[30] file transfer protocol servers (ftp),[31] the Usenet discussion groups, real-audio and real-video systems that can include live sound and image transmissions, and finally e-mail systems. These systems cannot be rated with such systems known as Platform for Internet Content Selection (PICS) or Recreational Software Advisory Council on the Internet (RSACi) and therefore the assumption that rating systems would make the Internet a 'safer environment' for children is wrong as the WWW content represents only a fraction of the whole of the Internet content.

Even when the rating technology is applicable, it is not clear what the regulators have in mind when it comes to what sort of content should be rated. For example, according to the UK Internet Watch Foundation, there is 'a whole category of dangerous subjects' that require ratings and these include information related to drugs, sex, violence, information about dangerous sports such as bungee-jumping, and hate speech material.[32] This kind of content would certainly include such publications as *The Anarchist Cookbook* (Powell, 1989)[33] that can be downloaded from not only WWW sites but also can be obtained through ftp servers or through the use of automatic e-mail services apart from its availability through well-known bookshops within the UK. Therefore, rating systems would not in any way be a complete solution to content deemed to be harmful to minors.

Furthermore, if the duty of rating is handed to third parties, this would pose free speech problems and with few third-party rating products currently available, the potential for arbitrary censorship increases (note that no UK-based third party rating body currently exists). This would mean that there would be no space for free speech arguments and dissent because the ratings would be done by private bodies and the governments will not be involved 'directly'. When censorship is implemented by government threat in the background, but run by private parties, legal action is nearly impossible, accountability difficult, and the system is not open or democratic. In fact, none of the criticisms in relation to these issues were taken into account by the IWF (Cyber-Rights and Cyber-Liberties (UK), 1997, 1998).

Another downside of relying on such technologies is that these systems are defective and in most cases they are used for the exclusion of socially useful web-sites and information. The general excuse remains the protection of children from harmful content and also the duty of the industry to give more choices to the consumers. Filtering software and rating systems will be used to exclude minority views and socially useful sites rather than protecting children from anything.[34]

Furthermore, while children's access is the most cited excuse for the regulation of the Internet, in fact, it is not possible for children to have their own Internet accounts without the involvement of an adult, as it is not possible to get an Internet account through an Internet Service Provider before the age of 18 in almost all countries. Therefore, there is always a role to play for the adults and parents in relation to the children's access to the Internet and adults should act responsibly towards children's Internet usage rather than relying on technical solutions that do not fully address the problems that may be raised by some Internet content.

Furthermore, any regulatory action intended to protect a certain group of people, such as children, should not take the form of an unconditional and universal prohibition on using the Internet to distribute content that is freely available to adults in other media. The US Supreme Court stated in the case of *Reno v ACLU*,[35] that 'the Internet is not as "invasive" as radio or television and confirmed the finding of the US Court of Appeal that 'communications over the Internet do not "invade" an individual's home or appear on one's computer screen unbidden'.

It should be noted that current solutions offered at various fora, such as the development of rating and filtering systems, may not be the real answers and solutions for the existing problems and may result in the censorship of Internet content that is not illegal at all. Furthermore, as the Economic and Social Committee of the European Commission has pointed out, it is highly unlikely that the proposed measures will in the long term result in a safe Internet with the rating and classification of all information on the Internet being 'impracticable' (EcoSoc, 1998, pp. 29–32). The Committee, therefore, concluded that there is 'little future in the active promotion of filtering systems based on rating' (Walker and Akdeniz, 1998b, pp. 5–19).

Policing the Internet and Privacy Concerns

With the advancement of technology, the police have been facing formidable difficulties in dealing with crimes where computer systems are involved. So far the lack of experience, training and technical resources to keep up with the accelerating development of a sophisticated information society has exposed the law enforcement agencies to criticism from an anxious public. In particular, for failing to control the use of the Internet by cyber-criminals including paedophiles,[36] stalkers, hackers, and terrorists (Ellison and Akdeniz, 1998, pp. 29–48).

Calls for the regulation of the Internet were initially made in the summer of 1997, following a 10-month study by the NCIS[37] into the use of the Internet by professional criminals, terrorists and political extremists. NCIS allegedly requested urgent action to introduce laws enabling police to intercept and monitor e-mails.[38]

In November 1997, the Association of Chief Police Officers (ACPO) Computer Crime Unit together with the Internet Service Providers established the ACPO/ISPs Government Forum with the objective of developing good practice guidelines between law enforcement agencies and the Internet Service Providers industry, describing what information can lawfully and reasonably be provided to law enforcement agencies, and the procedures to be followed. Given the concern over cyber-crimes and cyber-criminals it is entirely understandable that the police and the ISPs should wish to develop mutual understanding and support, and to establish working relationships (Akdeniz and Bohm, 1999, pp. 20–24). For fighting Internet related crimes, the law enforcement agencies need to collaborate with the ISP industry to obtain evidence in relation to their investigations. However, it is argued that the legal rules on obtaining evidence through the ISPs are not so clear in addition to legal requirements for interception of Internet communications and therefore the Forum is working on these issues.

However, this initiative has caused considerable concern among the British Internet users and media.[39] According to Akdeniz and Bohm, 'any reader who finds this puzzling should try the thought experiment of reading the Forum's aims and objectives while replacing references to the ISPs with references to the Banks' (1999, p. 23). The main fear from a civil libertarian perspective was the fact that the law enforcement bodies and the Internet industry were not representing the rights and liberties of individual Internet users within the UK. Furthermore, the Forum did not consider at all the impact of the Human Rights Act 1998, which has incorporated the European Convention on Human Rights into the English legal system. Other legal issues that may prevent law enforcement agencies accessing the personal data of Internet users through the Internet Service Providers have also been incorporated. Article 8 of the European Convention refers to a 'right to respect for private life' and it states that:

(1)   Everyone has the right to respect for his private and family life, his home and his correspondence.

(2)   There shall be no interference by a public authority with the exercise of this right except such as is in accordance with the law and is necessary in a democratic society in the interests of national security, public safety or the economic well-being of the country, for the prevention of disorder of crime, for the protection of health or morals, or for the protection of the rights and freedoms of others.

It should be noted that Article 8 expressly incorporates a right to privacy in 'correspondence', and this has long been interpreted by the European Court of Human Rights as including privacy in relation to communications via telecommunications networks.[40]

As a result of concerns expressed about these issues, Cyber-Rights and Cyber-Liberties (UK) has developed a 'privacy letter'[41] to be sent from a subscriber to an ISP addressing the position from the subscriber's point of view. A number of ISPs have replied as they are responsive to these concerns, but further evidence is needed before conclusions can be drawn.[42] It should also be noted that the approach Cyber-Rights and Cyber-Liberties (UK) have taken with the development of the 'privacy letter' is consistent with the February 1999 Recommendation of the Council of Europe 'for the Protection of Privacy on the Internet'.[43]

Furthermore, a Cyber-Rights and Cyber-Liberties (UK)'s report entitled *Who Watches the Watchmen: Part III – ISP Capabilities for the Provision of Personal Information to the Police*, (1999), showed that there were legitimate concerns in relation to privacy issues involving the Internet Service Providers and law enforcement bodies.

Encryption Debate

In addition to the privacy concerns raised by the desire of the law enforcement agencies to access personal data and Internet communications, the policy initiatives in relation to the use of encryption technology to secure electronic communications do involve important privacy issues. The government is currently trying to formulate an Electronic Commerce Bill, (see Chapter 8). This piece of legislation and the various proposals and initiatives through the Department of Trade and Industry do balance the need for a regulatory framework for electronic commerce with the need of the law enforcement agencies to deal with cyber-crimes.[44] The government view is that access to encryption keys is vital as far as access to encrypted communications are concerned, even though there is no substantial evidence that the use of encryption technology is creating problems for the law enforcement (Cyber-Rights and Cyber-Liberties, 1999). In any event, strong encryption systems without backdoor capabilities are currently available and easily obtainable and it would be fanciful to expect that criminals will use the government mandated encryption systems.

A survey of recent Internet-related papers including the most recent March 1999 consultation paper[45] issued by the DTI would strongly suggest that privacy is not one of its prime concerns. So far, privacy issues in relation to the use of strong encryption systems have never been addressed fully by the government. This silence is especially remarkable in the light of other governmental initiatives such as the above-mentioned Human Rights Act 1998 (Akdeniz, *et al*, 1999). Furthermore, according to the European Commission (1997):

> International treaties, constitutions and laws guarantee the fundamental right to privacy including secrecy of communications. Therefore, the debate about the prohibition or limitation of the use of encryption directly affects the right to privacy, its effective exercise and the harmonisation of data protection laws in the Internal Market. [46]

Indeed, the United Kingdom has already been found to be in breach of Article 8 of the European Convention on Human Rights (ECHR) on several occasions for failing to pay adequate attention to the value of privacy.[47] Therefore there is a substantial risk that Internet-related proposals emanating from the DTI are in danger of repeating this error.

These national and international developments, which express significant support for data privacy, should have important implications for the treatment of encryption and privacy of communications. The use of privacy-enhancing technologies such as encryption should be *prima facie* respected and even encouraged. By contrast, the government approach should be criticised as being fixated on the value of encryption solely in connection with commerce and ignoring wider political and social uses of information technology that might legitimately require the use of encryption.

Conclusions

The Internet as a global medium does not recognise boundaries and with this new reality comes an evermore pressing need to align national strategies with the rest of the world toward a global information society that respects fundamental human rights such as freedom of expression and privacy. The enactment of the Human Rights Act 1998, which incorporated the European Convention on Human Rights into the English legal system is a major step towards a new era in which 'the result will be the beginning of the strong development of a human rights culture in this country'.[48]

It is necessary to emphasise the importance of some of the fundamental principles to be observed and taken into account while decisions are taken by government and government bodies in relation to Internet policy-making. All policy initiatives (including those by quasi-regulatory bodies such as the IWF) should be compatible with the Human Rights Act 1998.

Furthermore, all policy initiatives and those who are involved with the policy making process should take into account the Nolan Committee principles on good standards in public life, which established the 'Seven Principles of Public Life'[49] and which apply to all aspects of public life. The Committee has set them out for the benefit of all who serve the public in any way. In addition to the Nolan Committee principles, the Better Regulation Task Force's[50] Principles of Good Regulation[51] can provide further guidance for initiatives in Internet-related policy issues.

The Task Force defines regulation 'as any government measure or intervention which controls the behaviour of individuals or groups. Government regulation can both promote the rights and liberties of citizens, and restrict the behaviour of citizens' (1998, p. 1) and according to the Task Force 'whilst recognising such philosophic differences, governments should be satisfied that regulations are necessary, fair, effective, balanced, and enjoy a broad degree of public confidence' apart from the regulatory process being transparent and open.

The government and its agencies therefore should respect the fundamental rights of its citizens such as freedom of expression and privacy under the Human Rights Act 1998 and should take into account the other principles described above while formulating its Internet-related policies. The government should also support the 'active and accelerated promotion of the Internet as a vital engine of social and economic development' (House of Commons Select Committee on Culture, Media and Sport, 1998).

According to this House of Commons Select Committee, international initiatives will have an important impact on national Internet regulation but at the same time 'the question is whether such attempts at regulation can be anything more than optimistically indicative rather than genuinely effective' (House of Commons Select Committee on Culture, Media and Sport, 1998, Vol. I, para. 108). This is true and the global nature of the Internet should be taken into account while policies are fostered as the Internet is too widespread to be easily dominated by any single government and with technologies that increasingly destroy distance, the challenge of seizing the opportunities of the new age are not merely national, but global in nature. This is not to mean that the Internet should be outside the domain of governmental regulations and that there should be no laws governing the Internet. However, unnecessary restrictions would make Britain a second-class nation for network development or for any other high-tech industry and investment in the Information Age, despite the government's commitment to the development of the Internet. Moreover, government-imposed censorship, over-regulation, or service provider liability[52] will do nothing to keep people from obtaining 'undesirable material'. Such objectionable Internet content will continue to be accessible on servers in other countries, as happened with the availability of the JET Report on 37 different web-sites on the Internet outside the UK (Akdeniz, 1997a), and more recently with the publication of an MI6 directory including over 100 names of active British spies over the Internet newsgroups and World Wide Web pages.[53]

Procedures can only be properly designed within a legal context that takes due account of individual rights and liberties. Such procedures are a matter of legitimate public interest, especially to Internet users. Accountability, effectiveness and openness will be the key elements of a democratic and healthy regulatory environment for Internet regulation and policies can only be developed within such a framework to achieve digital democracy in the Information Age.

Notes

1. See Prime Minister Launches Strategy for the Information Age, at 16 April, 1998 at http://www.number-10.gov.uk/textsite/info/releases/publications/infoagefeat.html.
2. Speech at the Labour Party Conference September 1997. See UK NetYear project at http://www.uknetyear.org/.
3. April 1999. For up to date information about the UK government encryption policy visit the Cyber-Rights and Cyber–Liberties (UK) at http://www.cyber-rights.org.
4. See http://www.dti.gov.uk/CII/ana27p.html.

5. Department of Trade and Industry, 'Building Confidence in Electronic Commerce', 5 March, 1999, at http://www.dti.gov.uk/cii/elec/elec_com.html. See also DTI and Home Office Press Release, 'Building Confidence in Electronic Commerce: Government Consults on Proposals to Make UK Best Place to Trade Electronically', P/99/200, 5 March, 1999, and BBC News, 'Encryption: the Civil-libertarian View', 5 March, 1999, and Cukier, K.N., 'UK Challenges Industry to Give Police Access to Crypto 'Key-Escrow' Introduced Unless Alternatives Found', *Communications Week International,* 15 March 1999, p. 1.

6. DTI, Net Benefit: The Electronic Commerce Agenda for the UK, DTI/Pub 3619, October 1998, at http://www.dti.gov.uk/CII/netbenefit.html. See also the associated Press Release, Net Benefit: Barbara Roche Sets Out Britain's Electronic Commerce Agenda, P/98/755 6 October 1998.

7. BBC News Online, 'Boost for Net Learning', 6 November 1998; BBC News Online, 'Super Grid Offers Fast Track for Colleges', 9 November 1998. See also the National Grid for Learning web-site at http://www.ngfl.gov.uk/.

8. See 'Prime Minister Launches Strategy for the Information Age', at 16 April 1998 at http://www.number-10.gov.uk/textsite/info/releases/publications/infoagefeat.html.

9. Ibid.

10. See generally the Special Edition of the *Criminal Law Review* entitled 'Crime, Criminal Justice and the Internet', December 1998.

11. Under section 1(1) of the Official Secrets Act 1989, 'A person who is or has been – (a) a member of the security and intelligence services, or (b) a person notified that he is subject to the provisions of this subsection, is guilty of an offence if without lawful authority he discloses any information, document or other article relating to security or intelligence which is or has been in his possession by virtue of his position as a member of any of those services or in the course of his work while the notification is or was in force'. See the following articles: Sprenger, P., 'Britain Shuts Down Spy Sites', *Wired News*, 13 May 1999; 'TRAITOR: Ex-spy puts Names of MI6 Agents on Internet in Revenge for Getting the Sack', *The Mirror*, 13 May, 1999; Arthur, C., and Lashmar, P., 'Dozens of British Agents Exposed on Net', *The Independent*, 13 May 1999.

12. For a critique of such initiatives see Cyber-Rights and Cyber-Liberties (UK) 1997, 1998.

13. See Safety-Net proposal, 'Rating, Reporting, Responsibility, For Child Pornography & Illegal Material on the Internet' adopted and recommended by the Executive Committee of ISPA – Internet Services Providers Association, LINX - London Internet Exchange and the Internet Watch Foundation at http://dtiinfo1.dti.gov.uk/safety-net/r3.htm.

14. See Communications Decency Act 1996 (47 USC s.223); ACLU v Reno (1997) 117 S. Ct. 2329.

15. Both pieces of legislation were amended by the 1994 Criminal Justice and Public Order Act to take into account technological developments. See further Akdeniz, Y. (1996b).

16. Operation Starburst and Operation Cathedral are among many other police investigations into the use of the Internet by paedophiles.
17. See the Local Court (Amtsgericht) Munich the Criminal case of Somm, Felix Bruno, File No: 8340 Ds 465 JS 173158/95,. An English version of the case is available at http://www.cyber-rights.org/isps/somm-dec.htm.
18. See Mrs Barbara Roche, DTI, Internet, Commons Written Answers, 26 June 1997.
19. See http://www.internetwatch.org.uk/hotline/report.html.
20. See the IWF statistics at http://www.internetwatch.org.uk/stats.html and the annual report at http://www.internetwatch.org.uk/annual.html.
21. 'Action taken' counts those reports which IWF has judged to contain potentially illegal material.
22. For the consultation paper and associated press releases see http://www.internetwatch.org.uk/rating/rating_r.html.
23. Adjournment Debate, HMG Strategy for the Internet: Memorandum by the Hon John Battle MP, Minister for Science, Energy and Industry, House of Commons, 18 March 1998, at http://www.dti.gov.uk/Minspeech/btlspch3.htm.
24. According to Mr. Alun Michael, Home Office, Commons Written Answers, 2 March 1998.
25. According to Mr Michael, Home Office, Commons Written Answers, 18 February 1998, Column: 678. See also Mr Michael's statement, Home Department (Internet), Commons Written Answers, 25 June 1997, Column: 510 [4902]. See for further support to the rating and filtering systems by Lord Clinton-Davis, The Minister of State, Department of Trade and Industry, Written Answers on Internet: Addiction, House of Lords, 1087, 27 March 1998.
26. Prime Minister Commons Written Answers 8 June 1998, Child Pornography. Similar statements were given through the UK Parliament within the last two years and the 'Net Benefit: The Electronic Commerce Agenda for the UK' document by the DTI also refers to the activities of the IWF. See DTI, 'Net Benefit: The Electronic Commerce Agenda for the UK', DTI/Pub 3619, October 1998, at http://www.dti.gov.uk/CII/netbenefit.html.
27. The DTI recently reviewed the IWF through a study by KPMG/Denton Hall and the government is pleased with this self-regulatory scheme. See the 'Review of the Internet Watch Foundation: A Report for the DTI and Home Office' by KPMG/Denton Hall, February 1999, at http://www.dti.gov.uk/CII/iwfreview/.
28. The INCORE (Internet Content Rating for Europe) project was set up by a group of European organisations including the UK's Internet Watch Foundation with common interest in industry self-regulation and rating of Internet content. It is now focused on a project that aims to create a generic rating and filtering system suitable for European users. This is being funded by the European Commission in 1999 under the Commission's Action Plan on promoting safer use of the Internet by combating illegal and harmful

content on global networks, Decision No. 276/1999/EC of the European Parliament and of the Council of 25 January 1999.

29. The IWF is also involved with the Internet Content Rating Alliance (ICRA) project with the mission 'to develop an internationally acceptable rating system which provides Internet users world wide with the choice to limit access to content they consider harmful, especially to children'. See the IWF Press Release, 'Consultations on International Internet Self-Rating System launched', 7 October 1998.

30. Interactive environments such as chat channels cannot be rated as the exchange and transmission of information takes place live and spontaneously.

31. Estimated amount of ftp servers on the Internet is about one million. Some of these on-line libraries may have offensive content or legal content that may be considered harmful to children.

32. *Wired News*, 'Europe Readies Net Content Ratings', 7 July 1997.

33. In fact, there are many similar books available through various bookshops and libraries including Harber, D. (1990), *The Anarchist Arsenal : Improvised Incendiary and Explosives Techniques*; Feral, R. (1983), *Hit Man: A Technical Manual for Independent Contractors*, and Hutchinson, M. (1988) *The Poisoner's Handbook.*

34. See Gay and Lesbian Alliance Against Defamation report, *Access Denied: The Impact of Internet Filtering Software on the Lesbian and Gay Community*, New York, December 1997, at http://www.glaad.org/glaad/access_denied/index.html.

35. *Reno v ACLU* (1997) 117 S. Ct. 2329.

36. A letter (including a list of newsgroups allegedly carrying illegal content) from the Metropolitan Police Clubs and Vice unit was sent to the UK ISPs on 9 August 1996, which requested them to remove these newsgroups. The industry reaction was to set up the Internet Watch Foundation in September 1996. See generally Akdeniz, Y. 1997a, pp. 223–41 and the letter from the Metropolitan Police to the UK ISPs, August 1996, at http://www.cyber-rights.org/themet.htm.

37. In October 1996, NCIS launched Project Trawler to study the extent of criminal misuse of information technology and the methods that law enforcement officials should use.

38. See Uhlig, R. and Hyder, K., 'E-mail Open to Police Scrutiny', *The Daily Telegraph*, 9 June 1997.

39. 'Concerns Raised over Police Move to Read Private E-Mail', *The Scotsman*, 12 August 1998; 'Police Tighten the Net', *The Guardian, Online*, 17 September 1998; 'Civil Liberties Organisations Condemn Talks Between Internet Providers and Police', 18 September 1998 at http://www.cyber-rights.org/press/; Campbell, D. 'Personal Privacy Versus Crime Fighting on the Electronic Frontier', *Computing*, 7 October 1998; 'The Police State Their Clear Intentions', *Computing*, 28 October, 1998.

40. See for example *Klass v Germany*; Judgment of 6 September 1978, A.28; [1979] 2EHRR 214; *Huvig v France*, [1990] 12 EHRR 547; *Valenzuela Contreras v Spain*, [1998] ECHR Judgment of 30 July 1998, – V; *Kopp v.*

Switzerland [1998] ECHR Judgment of 25 March 1998, – II; *Lambert v. France,* ECHR Judgment of 24 August 1998, not yet published.

41. See the Cyber-Rights and Cyber-Liberties (UK) privacy letter at http://www.cyber-rights.org/ privacy/letter.htm. This letter was drafted by Yaman Akdeniz and Nicholas Bohm and has been finalised following extensive discussion within the Cyber-Rights-UK Mailing List in November 1998.

42. The responses are available from the above pages.

43. See Council of Europe Recommendation No. R (99) 5 of the Committee of Ministers to Member States, at http://www.coe.fr/cm/ta/rec/1999/99r5.htm.

44. First, the US FBI insisted on access to encryption keys and on a key escrow (or key recovery) mechanism for protection against terrorism, violent crime, foreign threats, drug trafficking, espionage, kidnapping and other crimes. NCIS took a similar position in January 1999. See National Criminal Intelligence Service Press Release, 'NCIS calls upon Government to Ensure Law Enforcement Powers do not Fall Behind Technology in Fight Against Crypto Criminals', No. 02/99, 26 January 1999.

45. DTI, 'Building Confidence in Electronic Commerce', 5 March 1999, at http://www.dti.gov.uk/cii/elec/elec_com.html. See also DTI and Home Office Press Release, 'Building Confidence in Electronic Commerce: Government Consults on Proposals to Make UK Best Place to Trade Electronically', P/99/200, 5 March 1999, and BBC News, 'Encryption: the civil-libertarian view', March 5 1999, and Cukier, K.N., 'UK Challenges Industry to Give Police Access to Crypto 'Key-Escrow' Introduced Unless Alternatives Found', *Communications Week International*, 15 March 1999, p. 1.

46. See Principle 5 of the OECD Guidelines on Cryptography Policy (March 1997); Article 12, Universal Declaration of Human Rights; Article 17, International Covenant on Civil and Political Rights; Article F(2) Treaty on European Union, and the EU Data Protection Directive.

47. See *Malone v U.K.* Appl no. 8691/79, Ser. A. vol. 82, [1984] 7 EHRR 14; *Govell v United Kingdom* App.no. 27237/95 [1997] EHRLR 438; *Halford v UK*, Appl. no. 20605/92, 1997-III, [1997] 24 EHRR 523.

48. According to the then Parliamentary Under-Secretary of State for the Home Department, Mr Mike O'Brien, House of Commons Hansard Debates for 21 October 1998, Column 1322.

49. These are: selflessness, integrity, objectivity, accountability, openness, honesty, and leadership. See The Seven Principles of Public Life, at http://www.official-documents.co.uk/document/parlment/nolan3/7-prncpl.htm.

50. The Better Regulation Task Force is an independent advisory group and was appointed by the Chancellor of the Duchy of Lancaster in September 1997 to advise government on action that improves the effectiveness of government regulation by ensuring that it is necessary, fair and affordable, and simple to understand and administer.

51. See Cabinet Office Press Release, 'Better Regulation Task Force published "Critics Guide" to Good Regulation', 21 January 1998, at http://www.open.gov.uk/co/bru/prnotice/210198.htm. A copy of this leaflet is available through http://www.open.gov.uk/co/bru/prin.htm.

52. See *Local Court of Munich v. Somm, Felix Bruno*, Local Court [Amtsgericht] Munich, File No.: 8340 Ds 465 Js 173158/95, at http://www.cyber-rights.org/isps/somm-dec.htm.

53. BBC News Online, 'Renegade Spy Rejects Damage Claim', 13 May, 1999; Campbell, D., 'More about Spies on the Internet', *The Guardian*, 14 May 1999.

10 The Political Impact of the Internet: The American Experience

RICHARD DAVIS

It is easy to forget how new the Internet really is. In April 1994, a Louis Harris survey found that two-thirds of Americans had never heard of the information superhighway (Pavlik, 1996, p. 140). Nor is this growth in the Internet hardly an American phenomenon. One recent estimate had the number of Internet users reaching 1 billion people world-wide by the year 2003.[1]

How can an innovation so new have such an extensive reach across the globe in less than a decade? Even more importantly, what does the emergence of this new technology mean for the future?

Clearly, Americans have adjusted their lives to accommodate the Internet. Since the US experience of broad acceptance and usage of the Internet has preceded that of many other nations, even industrialised nations, it offers a model of the impact of that transformation elsewhere. Analysing Internet impact on US politics may prove valuable for predicting the political role of the Internet in the United Kingdom, where usage is growing quickly. Obviously the differences in political system composition make this task somewhat problematic. However, looking at the US model may be beneficial in anticipating some of the effects of the Internet on British politics.

The purpose of this chapter is to do just that. First we will examine the influence of the Internet on US life, particularly politics. Then we will hone in on the role of the Internet in US elections and public policy-making. Finally, we will draw conclusions about that impact and speculate whether a similar scenario may unfold in the UK.

The Internet and US Political Life

The Internet has sparked extensive debate particularly about the political consequences of this new communications technology. Visions of the future have imbued the Internet with a capability to restructure relations between people on the planet and solve vexing economic, social and political problems. Repeatedly, US Vice President Al Gore has painted a bright political future with the Internet, or 'Global Information Infrastructure', as a world-wide communications device:

> These highways... will allow us to share information, to connect, and to communicate as a global community. From these connections we will derive robust and sustainable economic progress, strong democracies, better solutions to global and local environmental challenges, improved health care, and – ultimately – a greater sense of shared stewardship of our small planet... The Global Information Infrastructure will help educate our children and allow us to exchange ideas within a community and among nations. It will be a means by which families and friends will transcend the barriers of time and distance. It will make possible a global information marketplace, where consumers can buy or sell products (Gore, 1995, p. 621).

Sheer numbers suggest that the USA is implementing the Global Information Infrastructure at a rate faster than other nations. For example, while an estimated 36 per cent of Americans go on the Internet, 16 per cent do so in the UK.[2] Americans have embraced the Web. The most coveted activity of most Americans – leisure – increasingly has included time on the Web. Time spent on-line by Americans has increased dramatically. By 1997, 85 per cent of users said they went on-line at least daily.[3] In 1997, America Online, the first major on-line service, was severely criticised and even sued by some of its customers for dumping millions of disks in direct mail campaigns and offering unlimited access time without sufficiently increasing their ability to handle new customers.[4] On-line services are rushing to increase telephone connections to meet the growing demand.

Although initial use centred on the workplace, where corporate or academic users utilised the Internet for business or research purposes, home use by Americans has exploded. Now people are more likely to go on-line at home than at work.[5] The Internet has gone from a tool for labour to a leisure activity (Pavlik, 1996, pp. 55-6). Since the amount of leisure time has not increased, many people are logging on in lieu of other past activities. For example, 37 per cent of Internet users say that they go on-line instead of watching television.[6]

A portent of its future role is the age group to which it most appeals. The Internet has caught the attention of younger Americans in particular. According to one *Newsweek* survey, 61 per cent of teenagers say that they surf the Net.[7] This fact may be related to the integration of the Internet into colleges and, increasingly, elementary and secondary schools. At many higher education institutions students are expected to own personal computers. Not surprisingly, people under 30 are the most likely to have access to the Internet.[8]

A prerequisite for such growth outside the workplace is the flourishing use of home computers. According to the US Census Bureau, the number of American households with computers grew from 6.9 million in 1984 to over 40 million by 1997 or approximately 43 per cent of US households. Also over 50 per cent of households with children had a computer in the home.[9] Sales of computers for home use have increased at a rapid rate. In 1997, sales jumped 76 per cent for that market.[10]

Dramatic growth may continue with the introduction of Web TV.[11] The change to digital television required under US law by the year 2005 will force television set owners to purchase new receivers. That transition could stimulate Internet use if new sets are accessible to Web TV.

Does this growth have a political relevance? Are Americans using the Web for political purposes? The answer is yes and no. Most Americans actually go on-line for non-political purposes, such as sending e-mail, shopping, or getting information about entertainment or leisure activities. However, one highly relevant piece of information is the number of people now going on-line to get news. That figure has mushroomed in recent years. Between 1996 and 1998 the number of Americans going on-line for news rose from 11 million to 36 million.[12]

The Internet in US Elections

During his first of two debates with President Bill Clinton, Republican challenger Bob Dole invited viewers to visit his web-site. The offer was significant. A presidential candidate was inviting potential viewers to view him or her from a new perspective – cyberspace.

The 1990s have seen US candidates from president to sheriff initiating cyberspace campaigning. The Clinton campaign in 1992 was the first to establish an Internet site and disseminate electronic information about the candidate.

Since then, a growing number of candidates for federal office have established Web pages. A 1998 survey of candidate web-sites on *democracy.net* found that 36 per cent of candidates for federal office had web-sites. One-third of House of Representatives' candidates had sites, compared to 49 per cent of those running for the US Senate.[13]

Candidates established web-sites because they did not want to be left out of the rush to new technology. One campaign aide explained that 'having a Web-site these days is like having a mailbox. You gotta have one. You can argue about how important it is. But it's just seen as a greens fee that you have to pay'.[14]

However, in addition they were responding to the perception that an audience beckoned. Not only were many people on-line, as noted above, but a growing percentage of users went on-line specifically for election news. According to one study, 22 per cent of on-line users said that they went on-line to read news about the 1996 election.[15]

However, it is important to note that the role of on-line information sources is one of supplementing not supplanting other information sources such as newspapers or television. For example, 77 per cent of on-line users also read a newspaper while 56 per cent also watch local television news (Davis and Owen, 1998, p. 141).

The on-line audience is like no ordinary group. Internet users were a particularly useful audience for candidates because they included a larger-than-average proportion of actual voters. In 1996, over two-thirds of Internet users said that they would vote. In fact, the proportion of intended voters was even higher among people who used the Internet for political information (Muzzio and Birdsell, 1997, pp. 42-43). Contrast this with less than 50 per cent of the American electorate who actually voted that year.

Does the Internet have any effect on the campaign? One anticipated effect would be a levelling of the playing field among candidates. The speculation was that voters could just as easily gain information about an unknown challenger as they could about the well-established incumbent. Since all sites are equally accessible, minor parties such as the Greens or the Libertarians would be treated as seriously as the Democrats and Republicans. One analyst even suggested that, with the aid of the Internet, the playing field will be levelled to such an extent that 'in the future the political system may no longer be dominated by the Democratic and Republican parties' (Corrado and Firestone, 1997, p. 12).

As a result, minor party sites have flourished. The Reform Party, Natural Law Party, the Green Party, the Libertarian Party, and the US Taxpayers Party all created their own sites for the 1996 presidential election. So did many Congressional candidates who represented these parties.

Yet, the Web did not convey equality. In 1996, a search of three Web candidate lists of congressional candidates immediately following the November general election found that 72 per cent of the web-sites were put up by incumbents while only 22 per cent were challenger sites. Incumbents were far more likely than challengers to have a Web presence. Moreover, members of Congress can maintain web-sites at the taxpayers' expense. A total of 93 per cent of the incumbent web-sites were official sites set up by the US Congress, but containing content selected by the incumbent.

By 1998, many incumbents also set up their own candidate Web pages separate from the official page due to some restrictions on overt campaigning on official sites. As a result, incumbents can double their presence on the Web. The incumbent's advantages apparently carry over to the Internet as well.

Minor parties experience the same frustration with the expected equality. Many voters learn about candidate web-sites through the news media. This is particularly true of minor party candidates who do not have the resources to campaign extensively off-line. Yet, news media coverage of Web-sites during campaigns has favoured the well-known candidates and excluded minor party candidates. One Libertarian candidate complained that the news media wrote articles about the web-sites of the major parties but would not mention those of Libertarian candidates.[16] Moreover, resource-rich candidates could advertise their sites through other means – broadcast or print advertisements or billboards. Other candidates relied on the news media to advertise their sites. However they were disappointed. One webmaster for a minor party candidate found that journalists would 'look at [the candidate's web-site] and see if they could get some more information for their article (about candidates), but they wouldn't advertise it in the paper'.[17]

However, the advantage for the major party candidates and incumbents in particular rests largely with voter behaviour. Name recognition advantage and a low level of voter interest limit use of the Internet to gain more information about other candidates.

Name recognition clearly favours the established parties and candidates. For example, incumbents were more likely to be found and seen by voters since they were linked to other official government sites. Also, voters were more likely to know an incumbent by name and be able to conduct a search for the candidate's site if they did not have a URL address. Presidential candidates such as Texas Governor George Bush, Jr. or Vice-President Al Gore, who already have broad name recognition, are going to attract to their candidate sites more users than other candidates who are less well known or supported.

Another advantage for established candidates is voter approach to candidate information. It is more likely that voters manage Internet information in the same way they do other media sources, i.e. not as a means for challenging their preconceived notions but as a reinforcement of their ideological or partisan views. As a result, voters will focus more often on the sites of candidates or parties with whom they think they agree. Admittedly, supporters of minor parties or resource-poor candidates may visit their respective sites more frequently due to the need for stronger reinforcement.[18] However, such behaviour obviously does not aid minor parties and lesser-known candidates. In summary, for the most part, voters are not going to gravitate to sites of parties or candidates whom they have never heard of, do not agree with, and assume will not win. Why should they do so?

Even if a voter happens upon a candidate's site, voter interest in the site dictates whether the voter stays on the site and/or comes back later. Site appeal attracts users in the first place but also maintains their interest. An engaging, informative, visually entertaining and frequently updated site will lure potential voters initially and repeatedly.

Yet, there are significant differences between rich and poor candidates regarding the ability to develop such a site. Resource-rich candidates can devote part of their vast resources to a well-developed Internet site and still retain sufficient funds for other off-line activities. Meanwhile, resource-poor candidates must choose to have a simple site or no site at all.

Clearly candidates have adapted to the Internet, and many more of them will do so in the future – both major and minor party candidates, both the viable and the not so viable. However there will be a difference. The main beneficiaries on-line will be the same candidates who have benefited off-line. Such benefits have nothing to do with the Internet; they stem from party affiliation, organisation, candidate background and money. This new technology will not revolutionise who gets elected; it will change the way in which campaigns are run. Candidate communication via the Internet will become staple, but that will not alter the balance of power in favour of candidates and parties who fail to attract voter support now.

Governance and the Net

According to the predictions concerning its political role, the Internet holds great promise as a medium for stimulating and expressing a public role in governance. *Newsweek* columnist Howard Fineman called it 'the new Louisiana Purchase, an uncharted west'. The political role of new communication technology has been termed a 'great transformation' (Grossman, 1995, p. 149).

The Internet is viewed as a vehicle for educating individuals, stimulating citizen participation, measuring public opinion, easing citizen access to government officials, offering a public forum, simplifying voter registration, and even facilitating actual voting (Corrado and Firestone, 1997; Pavlik, 1996, p. 313). It has been termed as a 'powerful technology for grassroots democracy' and one that by 'facilitating discussion and collective action by citizens, strengthens democracy' (Klein, 1995). It also has been called potentially 'the most powerful tool for political organising developed in the past fifty years' (Schwartz, 1996, p. 5).

However, has the Internet, in reality, fulfilled or even begun to fulfil this vision? Let us answer that question by examining the Internet's usage in the public policy-making process. When Newt Gingrich became Speaker of the US House of Representatives in January 1995, he outlined his vision of a technological future for the House, promising that 'every amendment, every conference report', would be on-line and accessible to the country.[19] Gingrich envisioned the Internet making the legislative process more open and accessible to the American public.

However, the US Congress rarely acts rapidly and the same is true in its approach to new communications technology. Congressional offices are still adapting to the Internet's capabilities. Members of Congress have not been quick to go on-line personally, although all now have Web pages and e-mail addresses. Congress has been willing to disseminate public information over the Internet. The Library of Congress has an extensive legislative information site in THOMAS, which allows site visitors to access bill texts, read the minutes of floor debate, and even look up scheduled committee and floor activity. The amount of information available to any Internet user about government has been greatly expanded. Moreover, use of that information has also been facilitated by easing the process of information retrieval.

Yet, realising that information dissemination potentially can shift the balance of power, policy-makers have not relinquished control over that task even in the Internet age. Congress has attempted to limit citizen access to this information via the Internet. For example, in a dispute over whether committee reports should be placed on-line, the chair of a Congressional committee said that he had the power to determine which committee documents could be placed on the Internet. Also, users seeking to access the minority party views on a Congressional committee must access them through the site controlled by the majority party (Davis, 1999, p. 125). In another instance, the White House issued a news release in January 1994, attacking a *New Republic* article criticising the administration's health care reform plan. However, the administration toned down the electronic version before placing it on the Web. As justification, the White House press secretary claimed that the White House could 'reserve the right to edit' (Maxwell, 1996, p. 4).

Individual members of Congress also are utilising the Web to shape the information transmitted to their constituents about the member's activity, using it to further their 'homestyle' or convey constituent communication designed to soothe constituents into believing that the member is worthy of their continued support.[20] If a user calls up the site of their individual member, they will find positive accounts of the member's activity. Individual member sites have become advertising tools for the members in their re-election bids. In accordance with David Mayhew's (1974) conclusion of a tripartite activity of members – advertising, credit claiming, and position taking – the Internet has become a low-cost mechanism for members to maintain a home presence. They can place their news releases and self-congratulating statements in homes and offices throughout the district, particularly without the filter of the news media.

For example, Connecticut Congressman Sam Gejdenson's on-line biography calls him 'a passionate advocate for children, senior citizens, and working families', and continues that 'Gejdenson has fought to make education more available and affordable, expand and enhance retirement security, protect the environment for future generations to enjoy, and create jobs and economic opportunity here at home by promoting American-made goods and services in new markets overseas' (Davis, 1999, p. 131). Other 'homestyle' messages are primarily personal. Many members want to communicate an affinity with their constituents. The web-site of Representative Richard Armey, the House Majority Leader, relates that Armey and his wife 'attend Lewisville Bible Church. They have five children. Armey is an avid bass fisherman and believes in the restorative powers of fishing, where he can put aside the pressures of work and spend time with his wife and children'. The biography is accompanied by a photograph of Armey kissing a fish.

This use of the Internet is a far cry from what was envisioned as a potentially revolutionary medium. Using Internet sites funded at government expense much like constituent newsletters, members of Congress have been able to turn a potentially interactive medium into one that plainly furthers their re-election efforts. In essence, rather than reallocating power away from the elected member of Congress, an outcome widely promised, the Internet is far more likely to reinforce it by giving the member another tool to communicate their messages and acquire an additional advantage over potential challengers.

What is missing from governmental sites is what Internet proponents suggest is its strongest trait – interactivity. Interactivity on the most popular US political sites is primarily an illusion. Candidates, party organisations, and elected officials seek to use the Web for information dissemination, but they are rarely interested in allowing their sites to become forums for the opinions of others. Few candidates use their sites to poll constituents on their views on issues. E-mail does not serve that purpose. Members of Congress often request that e-mail correspondents send them their postal mail addresses so that they can screen non-constituents. Thus, what communication takes place often occurs off-line. Federal executive agencies often do not even encourage e-mail to policy-makers. Site visitors are asked to contact the webmaster instead.

This reluctance towards interactivity is not surprising. Ithiel de Sola Pool, (1990, p. 261), correctly prophesied that interactivity would be mediated: 'Somehow, by a combination of devices and customs, a protective shell will be created as fast as the flow of communication threatens to become overwhelming'. However, is interactivity available anywhere? Doesn't electronic communication affect legislative decision making?

The ideal of cyberspace, particularly via e-mail, would be the ease of constituent expression and, consequently, the facilitation of policy-maker knowledge of public will. Former PBS president Lawrence Grossman concludes that this ideal is not far off. 'By pushing a button, typing on-line, or talking to a computer, they will be able to tell their president, senators, members of Congress, and local leaders what they want them to do and in what priority order' (Grossman, 1995, p. 149). Is this ideal becoming reality?

Certainly the volume of e-mail to elected officials has soared. One survey of Congressional offices found that most members receive 175 or more e-mail messages per week (Davis, 1999, p. 127). However, those numbers increase dramatically during particular legislative debates. President Clinton gets an average of 1,800 messages daily, but has received as many as 5,500 in one day.[21]

However, the ideal has eluded reality. One example for members of Congress has been the non-constituent problem. While members usually receive regular mail from their own constituents, e-mail also enables anyone with an e-mail account to 'spam' the offices of members of Congress. The vast majority of e-mail comes from non-constituents, and

Congressional offices have a new challenge of sorting genuine constituent messages from those sent by non-constituents (Davis, 1999, p. 128).

Even constituents may become a problem for Congressional offices, given the greater ease of initiating mail. 'What's happening is that with the new software programs today', explains Representative Gejdenson, '16,000 kids at a college can send me a letter with a push of a button. I don't have the ability to go through all of that'.[22] A single constituent can deluge or disrupt the e-mail system of a member. According to one Congressional e-mail system analyst, 'Congressional offices are already so stretched out, and their people are so stressed out. There's the fear that this will take those offices to a whole new level of dealing with the constituent computer hacker'.[23]

However, even if there was an outpouring of genuine public expression from constituents, some have expressed concern that such expression would not be healthy. There is the fear that public reaction via e-mail is too quick in a representative democracy. One journalist sees the new style of letter writing (via electronics) as potentially less temperate. 'Most of us have either sent or received an electronic jolt that would have benefited from the cooling-down period afforded by the traditional drawer-yanking search for an envelope and fumble for a stamp'.[24] The time period between initial reaction and expression of that reaction to a public official has been significantly reduced.

However, the fear that e-mail senders will be more vitriolic because they take less time to ponder the consequences of their messages is not borne out in Congressional e-mail, according to a survey of Congressional offices. The survey of Congressional offices concluded that while more Congressional webmasters felt the tone of Congressional e-mail was negative rather than positive (24 per cent versus 19 per cent), the majority (57 per cent) felt that there was no difference in tone between e-mail and regular mail (Davis, 1999, pp. 126-7).

Yet, that finding does not answer the question of whether members are more inclined to respond to e-mail than to regular mail. Do members pay more attention to it than they do to regular mail? The answer, surprisingly, may be the opposite. Many members have become so disgusted by the 'spamming' by individuals and groups that e-mail may actually be devalued. One Congressional staff member concluded that 'the e-mail address for the Congressman has to be one of the biggest wastes of taxpayers' dollars – the whole thing is a real headache for staff and of no value to the actual constituents' (Davis, 1999, p. 129).

Ithiel de Sola Pool predicted this outcome nearly 20 years ago when he suggested that someone who 'now laboriously writes a letter to his

Congressman could on a computer network send an instantaneous personalised message to every member of Congress. It would, of course, not be listened to; it would perhaps have less effect than his present letter' (1990, p. 261). Some policy-makers initially expressed enthusiasm about the ideal of e-mail communication with constituents. However, even their enthusiasm has been dampened by the reality of e-mail interaction.

Conclusion

The Internet has affected American politics. Citizens are finding another mode for acquiring information about candidates and elected officials. Candidates and elected officials are using the Internet to send the same messages that they have sought to communicate off-line. Increasing numbers of on-line users are sending e-mail messages to their elected officials. All parties are supplementing other sources of information or communication.

Nevertheless it is important to note what has not happened. The balance of power has not shifted towards resource-poor organisations or individuals or the public. Candidates and elected officials have not lost control of the agenda. They have not been displaced by direct democracy. Less influential players, such as resource-poor candidates or minor parties, have not acquired greater importance. In fact, the opposite is true. Increasingly, established players have adjusted nicely to the new medium. They have embraced the Web with publicity-oriented sites. They have used their resources to turn the on-line audience towards their messages. Others messages are still there, but, as with their off-line experience, they find it difficult to be noticed.

Will the Internet upset the existing balance of power in the UK? Will it upset existing power structures leading existing political organisations and even political institutions to be replaced? Will we see the rise of the age of 'Internet democracy', a period when the public will suddenly become political activists due to their new capability to acquire information, register opinions and therefore directly make public policy?

This chapter has demonstrated that none of this has occurred in the USA, nor will it in the UK. The point is that computer-assisted politics will not be radically different to today's politics (Schwartz, 1996). Existing dominant players will adapt to the Internet and transform it into a vehicle for their own continuance in power. The party organisations and institutions in the UK have already gone on-line with the same kinds of information about party organisations and individual candidates, as well as the national government branches, as in the USA.

However, the potential for the Internet to effect even the changes that have occurred in the USA is low. One reason is technical. While local telephone calls in the USA are free, that is not true in the UK. The cost of going on-line is higher for Britons and limits their access to the Internet. Staying on the Internet for any period of time in order to e-mail political officials, participate in newsgroups, or acquire political information becomes costly for many Britons. This cost explains why Internet access is low and is unlikely to grow quickly in the UK in the near future. According to a Guardian, ICM survey, while 14 per cent of Britons said they have access to the Internet at home only 4 per cent more believed that they would have Internet access at home in the next year.[25]

Another factor is due to the systemic differences between the two political systems. The US electoral system is more porous than that of the UK. Candidates for federal office, from President to a member of Congress, must campaign to masses of voters even to secure a party nomination. Then, once in a general election campaign, they cannot rely as much as in the past on party cue or party organisational support in order to acquire electoral victory. Such candidates have an incentive to use the Internet as a forum to reach voters.[26] The same is true for individual members of Congress. Even despite the increasing partisanship of Congress in the 1990s, the US Congress is still highly decentralised. As a result, members are more likely to be entrepreneurs than party adherents. They also are increasingly tied to their individual constituencies and less beholden to a party organisation.[27] Individualism is especially strong in the US Senate. Therefore members of Congress seek to use the Internet in order to achieve re-election.

Candidates for Parliament lack those incentives for employing the Internet as a communications tool. Members of Parliament similarly lack the kind of reliance on the local constituencies that would stimulate reliance on another communications tool for re-election purposes.

The relevance for British politics of this look at the USA is that the Internet has the potential not for causing a political revolution where a populist wave transforms representative democracy into direct democracy, but for becoming another tool for existing players to maintaining power in the political system. Moreover, the public – either in the USA or the UK – does not want the Internet to create a system without filters. Public involvement requires the organisation of public debate. Ian McLean addresses the problem that arises if agenda setting is assumed to be held in abeyance:

> Today we will vote on how much to spend on the NHS (National Health Service), tomorrow on how to divide it up between hospitals, GPs (general

practitioners), and anti-smoking propaganda, on Wednesday we will vote on animal experiments, and on Thursday we will vote on the Sunday trading laws... What can we do about the awkward character who says, 'The issues are wrongly posed. I think it is worth spending a lot on hospitals only if the State permits medical experiments on animals to continue'. So I cannot vote on Monday because I do not know the outcome of Wednesday's vote. It is no use reversing the order, because then another awkward customer will say 'I favour animal experiments if and only if NHS spending is high enough to allow the results to be used in a socialized health system (1989, p. 11).

Structuring the debate through setting the agenda and framing the options will remain in the hands of established players. Obviously such framing will carry with it its own biases. For example, during the 1996 US debate over term limits for members of Congress, Missouri Senator John Ashcroft invited visitors to his site to register their opinions on the topic. The hot link for supporting term limits was much larger and more prominent than the one for opposition. Not surprisingly, 80 per cent of votes registered were for term limits.[28]

In addition, the choice of who participates will not be left unfulfilled. Rather, mediation of public input will still occur and in fact will be imperative to allow any expression at all. However, the bottom line is an eventual filtering of public input. For example, when Vice President Al Gore visited a CompuServe chat room approximately 900 people tried to join the conversation but only 10 were able to put a question to the Vice President (Diamond and Silverman, 1995, p. 148). Who determines those who are successful and those who are not? It is not the users who do so.

Refuting the idea that new communications technology sweeps away mediating institutions, Mulgan argues that such technology 'is not an end to mediation, but rather the emergence of more complex structures of mediation' (1991, p. 7). The same can be said for the Internet. Those 'more complex structures of mediation' are important to examine and that is what this book is designed to do.

Notes

1. Speech by Steve Case, President of America Online, at the National Press Club, 14 December, 1998.
2. 'Internet News Takes Off', Pew Research Center for the People & the Press, 8 June, 1998; See also Chapter 6.
3. Eighth WWW User Survey, Graphic, Visualization, & Usability Center, Georgia Tech University, December 1997.

4.   Jackson, D.S, 'AOL Buys Some Time', *Time*, 10 February, 1997, p. 50; and McAllester, M. 'New Scrutiny for Troubled AOL', *Newsday*, 24 January, 1997, p. A6.

5.   'One-in-Ten Voters Online for Campaign '96', Pew Research Center for the People & the Press, Technology '96. Summary available at *http://www.people-press.org/tech96sum.htm*.

6.   Sixth WWW User Survey, Graphic, Visualization, & Usability Center, Georgia Tech University, December 1996.

7.   Pew Research Center for the People & the Press survey, 23 January, 1998; Harris Poll, 18 February, 1998.

8.   'Survey Profiles Voters' Use of Media', Media Studies Center, Freedom Forum News Advisory, at *http://www.mediastudies.org/new.html*.

9.   US Census Bureau, 'Computer Use and Ownership', *http://www.census.gov/population/www/socdemo/computer.html*; 'Going Mainstream: The Internet and the US Mass Market', *Computer Industry Report*, 15 January, 1998, p. 4.

10. Niemara, M.P., 'What's Hot, What's Not: A Look at Consumer Buying Patterns', *Chain Store Age*, 1 April, 1998, p. 30.

11. Sixth WWW User Survey, Graphic, Visualization, & Usability Center, Georgia Tech University, December 1996.

12. 'Internet News Takes Off', Pew Research Center for the People & the Press, 8 June, 1998.

13. The survey was conducted in December 1998. It is possible that some of the sites were disbanded immediately after the election, which would mean that the number of sites actually could have been larger.

14. Telephone interview with Michael Armini, Press Secretary to former Representative Peter Torkildsen (R-Massachusetts), 20 November, 1996.

15. 'One-in-Ten Voters Online for Campaign '96', at *http://www.people-press.org/tech96sum.htm*.

16. Telephone interview with Richard Osness, Minnesota State Senate candidate, 22 November, 1996.

17. Telephone interview with Eric Woolhiser, webmaster for Susan Gallagher for US Senate Campaign in Massachusetts, 14 November, 1996.

18. This is one reason that the number of 'hits' is an inaccurate measure of user interest because avid candidate or party supporters frequently visiting the site for campaign updates or just reinforcement effectively boosted the numbers.

19. *Congressional Record*, 4 January, 1995, vol. 141, (1), p. 1400.

20. For a discussion of Congressional homestyle, see Fenno 1978; and also Parker, 1986.

21. E-mail message from Stephen K. Horn, Director, Presidential e-mail, White House Office of Correspondence, 14 August, 1997.

22. Quoted in Browning, G., 'Return to Sender', *National Journal*, 1 April, 1995, p. 794.

23. Ibid, p. 797.

24. McGrath, C., 'The Internet's Arrested Development', *New York Times Magazine*, 8 December, 1996, p. 85.
25. 'Poll Points to Lift Off for Internet', *The Guardian*, 11 January, 1999, p. 1.
26. For a sample of the discussion of Congressional campaigning, see Jacobson, 1997; Herrnson, 1998. For a discussion of presidential candidate campaigning, see Polsby and Wildavsky, 1996; Kessel, 1992.
27. See for example, Fenno, 1978; Parker, 1986; and Davidson, 1992.
28. Starobin, P., 'On the Square', *National Journal*, 25 May, 1996, pp. 1145-49.

11 Conclusions: Modernising without Democratising?

RACHEL GIBSON AND STEPHEN WARD

This final chapter attempts to draw these contributions together, and does so by asking three central questions: (1) are there any discernible trends or patterns in the adaptation and utilization of new ICTs by UK institutions and organisations?; (2) can inter-group and institutional comparisons be made that indicate greater or lesser receptivity to the new technologies and what might explain such differences?; and (3) overall what have the chapters revealed to us about the prospects of a different style of politics on the horizon, are we on course to erosion of the established structures of liberal democracy, their reinvigoration, or, in fact, is it really the case that the more things change, the more they stay the same?

Utilisation: Slow Adaptation

Perhaps Clive Walker's comment in Chapter 5 best summarises one of the key trends to emerge from the book when he refers to modernisation, not democratisation as the chief aim and end point of judicial adaptation to the new media. This is a story echoed in all the chapters of the book. The organs of UK democracy are clearly moving into the digital age, but with an eye to efficiency and internal reform rather than as a means for greater public consultation and debate. If one considers the breadth of possibilities offered by the new ICTs, given their essential properties (see Chapter 1), the consensus seems to be that they are not being exploited. So far, much of the debate in the governmental sphere has concerned the benefits of e-commerce and the need for businesses to adapt for reasons of economic competitiveness. Discussions concerning the new media's ability to facilitate greater civic engagement have been much lower on the agenda. While Parliament, local government, the parties and pressure groups have all captured the downward flows of information and service provision, a concomitant commitment to upward feedback does not materialise.

As Stephen Coleman points out, Parliament has transferred a number of its internal functions onto computerised systems. Most MPs, or at least their staffs, use e-mail to communicate and all are kept informed by the video and data network. However, the possibilities for more direct solicitation of constituency opinion through regular virtual surgeries or sponsoring independent deliberative polling of citizens' views are not being taken up. Similarly, Walker contends that compared to other countries, most notably the USA, the British judiciary have been very timid in their use of new ICTs to open up the judicial process. Options such as recruiting judges, advertising open days, allowing for certain cases to be resolved on-line and organising a citizens' resource centre of previous judgements and background information are not being offered via the Internet.

More surprisingly, and perhaps more damningly, the organisational chapters offer similar criticism. Both main parties and it appears pressure groups are failing to exploit the democratic and participatory potential of this media, largely as a result of a combination of timidity and ignorance. Smaller parties, however, such as the SNP or the Greens have displayed a more imaginative feel for the new technology, although until a wider public start to use the media the effects of such innovation will go unrewarded. For the most part though, political organisations are largely trying to utilise the Internet in the same manner in which they use the traditional media. The chapters by Nixon and Percy-Smith reinforce this judgement, in the context of both central and local government.

Of course innovative and enthusiastic use of the Internet is not entirely without pitfalls. A second key theme to emerge from these analyses is an understanding of the double-edged nature of this technology when applied to democratic politics. While there is a general chiding of the government and representative bodies for failing to deploy the technology to a more interactive end, the dangers of such 'technopopulism' are squarely pointed out by the authors. Some of the 'cons' to e-democracy raised here encompass giving voice to instantaneous prejudice, two-tiered access systems, the removal of the pressures of 'real-time' court proceedings, and demand overload leading to declines in public perceptions of government efficiency. Such dangers are real. Do we really want to be ruled by plebiscite? How can it be ensured that everyone would have an equal role, if some individuals are unable to access information and services from their home? Does the removal of 'face-time' from judicial and policy debates in general crucially undermine that process? The technology may allow more voices into the political process, but it does not guarantee that we listen to one another, or indeed that policy-makers will listen at all. Even if it were possible to resolve these issues, how far should, or indeed could, the government go toward resolving them.

As Akdeniz and Wheeler's discussions make clear, even if our policy-makers decided to take a more interventionist stance to facilitate wider use of the Internet, problems arise from conflicting imperatives. Economic incentives require stronger security measures to be put in place, but equally regulatory restrictions can engender greater inefficiencies. From a political viewpoint, open exchanges of opinion may be best fostered by anonymity, but such privacy can provoke a more hostile and aggressive exchange of views, detrimental to the social fabric. The defenders of Civil liberties are no doubt pleased with the retrenchment of the UK government and the EU in general from stronger surveillance and regulation. However, civil rights promoters, and those arguing family-centric concerns are clearly alarmed at the level of hate mongering and pornographic images available through an uncontrolled Internet. Aside from the deeper moral conundrum that Internet regulation poses, the practicalities of such a process as Akdeniz makes clear are seemingly infinite. Issues of jurisdiction and conflicting obscenity laws are all required to be addressed first before any steps can be taken towards state-imposed control.

A third broad argument to emerge from the book is the extent to which the technological determinist viewpoint is weakened by the evidence from the UK. While this might be expected from a work that makes institutional and organisational adaptation its focal point, the extent to which the authors exhort or recommend a more imaginative response to the new media challenge is notable. Given the evidence of declining conventional participation in terms of voting, organisational membership, and decreasing confidence in governing institutions, the opportunities for re-engagement with the public that new ICTs offer are strongly lauded by these observers. The key is, however, that such ends will be not be reached inevitably. While new and more 'high tech' legislative bodies may be set up such as the Scottish Parliament, this in itself will not bring about a change in the level of consultation. More channels of communication do not equate automatically with more democracy. Citizens need to engage with the issues and believe that their participation is meaningful. To ensure this, wider political and institutional reforms and civic education are necessary. The optimism of the government's White Papers on modernising central and local government in 1998 and 1999, as Nixon and Percy-Smith point out, cannot be realised without a root and branch change in institutional culture. Traditional hierarchical structure is incompatible with seamless Web service from common delivery points. The reports, as they indicate, are over-reliant on technology as the solution, and skate over the crucial nexus of social inequality and power relations from whence the information age must spring. Nixon, however, does provide a pause for thought in this process. The way information is collected, he points out, and what is collected, structures the government-citizen relationship. Joining up government departments, offering quicker and expanded services, could serve to create additional and perhaps burdensome demands. Alternatively, it might promote a greater autonomy and questioning of existing authorities on the part of the public. As Walker points out, access to legal documents and court decisions could re-empower the parties in the case. With information more freely available and no longer in the hands of 'gatekeepers', reliance on judges or experts in other fields would be reduced. For organisations, too, the onus lies very much with them to take a bolder stance in harnessing the new communication possibilities. According to the accounts contained here, at present it is very much a value-added approach that is taken towards the new media.

Institutional and Organisational Comparison: Capacity and Incentives

When contrasting institutional and organisational deployment of new ICTs, clearly capacity and resources (finance and skilled staff) are important, as Gibson and Ward's comparison of minor and major parties reveals in Chapter 6. However, this study indicates that further dimensions need to be considered in understanding adaptation to the new media – institutional or organisational incentives such as: ideology, culture, target audience and access to the traditional media. Currently, these may be even more important than resources in stimulating proactive Internet strategies. Hence, those organisations with a pre-existing commitment to enhancing direct democracy which cannot rely on the traditional media to communicate their message and can identify an on-line audience are the most likely to utilise the technology. Alternatively, as Nixon's chapter indicates, while Whitehall may have the capacity to engage in innovative uses of technology, the cautious bureaucratic culture and the reliance on traditional methods has hindered uptake of new technology.

The general trends therefore, seem to point to a failure in some sense on the part of the political system to rise to the challenge of the new politics. However, there does appear to be certain areas of innovation and change within this overall picture. Most notably the internal life of the structure studied here does appear to be in transition. While the benefits of the wiring up of legislatures, parties and government departments may not be extended to the public sphere, the opportunities for expansion of intra-organisational and intra-institutional debate and discussion have become greater. Again, simply putting the lines of communication in place, however, is no guarantee that they will engender greater levels of internal democracy.

It is clear from these chapters, however, that these reprimands should be meted out with differing levels of harshness. In particular, the Courts appear to have embraced the power of new ICTs with a series of initiatives from the Lord Chancellor's Department and the legal profession itself. The large number of groups formed to put forward suggestions for utilising digital technologies that Walker lists, and the suggestions made in the 1998 consultation paper (Lord Chancellor's Department, 1998b), such as putting decisions on the Internet, point to the judiciary as a leader in the field. Walker's comments that the movement toward the 'dematerialisation' of the court service, has come from the senior judiciary and uptake by solicitors and barristers, underscores once more the centrality of the political actors in this process. Beyond the courts, clearly some of the parties have been attempting to use the technology in innovative ways. Although in general parties show a considerable degree of staidness, the Liberal Democrats established their own internal talking shop or intra-net for members to chat and exchange ideas as early as 1992. The Greens have also adopted a number of member-based e-mail discussion fora since the mid 1990s.

While the study of pressure groups presented here speaks to a very particular case, the Lyminge Forest protest, it shows that the more creative and adventurous approach to the Net is taken by those in a less institutionalised setting. Although not used as a method of participation in itself, it is the medium's impact on off-line participation where we can glean traces of a revolutionising potential. The e-mail networks to request support, circulate alerts on eviction, and provide maps, links, and contacts, outlined by Pickerill, in Chapter 7 all highlight the Internet's invaluable co-ordinating ability. Clearly the issues of publicising the site, the practical difficulties of ensuring updates, recruiting IT literate personnel, and its impersonalisation as a method of campaigning pose barriers to more widespread use. Given more recent instances of the Internet's use for organising spontaneous demonstrations at the global level, however, such as the June 1999 Carnival against Capitalism in London, it is clear that these barriers are not insurmountable. The greatest impact of the new media, therefore, may be that it provides a degree of organisational coherence and thus mobilisation of power for those who would otherwise be unable to orchestrate a campaign of protest. Indeed, one noticeable impact already has been the ability to globalise protest almost instantaneously and internationalise even small locally-based campaigns. In short, as Web technology becomes more widespread it seems likely that we will witness more and more transitory, *ad hoc*, protest networks forming and organising largely in cyberspace.

Prospects: 21st Century Politics

In terms of the third set of questions that this chapter set itself to address – what do the chapters project for the future style of politics and its institutional frameworks? – Davis's chapter in particular offers some clues. Based on the American experience, he predicts that the Internet will not result in radical political changes in the UK. The major political players will adapt successfully to the Internet era. Most of the other chapters would concur with this viewpoint. It would seem therefore that claims of institutional erosion are not supported. While this argument does have a 'straw man' quality to it, at least at this early juncture few signs of weakening or decline in the major political players are detectable. Although they have not proved immutable to change, Parliament, Whitehall, local government and the party system all appear to be standing firmly in place against any levelling of hierarchy. In fact, if anything, it is these actors that are shown to be in the driving seat, exercising strategic control over how far the Internet and its related technologies are used by the British public and to what ends.

The picture is not one of unadulterated continuity, however. It does appear that in certain sectors reformist tendencies are emerging. In broad terms, the government's agenda for reform of government services is indeed sweeping. The prospect of all citizen-state transactions being on-line by 2008 is an ambitious one, and one that will clearly alter the structure and functioning of government and its relationship to the public. Changes to the policy-making process will be far reaching as old department fiefdoms are redrawn. Such restructuring clearly brings with it the enhancement of key governing bodies such as the Exchequer and the Cabinet Office, since co-ordination of information holdings, budgetary constraints and expenditure levels will all be accessible at the click of a mouse.

Such changes, without new fora for government-citizen consultation to facilitate widespread and meaningful debate, however, raise the spectre of a move toward a consumerist model of democracy (Bellamy and Taylor, 1998). Government provides increasingly better and faster services, people are consulted on their levels of satisfaction but not for setting the long-term or even short-term social and economic agenda. Electronic voting will undoubtedly be facilitated and referenda may be held on topics of national interest but increasing individualisation of information control will allow a greater diversification of tastes, and ultimately a more fragmented polity.

Thus, based on present trends, while reform may be forthcoming, it will not necessarily be focused on the rebirth of idealised democratic practice, greater transparency and accountability. Indeed, any redistribution of power seems more likely to be in the direction of the centre away from the peripheries, rather than the reverse. Instead of a move to a form of leaner, mediated direct democracy the shift appears to be toward a less politicised management of popular demand.

Bibliography

Abramson, J., Arterton, C. and Orren, G. (1988), *The Electronic Commonwealth*, Harvard University Press, Cambridge,MA.

Adams, P., (1996), 'Protest and the Scale of Politics of Telecommunications', *Political Geography*, vol 15 (5), pp. 419–41.

Akdeniz, Y. (1996a), 'Section 3 of the Computer Misuse Act 1990: an Antidote for Computer Viruses!', *Web Journal of Current Legal Issues*, issue 3, available at http://webjcli.ncl.ac.uk/1996/issue3/akdeniz3.html

Akdeniz, Y. (1996b), 'Computer Pornography: A Comparative Study of the US and the UK Obscenity laws and Child Pornography Laws in Relation to the Internet', *International Review of Law, Computers and Technology*, vol. 10 (2), pp. 235-61.

Akdeniz, Y. (1997a), 'Governance of Pornography and Child Pornography on the Global Internet: A Multi-Layered Approach', in L. Edwards and C. Waelde (eds), *Law and the Internet*, Hart Publishing, Oxford, pp. 223–41.

Akdeniz, Y. (1997b), 'UK Government Encryption Policy' *Web Journal of Current Legal Issues, issue* 1, available at http://webjcli.ncl.ac.uk/1997/issue1/akdeniz1.html.

Akdeniz, Y. (1997c), 'Copyright and the Internet', *New Law Journal*, vol. 147 (6798), pp. 965–6.

Akdeniz, Y. (1998a), 'No Chance for Key Recovery: Encryption and International Principles of Human and Political Rights', *Web Journal of Current Legal Issues,* issue 1 available at http://webjcli.ncl.ac.uk/1998/issue1/akdeniz1.html.

Akdeniz, Y. (1998b), 'The EU and Illegal and Harmful Content on the Internet', *Journal of Civil Liberties*, vol. 3 (1), pp. 31–6.

Akdeniz, Y. (1999), *Sex on the Net? The Dilemma of Policing Cyberspace*, South Street Press, Reading.

Akdeniz, Y., Clarke, O., Kelman, A. and Oram, A. (1997), 'Cryptography and Liberty: Can the Trusted Third Parties be Trusted? A Critique of the Recent UK Proposals', *The Journal of Information, Law and Technology, issue 2, available at* http://elj.warwick.ac.uk/jilt/cryptog/97_2akdz/.

Akdeniz, Y. and Bohm, N. (1999), 'Internet Privacy: New Concerns about Cyber-Crime and the Rule of Law', *Information Technology and Communications Law Journal*, vol. 5, pp. 20–4.

Akdeniz, Y., Bohm, N. and Walker, C. (1999), 'Internet Privacy: Cyber-Crimes vs Cyber-Rights', *Computers and Law*, vol. 10 (1), pp. 34–9.

Alderdice, J. (1996), 'Politics and the Information Age', paper presented to the Annual Congress of European Liberal Democrats, 11 July, Vienna.

Anderson, R. (1993), 'The Impact of Information Technology on Judicial Administration: A Research Agenda for the Future', *Southern California Law Review,* vol. 66, pp. 1762–812.

Annis, S. (1992), 'Evolving Connectedness Among Environmental Groups and Grassroots Organizations in Protected Areas of Central America', *World Development*, vol. 20 (4), pp. 587–95.

Aurigi, A. and Graham, S. (1996), 'Virtual Cities, Social Polarisation and the Crisis in Urban Public Space', paper presented at the Cyberspace Divide Conference, , 11–12 September, Teeside University.

Auty, C. and Nicholas, D. (1998), 'British Political Parties and their Web Pages', *Aslib Proceedings*, vol. 50 (10), pp. 283–96.

Bangemann, M (1994), *Europe and the Global Information Society: Recommendations to the European Council*, European Commission, Brussels.

Barber, B., Mattson, K. and Peterson, J. (1997), *The State of Electronically Enhanced Democracy: A Survey of the Internet*, a report for the Markle Foundation, Walt Whitman Center for Culture and Politics of Democracy, New Brunswick, NJ.

Barbrook, R. (1997), Electronic Democracy, available at http://ma.hrc.wmin.ac.uk/ma.theory.4.5.db.

Barrett, N. (1997), *Digital Crime,* Kogan Page, London.

Becker, T. (1996), 'Televote: Interactive, Participatory Polling', in T.L. Becker and R.A. Couto (eds), *Teaching Democracy By Being Democratic,* Praeger, London.

Bellamy, C. and Taylor, J. (1996), 'New ICTs and Institutional Change: The Case of the UK Criminal Justice System', *International Journal of Public Management*, vol. 9 (4), pp. 51–69.

Bellamy, C., Horrocks, I. and Webb, J. (1995), 'Exchanging Information with the Public: From One-stop Shops to Community Information Systems', *Local Government Studies*, vol. 21 (1), pp. 11–30.

Bellamy, C. and Taylor, J.A. (1998), *Governing in the Information Age,* Open University Press, Buckingham.

Belt, V. (1998), 'New Communications Technologies, Modernity and Community', paper presented at Technology and the Spaces of Modernity Conference, 9–11 October, Gregynog, Wales.

Bessette, G. (1997), 'Empowering People Through Information and Communication Technology: Lessons From Experience?', *Journal of Development Communication*, vol. 1, pp. 1–26.

Bijker, W. (1995), *Of Bicycles, Bakelites, and Bulbs: Toward a Theory of Sociotechnical Change*, The MIT Press, London.

Bijker, W., Hughes, T. and Pinch, T. (eds) (1987), *The Social Constructions of Technological Systems: New Directions in the Sociology and History of Technology*, The MIT Press, London.

Bijker, W. and Law, J. (eds) (1992*), Shaping Technology/Building Society: Studies in Sociotechnical Change*, The MIT Press, London.

Bimber, B. (1998), 'Toward an Empirical Map of Political Participation on the Internet'. Paper presented at the American Political Science Association Conference, 3–6 September, Boston, MA.

Bonchek, M.S. (1995), 'Grassroots in Cyberspace: Using Computer Networks to Facilitate Political Participation', paper presented at the 53rd Annual Meeting of the Midwest Political Science Association, 6 April, Chicago, available at http://www.ai.mit.edu/people/msb/pubs/grassroots.html.

Bosso, C.J., (1991), 'Adaptation and Change in the Environmental Movement', in J. Ciger and B. Loomis (eds), *Interest Group Politics*, Congressional Quarterly Press, Washington DC, pp. 151–76.

Bosworth, K. (1991), 'Taking up Computer Expectations', *Yearbook of Law, Computers and Technology* vol. 5, Butterworths, London, pp. 58–64.

Bowden, C. and Akdeniz, Y. (1998), 'Cryptography and Democracy: Dilemmas of Freedom', in Liberty (ed), *Liberating Cyberspace: Civil Liberties, Human Rights and the Internet*, Pluto Press, London.

Brass, E. and Poklewski Koziell, S. (1997), *Gathering Force: DIY Culture - Radical Action for Those Tired of Waiting*, The Big Issue Writers, London.

Breheny, B.V. and Kelly, E.M. (1995), 'Note: Maintaining impartiality: Does Media Coverage of Trials Need to be Curtailed?' *St. John's Journal of Legal Commentary,* vol. 10, pp. 371–402.

Brooke, Lord Justice (1998), 'IT and the Courts of England and Wales: The Next Ten Years', paper presented at the 13th BILETA Conference, Dublin, available at http://www.bileta.ac.uk/.

Brown, R. and Svennevig, M. (1999), 'Waiting for the Great Leap Forward? New Information Communications Technologies and Democratic Participation', paper presented to the UK Political Studies Association, 23-25 March, Nottingham.

Budge, I. (1996), *The New Challenge of Direct Democracy*, Polity Press, Cambridge.

Burton, A. (1997), 'Why Bother with the Internet?', *Ethos*, vol 1, pp. 60–3.

Burton, M. (1998), 'How Well-connected Are You?' *Municipal Journal*, 13 November, p. 23.

Byrne, L. (1997), *Information Age Government. Delivering the Blair Revolution*, Discussion Paper 38, The Fabian Society, London.

Cabinet Office (1996), Green Paper *'government.direct'*: *A Prospectus for the Electronic Delivery of Government Services*, Cm 3438, HMSO, London.

Cabinet Office (1997), *The Government's Response to Comments on the Green Paper 'government.direct'*, HMSO, London.

Cabinet Office (1999), White Paper *'Modernising Government'*, Cm 4310, HMSO, London, also available at
http://www.documents.co.uk/document/cm43/4310/4310.htm.

Calabrese, A. and Borchert, M. (1996), 'Prospects for Electronic Democracy in the United States: Rethinking Communication and Social Policy', *Media, Culture and Society*, vol. 18, pp. 249–68.

Campos, G. (1998), 'Public Wants Clear Evidence of New Technology Benefits', *Municipal Journal*, 6 November.

Castells, M. (1996), *The Information Age: Economy Society and Culture*, vol. 1, *The Rise of the Network Society*, Blackwell, Oxford.

Castells, M. (1997a), *The Information Age: Economy Society and Culture*, vol. 2, *The Power of Identity*, Blackwell, Oxford.

Castells, M. (1997b), *The Information Age: Economy Society and Culture*, vol. 3, *End of Millennium*, Blackwell, Oxford.

Chakravati, A.K. and Krishnan, A.S.A. (1999), 'Electronic Government and the International Scenario', Seminar on Electronic Governance, 27 January, Jaipur, Rajcomp.

Chancellor of the Dutchy of Lancaster (1998), *Crown Copyright in the Information Age: A Consultation Document on Access to Public Sector Information*, Cm. 3819, HMSO, London.

Charlton, R., May, R. and Cleobury, T. (1995), 'NGOs in the Politics of Development: Projects as Policy', *Contemporary Politics*, vol.1 (1), pp. 19–42.

Chesterman, M. (1997), 'OJ and the Dingo: How Media Publicity Relating to Criminal Cases Tried by Jury is Dealt with in Australia and America', *American Journal of Comparative Law,* vol. 45, pp. 109–47.

Chomsky, N. (1994), *Keeping the Rabble in Line*, AK Press, Edinburgh.

Clapham, A. (1993), *Human Rights in the Private Sphere,* Clarendon Press, Oxford.

Cleaver, H. (1998), 'The Zapatistas and the International Circulation of Struggle: Lessons Suggested and Problems Raised', available at http://www.eco.utexas.edu/Homepages/faculty/Cleaver/lessons.html. Austin University Texas, USA.

Coleman, S. (1999a), *Electronic Media, Parliament and the People: Making Democracy Visible,* The Hansard Society, London.

Coleman, S. (1999b), 'Cutting Out the Middle-Man: From Virtual Representation to Direct Deliberation', in B.N. Hague and B. D. Loader, *Digital Democracy,* Routledge, London, pp. 193–210.

Coleman, S. (1999c), 'Can the New Media Invigorate Democracy?', *Political Quarterly*, vol. 70 (2), pp. 16–22.

Coleman, S. (1999d), 'Westminster in the Information Age', in S. Coleman, J. Taylor and W. van de Donk (eds), *Parliament in the Age of the Internet*, Oxford University Press, Oxford, pp. 9–25.

Collinge, A. (1999), 'Don't be a Mouse in Expanding On-line', *Local Government Chronicle,* 22 January, pp. 10–11.

Committee on the Administration of Justice (1992), *The Casement Trials*, Pamphlet no. 19, Committee on the Administration of Justice, Belfast.

Corrado, A. and Firestone, C.M. (eds), (1997), *Elections in Cyberspace: Toward a New Era in American Politics*, The Aspen Institute, Washington, DC.

Council of Chief Justices, (1997), *Electronic Appeals Initiative Project Plan*, available at http://www.hcourt.gov.au/pp.htm.

Court Service Information Services Division (1998), *Information Technology (IT) Strategy*, available at http://www.courtservice.gov.uk/itstrat.htm.

Cremin, M. (1999), *Local Government and Information Communications Technologies: What Promise the World Wide Web*, Working paper No.1, Faculty of Law and Social Sciences, University of Central England, Birmingham.

Crewe, I. (1996), *Citizenship and Civic Education*, Citizenship Foundation, London.

Cyber-Rights and Cyber-Liberties (UK) (1997), 'Who Watches the Watchmen? Internet Content Rating Systems and Privatised Censorship', available at http://www.cyber-rights.org/watchmen.htm.

Cyber Rights and Cyber Liberties (UK) (1998a), 'Who Watches the Watchmen? Part II – Accountability and Effective Self Regulation in the Information Age', available at http://www.cyber-rights.org/watchmen-ii.htm.

Cyber-Rights and Cyber-Liberties (UK) (1998b), 'Who Watches the Watchmen? Part III – ISP Capabilities for the Provision of Personal Information to the Police', available at http://www.cyber-rights.org/watchmen-iii.htm.

Dalton, R.J. (1994), *The Green Rainbow: Environmental Groups in Western Europe*, Yale University Press, New Haven.

Davenport, T.H. (1993), *Process Innovation: Re-engineering Work through Information Technology*, Harvard Business School Press, Cambridge MA.

Davidson, R. (ed), (1992), *The Postreform Congress*, St. Martin's Press, New York.

Davies, M., Croall, H. and Tyrer, J. (1998), *Criminal Justice: An Introduction to the Criminal Justice System of England and Wales*, 2nd edn, Longman, London.

Davis, D. (1998), 'Criminal Law and the Internet: The Investigator's Perspective', *Criminal Law Review*, December, pp. 48–61.

Davis, R. (1999), *The Web of Politics*, Oxford University Press, New York.

Davis, R. and Owen, D. (1998), *New Media and American Politics*, Oxford University Press, New York.

Dawson, H. (1997), 'In Touch with the Future', *Local Government Management*, Summer, pp. 7–9.

Denison, D. (1997), 'On-line for Local Services', *Municipal Journal*, 18 May, pp. 18–19.

Denison, D. (1998) 'Of Mice and Men', *Municipal Journal*, 9 January, p. 20.

Department of Justice, Equality, and Law Reform (Ireland) (1998), *Illegal and Harmful Use of the Internet*, Pn. 5231, Dublin.

DETR (1998), *Modern Local Government. In touch with the People*, Cm. 4014, HMSO, London.

Diamond, E. and Silverman, R.A. (1995), *White House to Your House: Media and Politics in Virtual America*, MIT Press, Cambridge, MA.

Do or Die! (1997), 'Lyminge Forest: The Spread of Syphilitic Suburbia', *Do or Die! – Voice from Earth First*, no. 6, pp. 72–3.

Dobson, A. (1997), *Green Political Thought*, Routledge, London.

Doherty, B (1996) 'Paving the Way: The Rise of Direct Action Against Road-building and the Changing Character of British Environmentalism', Working Paper 21, Keele University Politics Department.

Doherty, B. (1997), 'Direct Action Against Road-Building: Some Implications for the Concept of Protest Repertoires'. *Political Studies Association Annual Conference, Ireland, vol. 2*, PSAI, Dublin, pp. 147–55.

Doherty, B. (1999), 'Change the World Via e-mail', *New Statesman*, 1 November, pp. xviii–xix.

Doyle, T. and Kellow, A. (1995), *Environmental Politics and Policy Making in Australia*, Macmillan, Melbourne.

Doyle, T. and McEachern, D. (1998), *Environment and Politics*, Routledge, London.

DTI (1996), White Paper, *Regulatory Intent Concerning Use of Encryption on Public Networks*, HMSO, London.

DTI (1997), *Licensing of Trusted Third Parties for the Provision of Encryption Services*, HMSO, London.

DTI (1998a), *Secure Electronic Commerce Statement*, available at http://www.dti.gov.uk/CII/ana27p.html.

DTI (1998b), *Secure Electronic Commerce: Summary of Responses*, available at http://www.dti.gov.uk/CII/respons.html.

DTI, (1998c), *Moving into the Information Age: An International Benchmarking Study*, available at http://www.isi.gov.uk/isi/bench/mitia.

DTI (1998d), *Converging Technologies: Consequences for the New Knowledge-Driven Economy*, HMSO, London.

DTI (1998e), *Our Competitive Future: Building the Knowledge Driven Economy*, HMSO, London.

DTI (1998f), *Net Benefit: The Electronic Commerce Agenda for the UK*, available at http://www.dti.gov.uk/cii/netbenefit.html.

DTI and Department for Culture, Media and Sport (1998), *Regulating Communications: Approaching Convergence in the Information Age*, Cm. 4022, HMSO, London.

Dulio, D., Goff, D. and Thurber, J. (1999), 'Untangled Web: Internet Use During the 1998 Election', *PS*, XXXII (1), pp. 53–9.

Dutton, W. (ed). (1996), *Information and Communication Technologies: Visions and Realities*, Oxford University Press, Oxford.

Dutton, W., Taylor, J., Bellamy, C., Raab, C. and Peltu, M. (1994), *Electronic Service Delivery: Themes and Issues in the Public Sector,* Programme on Information and Communications Technology, Policy Research Paper No. 28, ESRC, Swindon.

EcoSoc (1998), 'Opinion on the Proposal for a Council Decision Adopting a Multiannual Community Action Plan on Promoting Safe Use of the Internet', *OJEC*, 98/C214/08, 10 July, Brussels, pp. 29–32.

Ellison, L. and Akdeniz, Y. (1998), 'Cyber-stalking: The Regulation of Harassment on the Internet', *Criminal Law Review*, December, pp. 29–48.

Encyclopaedia of Direct Action (1995), 'Demonstrations and Protests', available at http://envirolink.org/action/eda.html.

Ericson, R.V. (1995), 'The News Media and Accountability in Criminal Justice', in P.C. Stenning (ed). *Accountability for Criminal Justice,* University of Toronto Press, Toronto, pp. 135–161.

European Commission (1994), *Europe's way to the Information Society,* European Commission, Brussels.

European Commission (1996a), *Info 2000: Illegal and Harmful Content on the Internet,* Communication to the European Parliament, the Council, EcoSoc and the Committee of the Regions, European Commission, Brussels.

European Commission (1996b), *Illegal and Harmful Content on the Internet: Protection of Minors and Human Dignity,* Press Release, European Commission, Brussels.

European Commission (1997), *Green Paper on the Convergence of the Telecommunications, Media and Information Technology Sectors, and the Implications for Regulation: Towards an Information Society Approach,* COM(97)623, December, European Commission, Brussels.

European Commission (1998), *Globalisation and the Information Society: The Need for Strengthened International Co-operation,* Communication to the European Parliament, the Council, EcoSoc and the Committee of the Regions, CoM (98) 50, February, European Commission, Brussels.

European Council (1994), *Europe and the Global Information Society: Recommendations to the European Council,* European Council, Brussels.

Fenno, R. (1978), *Homestyle: Members in Their Districts*, Little Brown, New York.

Ferst, P and Linehan, A. (1998), 'Culture Matters: EFL goes ECO: an Account of Socio-cultural Learning Project', *Modern Language Teacher*, vol. 17 (1), pp. 53–7.

FITLOG (1994a), *In Touch. Using Technology to Communicate with the Public,* LGC Communications, Tonbridge, Kent.

FITLOG (1994b), *Under New Management. Innovation Through IT for Local Government*, LGC Communications, Tonbridge, Kent.

Frederick, H. (1997), 'Mexican NGO Computer Networking and Cross-border Coalition Building', in Bailie, Mashoed and Winseck (eds), *Democratizing Communication – Comparative Perspectives on Information and Power*, Hampton Press Inc, NJ, p. 255–286.

Freeman, R. (1997), *Democracy in the Digital Age*, Arguments 16, Demos, London.

Friis, C. (1996), 'Two Starting Points on the Study of the Internet', paper presented to the European Consortium of Political Research Joint Sessions, University of Olso.

Friis, C., Demchak, C. and LaPorte, T. (1998), 'What Can be Learned from a Home-page? Public Agencies in Cyberspace', paper presented to the European Consortium of Political Research joint sessions, 23-28 March, University of Warwick.

Froehling, O. (1997) ' The Cyberspace War of Ink and the Internet in Chiapas Mexico', *The Geographical Review,* vol. 87 (2), pp. 291–307.

Gibson, R. and Ward, S. (1998), 'UK Political Parties and the Internet: Politics as Usual in the New Media?', *Harvard International Journal of Press/Politics,* vol. 3 (3), pp. 14–38.

Gibson, R. and Ward, S. (1999a), 'Political Participation and the Internet in Europe: Who Wants and Wants-Not to Engage in Online Debate', paper presented to the UK Political Studies Association, 23-25 March, Nottingham.

Gibson, R. and Ward, S. (1999b), 'Party Democracy Online: UK Parties and New ICTs', *Information Communication and Society,* vol. 2 (3), pp. 340–67.

Giddens, A. (1990), *The Consequences of Modernity,* Polity Press, London.

Gill, H.S. and Yates-Mercer, P. (1998), 'The Dissemination of Information by Local Authorities on the World Wide Web', *Journal of Information Science,* vol. 24 (2), pp. 105–12.

Glendinning, C. (1990), *When Technology Wounds: The Human Consequences of Progress,* William Morrow, New York.

Gore, A. (1995), 'Speech by Vice-President Al Gore to the International Telecommunications Union', 21 March 1994, Reprinted in D.G. Johnson and H. Nissenbuam (eds), *Computers, Ethics & Social Values,* Prentice Hall, Englewood Cliffs, NJ., p. 621.

Gosling, P. (1998a), 'Opening the Airways', *Municipal Journal,* 22 May, pp. 16–17.

Gosling, P. (1998b), 'Councils in the Digital Age', *LG Voice,* January, pp. 16–17.

Goss, C. (1997), 'Information Pull', *Electronic Public Information,* April/May, p. 25.

Graham, A. (1998), 'Broadcasting Policy and the Digital Revolution', in J. Seaton (ed). *Politics and the Media; Harlots and Prerogatives at the Turn of the Millennium,* Blackwell, Oxford, pp. 30–42.

Greenleaf, G. and Mowbray, A. (1993), 'Information Technology in Complex Criminal Trials', Australian Institute of Judicial Administration, available at http://www.austlii.edu.au/au/other/aija/aija.html.

Griffiths, J. (1970), 'Ideology in Criminal Procedure or a Third 'Model' of Criminal Process', *Yale Law Journal,* vol. 79, pp. 359–417.

Grossman, L. (1995), *The Electronic Republic,* Penguin Books, New York.

Hague B.N. and Loader B.D. (eds). (1999), *Digital Democracy,* Routledge, London.

Hambleton, J. (1995), 'Take a Walk on the Web Side', *Court Technology Bulletin,* vol. 7 (3), available at http://www.ncsc.dni.us/NCSC/BULLETIN/v07n03.htm.

Hamilton, A. (1987) *The Judiciary Department,* Federalist Paper no.78, New York.

Hansen, A. (ed) (1993), *The Mass Media and Environmental Issues*, Leicester University Press, Leicester.

Harris, B.A. (1993), 'The Appearance of Justice: Court TV, Conventional Television, and Public Understanding of the Criminal Justice System', *Arizona Law Review*, vol. 35, pp. 785–827.

Heeks, R. (1998), *Information Systems and Public Sector Accountability*, Working Paper No. 1, Institute for Development Policy and Management, University of Manchester, Manchester.

Herrnson, P. (1998), *Congressional Elections: Campaigning at Home and Washington*, 2 edn., CQ Press, Washington DC.

Hill, K. and Hughes, J. (1998), *Cyberpolitics: Citizen Activism in the Age of the Internet*, Rowan and Littlefield, Lanham, MD.

Hoff, J. and Lofgren, K. (1997), 'Political Parties and Computer Mediated Communication in Denmark: General Use and Strategy', paper presented to the European Group of Public Administration Annual Conference, 9–13 September, Leuven, Belgium.

Home Office (1991), *Home Office Working Group on Pre-Trial Issues*, HMSO, London.

Home Office, (1996), *Protecting the Public*, Cm. 3190, HMSO, London.

Home Office (1997), *Review of Delay in the Criminal Justice System: A Report*, HMSO, London.

Home Office (1998), *Juries in Serious Fraud Trials*, Home Office, London.

Hook, F.C. (1998), 'Judicial Philosophy in Information Technology', available at http://www.netjustice.com.au/content/tchjus.html.

Horrocks, I. and Bellamy, C. (1997), 'Telematics and Community Governance: Issues for Policy and Practice', *International Journal of Public Sector Management*, vol. 10 (5), pp. 377–87.

Horrocks, I. and Hambley, N. (1998), 'The 'Webbing' of British Local Government', *Public Money and Management*, April–June, pp. 39–44.

Horrocks, I. and Webster, W. (1995), 'Wired Up', *Local Government Chronicle*, June, p. 46.

House of Commons Select Committee on Culture, Media and Sport (1998), *Media and Sport Fourth Report: The Multi-Media Revolution – Volume I*, HC 520-I, HMSO, London.

House of Lords, Select Committee on Science and Technology, (1996), *Information Society: Agenda for Action in the UK, 1995–6*, HL 77, HMSO, London.

Hunter, D. (1998), 'Town Hall Teleculture', *Government Computing*, June, pp. 31–3.

Hurrell, A. (1995), 'International Political Theory and the Environment', in K. Booth and S. Smith (eds), *International Relations Theory Today*, Blackwell, Cambridge, pp. 129–53.

INSINC (1997), *The Net Result. Social Inclusion in the Information Society*, IBM/Community Development Foundation, London.

Interdepartmental Working Group on the Treatment of Vulnerable or Intimidated Witnesses in the Criminal Justice System (1998), *Speaking Up for Justice,* Home Office, London.

Jacobson, G. (1997), *The Politics of Congressional Elections,* 4th edn, Longman, White Plains, NY.

Jellinek, D (1998) 'Technophobia Hinders a Revolution in Service Delivery', *Local Government Chronicle,* 27 November, p. 14.

Johnson, P.J. (1993), 'Introduction: Planning for the Next Century in the California Courts', *Southern California Law Review,* vol. 66, pp. 1751–60.

Kable (1995), *Tomorrow's Town Hall,* Kable/LGMB.

Kamark, E. (1999), 'Campaigning on the Internet in the Elections of 1998', in Kamark, E. and Nye, J. (eds), *Democracy.Com? Governance in a Networked World,* Hollis Publishing, New Hampshire.

Katsh, M.E. (1995), *Law in a Digital World,* Oxford University Press, Oxford.

Katz, R. and Mair, P. (1994), *How Parties Organise: Change and Adaptation in Party Organisations in Western Democracies,* Sage, London.

Katz, R. and Mair, P. (1995), 'Changing Models of Party Organisation and Party Democracy: The Emergence of the Catch-all Party', *Party Politics,* vol. 1 (1), pp. 5–28.

Kelly, M. (1998), 'Getting Support from Litigation Support', paper presented at the 13th BILETA Conference, Dublin, available at http://www.bileta.ac.uk/.

Kessel, J.H. (1992), *Presidential Campaign Politics,* 4th edn., Brooks/Cole, Pacific Grove, Ca.

Kircheimer, O. (1966), 'The Transformation of West European Party Systems', in J. Lapalombara and M. Weiner (eds), *Political Parties and Political Development,* Princeton University Press, Princeton NJ, pp. 177–200.

Klotz, R. (1997), 'Positive Spin: Senate Campaigning on the Web', *PS: Political Science and Politics,* vol. XXX (3), pp. 482–86.

Kuhn, R. (1997), 'So What's New? The Media and Electoral Politics in Britain', paper presented to the European Consortium of Political Research joint sessions, Berne.

Kyrish, S. (1994), 'Here Comes the Revolution – Again', *Media Information Australia,* November, no. 74, pp. 5–14.

Labour Coordinating Committee (1997), *New Labour: A Stakeholders' Party,* The Interim Report of the Labour Coordinating Committee's Commission on Party Democracy, Labour Coordinating Committee, London.

Lamb, R. (1996), *Promising the Earth,* Routledge, London.

Lawson, G. (1998), *NetState: Creating Electronic Government,* Demos, London.

Lawson, R. (1995), 'Defenders of the Earth'. *Net,* October, issue 11, pp. 42–45.

Le Vay, P. (1989), *Magistrates' Courts: Report of a Scrutiny,* Home Office, London.

Leadbeater, C. and Mulgan, G. (1997), 'Lean Democracy and the Leadership Vacuum', in G. Mulgan (ed), *Life After Politics: New Thinking for the Twenty First Century,* Fontana Press, London, pp. 246–59.

Lederer, F.I. and Soloman, S.H. (1997), 'Courtroom Technology – An Introduction To The Onrushing Future'. Paper presented at the Fifth National Court Technology Conference (CTC5), available at http://www.ncsc.dni.us/ctc5/ctc5arts.htm.

Lee, P. (ed). (1995), *The Democratization of Communication*, University of Wales Press, Cardiff.

Lipow, A. and Seyd, P. (1996), 'The Politics of Anti-Partyism', *Parliamentary Affairs*, vol. 49 (2), pp. 273–84.

Loader B.D. (ed). (1998), *Cyberspace Divide*, Routledge, London.

Lofgren, K. (1998), 'Scandinavian Political Parties on the Internet', *ECPR News*, vol. 10 (1), pp. 9–10.

Lord Chancellor's Advisory Committee on Legal Education and Conduct, (1997), *Lawyers' Comments to the Media*, Lord Chancellor's Department, London.

Lord Chancellor's Department (1995), *Reforming Defamation Law and Procedure*, HMSO, London.

Lord Chancellor's Department (1998a), *Consultation Paper: Resolving and Avoiding Disputes in the Information Age*, available at http://www.open.gov.uk/lcd/consult/itstrat/civindex.htm.

Lord Chancellor's Department (1998b), *Departmental Report*, Cm. 3909, HMSO, London.

Lord Chancellor's Department (1998c), *Modernising Justice*, Cm. 4155, HMSO, London.

Lowe, P. and Goyder, J. (1983), *Environmental Groups in Politics*, George Allen and Unwin, London.

Lubbers, E. (1998), 'The Brent Spar Syndrome: Counterstrategies Against On-line Activism', available at http://www.xs4all.nl/~evel/brenteng.htm.

Magarey, K. (1999), 'The Internet and Australian Parliamentary Democracy' in S. Coleman, J. Taylor and W. van de Donk (eds), *Parliament in the Age of the Internet*, Oxford University Press, Oxford, pp. 42–66.

Mander, M. (1993), 'The JUDITH Report', *International Journal of Law and Information Technology*, vol. 1, pp. 249–89.

Margolis, M., Resnick, D. and Chin-chang Tu. (1997), 'Campaigning on the Internet: Parties and Candidates on the World Wide Web in the 1996 Primary Season', *Harvard International Journal of Press/Politics*, vol. 2 (1), pp. 59–78.

Margolis, M., Resnick, D. and Wolfe, J. (1999), 'Party Competition on the Internet: Minor Versus Major Parties in the UK and USA', *Harvard International Journal of Press/Politics*, vol. 4 (4), pp. 24–47.

Martin, B. (1984), 'Environmentalism and Electoralism', *The Ecologist*, vol. 14 (3), pp. 110–18.

Marx, L. and Smith, M. (1994), 'Introduction', in M.R. Smith, and L. Marx (eds), *Does Technology Drive History? The Dilemma of Technological Determinism*, The MIT Press, Cambridge, MA, pp. ix–xv.

Maxwell, B. (1996), *How to Access the Federal Government on the Internet,* CQ Press, Washington, D.C.

Mayhew, D. (1974), *Congress: The Electoral Connection,* Yale University Press, New Haven.

McInnes R (1998), 'Bordertown and the Globalisation of Justice: Using Computers in an Australian Magistrates Court', *The Journal of Information,Law and Technology,* issue 2, available at http://elj.warwick.ac.uk/jilt/itpract/98_2mcin/.

McKie, D. (1999), *Media Coverage of Parliament,* Hansard Society for Parliamentary Government, London.

McLean, I. (1989), *Democracy and New Technology,* Polity Press, Cambridge.

Merchant, I. (1992), *Radical Ecology: The Search for a Liveable World,* Routledge, London.

Micossi, S. (1996), 'By the People, for the People?' *I & T Magazine,* no. 19, April, p.1.

Milner, E. (1999), 'The 'Problem' of Electronic Government', in B.N. Hague and B.D Loader (eds), *Digital Democracy,* Routledge, London, pp. 63–72.

Moar, M. (1996), *Political Parties and Party Systems,* Routledge, London.

Muid, C. (1992), 'New Public Management and Informatisation: A Natural Combination?' *Public Policy and Administration,* vol. 7, pp. 75–9.

Mulgan, G. (1991), *Communication and Control: Networks and the New Economies of Communication,* Polity Press, Cambridge.

Mulgan, G. and Adonis, A. (1994), 'Back to Greece: the Scope for Direct Democracy', *Demos Quarterly,* vol. 3, pp. 2–9.

Muzzio, D. and Birdsell, D. (1997), 'The 1996 Net Voter', *The Public Perspective,* December/January, pp. 42–3.

Negroponte, N. (1995), *Being Digital,* Coronet, London.

Newell, J. (2000) *Italian Parties and the WWW: Normalisation Here Too?* Working Papers in Contemporary History and Politics, European Studies Research Institute, University of Salford.

Nixon, P. and Johansson, H. (1999), 'Transparency Through Technology: The Internet and Political Parties', in B.N. Hague and B.D. Loader (eds), *Digital Democracy,* Routledge, London, pp. 135–53.

Noam, E.M. (ed) (1990), *Technologies Without Boundaries,* Harvard University Press, Cambridge, MA.

Norris, P. (1998), 'Who Surfs? New Technology, Old Voters and Virtual Democracy in America', paper presented to the John F. Kennedy Visions of Governance for the Twenty First Century Conference, 19-22 July, Bretton Woods.

Norris, P. (1999), 'Who Surfs Café Europa? Virtual Democracy in the US and Europe', paper presented to the Annual Meeting of the American Political Science Association, 1-5 September, Atlanta, GA.

Norris, P. (2000), *Virtuous Circle: Political Communication in Post Industrial Democracies,* Cambridge University Press, Cambridge.

Northern Ireland Office (1998), *Review of the Criminal Justice System in Northern Ireland*, available at http://www.nio.gov.uk/review.pdf.

OECD (1997), *Report on the Background and Issues of Crytography Policy*, OECD, Paris.

O'Flaherty, D. (1996), 'Computer-generated Displays in the Courtroom: For Better or Worse?', *Web Journal of Current Legal Issues*, issue 4, available at http://www.webjcli.ncl.ac.uk/1996/contents4.html.

O'Lear, S. (1996), 'Electronic Communication and Environmental Policy in Russia and Estonia', *The Geographical Review*, vol. 87 (2), pp. 275–90.

O'Lear, S. (1997), 'Using Electronic Mail Surveys for Geographic Research: Lessons from a Survey of Russian Environmentalists', *Professional Geographer*, vol. 48 (2), pp. 209–17.

Oram, A. (1998), 'British and Foreign Civil Rights Organisations Oppose Encryption Paper', Computer Professionals for Social Responsibility, available at http://www.cpsr.org/cpsr/nii/cyber-rights/web/cryptobrit.html.

Parker, G.R. (1986), *Homeward Bound: Explaining Changes in Congressional Behavior*, University of Pittsburgh Press, Pittsburgh.

Pavlik, J. (1996), *New Media Technology: Cultural and Commercial Perspectives*, Allyn and Bacon, Boston.

Percy-Smith, J. (1995), *Digital Democracy: Information and Communication Technologies in Local Politics*, CLD Research Report No. 14, Commission for Local Democracy, London.

Percy-Smith, J. (1996), 'Downloading Democracy? Information and Communication Technologies in Local Politics', *Policy and Politics*, vol. 24 (1), pp. 43–56.

Peterson, J. and Sharp, M. (1998), *Technology Policy in the European Union*, Macmillan, Basingstoke.

Plotnikoff, J. and Woolfson, R. (1993), 'Replacing the Judge's Pen? Evaluation of a Real-time Transcription System', *International Journal of Law and Information Technology*, vol. 1, pp. 90–106.

Polsby, N. and Wildavsky, A. (1996), *Presidential Elections*, 9th edn, Chatham House, Chatham, NJ.

Powell, W. (1989), *The Anarchist Cookbook*, Barricade Books, London.

Pratchett, L. (1994), 'Information Prospects for Democratic Government in the UK', paper presented to the European Group of Public administration Permanent Study Group in Informatisation in Public Administration, Bad Tatzmannsdorf, Austria.

Princen, T. and Finger, M. (1994), *Environmental NGOs in World Politics: Linking the Local to the Global*, Routledge, London.

Purnell, N. (1990), 'Technology and the Courtroom', *New Law Journal*, vol. 140, pp. 1064–66.

Quirk, B. (1997), 'The Lewisham Public Management Forum: Beyond Fragmented Public Service', *Local Government Policy Making*, vol. 23 (5), pp. 48–53.

Raab, C. (1997), 'Privacy, Democracy, Information', in B. Loader (ed), *The Governance of Cyberspace: Politics, Technology and Global Restructuring,* Routledge, London, pp. 155–74.

Raab, C. (1998), 'Electronic Confidence: Trust, Information and Public Administration', in W. van de Donk and I. Snellen (eds), *Handbook of Public Administration for the Information Age,* IOS Press, Amsterdam.

Raab, C., Bellamy, C., Taylor, J., Dutton, W.H. and Peltu, M. (1996), 'The Information Polity: Electronic Democracy, Privacy, and Surveillance', in W. Dutton (ed), *Information and Comunication Technologies: Visions and Realities.* Oxford University Press, Oxford, pp. 283–300.

Raine, J. and Wilson, M. (1993), *Managing Criminal Justice,* Harvester, Hemel Hampstead.

Raine, J., and Wilson, M. (1997), 'Beyond Managerialism in Criminal Justice', *Howard Journal,* vol. 36, pp. 80–95.

Raine, J.W. (1989), *Local Justice,* T&T Clark, Edinburgh.

Rash, W. (1997), *Politics on the Nets: Wiring the Political Process,* W.H. Freeman, New York.

Resnick, D. (1999), 'The Normalisation of Cyberspace', in C. Toulouse and T. Luke (eds), *The Politics of Cyberspace,* Routledge, London, pp. 48–68.

Rheingold, H. (1995), *The Virtual Community: Finding Connection in a Computerised World,* Minerva, London.

Richards, P. (1996), 'Reconnecting Voters', *Municipal Journal,* 2-8 February, pp. 29–30.

Richardson, J. (1994), *The Market for Political Activism: Interest Groups as a Challenge to Political Parties,* Jean Monnet Papers No.18, European University Institute, Florence.

Road Alert! (1997), *Road Raging: Top Tips for Wrecking Roadbuilding,* RoadAlert!, Berkshire.

Rodgers, J. (1998), 'NGO Use of Computer-Mediated Communication: Opening New Spaces of Political Representation?', paper presented to the International Studies Association Annual Convention, 18–21 March, Minneapolis, MN.

Roper, J. (1999), 'New Zealand Political Parties Online: the World Wide Web as a Tool for Democratisation or Political Marketing', in C. Toulouse and T. Luke (eds), *The Politics of Cyberspace,* Routledge, London, pp. 69–83.

Roskill, Lord Justice (1986), *Fraud Trials Committee Report,* HMSO, London.

Rüdig, W. (1995), 'Between Moderation and Marginalisation: Environmental Radicalism in Britain', in B. Taylor (ed). *Ecological Resistance Movements.* State University of New York Press, Albany, pp. 219–40.

Schauer, F. (1982), *Free Speech,* Cambridge University Press, Cambridge,

Schwartz, E. (1996), *Netactivism: How Citizens Use the Internet,* Songline Studios, Sebastopol, CA.

Scottish Office (1998), *Serving Scotland's Needs,* Cm. 3914, HMSO, London.

Seago, P., Walker, C. and Wall, D. (1995), *The Role and Appointment of Stipendiary Magistrates,* University of Leeds/Lord Chancellor's Department, Leeds.

Seyd, P. and Whiteley, P. (1992), *Labour's Grassroots,* Clarendon Press, Oxford.

Shapiro, A. (1999), 'The Internet', *Foreign Policy,* Summer, pp. 14–27.

Sieber, U. (1998), 'Legal Aspects of Computer Related Crime in the Information Society', Legal Advisory Board, European Commission, January, available at http://www2echo.lu/legal/en/comcrime/sieber.html.

Smith, C. (1998), 'Political Parties in the Information Age: From Mass Party to Leadership Organisation', in W. van de Donk and I. Snellen (eds), *Handbook of Public Administration for the Information Age,* IOS Press, Amsterdam.

Smith, C.F. and Gray, P. (1999), 'The Scottish Parliament in the Information Age' in S. Coleman, J. Taylor, and W. van de Donk (eds), *Parliament in the Age of the Internet,* Oxford University Press, Oxford, pp. 67–79.

SOCITM (1996), *The Renaissance of Local Government. The Dawn of a New Age for Information, Systems and Technology in Local Government,* SOCITM, Northampton.

SOCITM (1997), *Local Government IT Trends 1997,* SOCITM, London.

SOLACE/LGMB (1995), *Managing with Intelligence. A Strategic Approach to the Management of Information and Information Technology,* SOLACE/LGMB, Luton.

Southern, A. (1995), 'Local Authority Information Technology Strategies: A Preliminary Assessment', *Local Government Policy Making,* vol. 22 (3), pp. 26–33.

Steel, R. (1998), 'Nurturing an Electronic Public Information Strategy in Local Government', *Vine,* no. 102, pp. 20–4.

Steele, J. (1995), *Information and Citizenship in Europe. An Overview,* Policy Studies Institute, London.

Stefanik, N. (1993), 'Sustainable Dialogue /Sustainable Development: Developing Planetary Consciousness via Electronic Democracy', in J. Breacher, J. Brown, J. Childs, and J. Cutler (eds), *Global Visions: Beyond the New World Order,* South End Press, Boston.

Stone, B. (1996), 'Politics '96' *Internet World,* November, pp. 44–50.

Strand, R.G. (1991), 'The Computer Integrated Courtroom Harnessing Technology to Enhance the Justice System', *Yearbook of Law, Computers and Technology* 5, Butterworths, London, pp. 1–8.

Streck, J. (1999), 'Pulling the Plug on Electronic Town Meetings: Participatory Democracy and the Reality of Usenet', in C. Toulouse and T. Luke (eds), *The Politics of Cyberspace,* Routledge, London, pp. 18–47.

Street, J. (1997), 'Citizenship and Mass Communication', *Contemporary Political Studies,* Vol. 1, UK Political Studies Association, Belfast, pp. 502–10.

Susskind, R. (1996), *The Future of Law: Facing the Challenges of Information Technology,* Clarendon Press, Oxford.

Sweeting, D. and Cope, S. (1997), 'Modernising Local Democracy: Democratic Innovations in Local Government', *Local Government Policy Making,* vol. 23 (5), pp. 3–8.

Tanburn, S. (1998), 'Connections of the Herts', *Municipal Journal,* 16 October, pp. 22–3.

Tang, P. (1998), 'Managing the Cyberspace Divide: Government Investment in Electronic Information Services', in B.D. Loader (ed), *Cyberspace Divide,* Routledge, London.

Tantum, M. (1991), 'The Lawyer and the War', *Yearbook of Law, Computers and Technology* 5, pp. 65–73.

Tapscott, D. (1996), *Digital Economy,* McGraw Hill, New York.

Taylor, J.A. (1998), 'Governance and Electronic Innovation: Whither the Information Polity?' *Information Communication and Society,* vol. 1 (2), pp. 144–62.

Taylor, J.A. and Webster, W.R. (1996), 'Universalism: Public Services and Citizenship in the Information Age', *Information Infrastructure and Policy,* vol. 5, pp. 217–33.

Tranvik, T. and Selle, P. (1998), 'Sand and Democracy: The Politics of Digital Networks in Norway', paper presented to the European Consortium of Political Research Workshops, March 23-28, University of Warwick.

Tsagarousianou, R., Tambini, D. and Bryan, C. (eds) (1998), *Cyberdemocracy: Technology, Cities and Civic Networks,* Routledge, London.

Turner, S. (1998), 'Wiring the Public into Local Services', *Municipal Journal,* 26 June, p. 20.

Upton, R. and Swinden, K. (1998), *Information Age Government - What's In It For Us?,* Kable, London.

Voerman, G. (1998), 'Dutch Political Parties on the Internet', *ECPR News,* vol. 10 (1), pp. 8–9.

Walker, C. and Akdeniz, Y. (1998a), 'UK Government Policy on Encryption: Trust is the Key?', *Journal of Civil Liberties,* vol.3 (2), pp. 110–16.

Walker, C. and Akdeniz, Y. (1998b), 'The Governance of the Internet in Europe with Special Reference to Illegal and Harmful Content', *Criminal Law Review,* December, pp. 5–19.

Walker, C., and Akdenix, Y. (1998c), 'UK Law Online', *Amicus Curiae,* vol. 11, pp. 6–7.

Walker, C., and Akdeniz, Y. (1998d), 'Virtual Democracy', *Public Law,* p.489.

Wall, D. (1998), 'Policing and the Regulation of the Internet', *Criminal Law Review,* December, pp. 79–90.

Wall, D.S. and Johnstone, J. (1997a), 'Lawyers, Information Technology and Legal Practice: The Use of Information Technology by Provincial Lawyers', *International Review of Law, Computers and Technology,* vol. 11 (1), pp. 117–28.

Wall, D.S. and Johnstone, J. (1997b), 'The Industrialization of Legal Practice and the Rise of the New Electric Lawyer', *International Journal of the Sociology of Law*, vol. 25 (2), pp. 95–115.

Wallace, J. and Mangan, M. (1996), *Sex, Laws and Cyberspace: Freedom and Censorship on the Frontiers of the Online Revolution*, Henry Holt, New York.

Ward, S. and Gibson, R. (1998), 'The First Internet Election? UK Political Parties and Campaigning in Cyberspace', in I. Crewe, B. Gosschalk and J. Bartle (eds), *Political Communications: Why Labour Won the General Election of 1997*, Frank Cass, London, pp. 93–112.

Warf, B. and J. Grimes (1997), 'Counterhegemonic Discourses and the Internet', *The Geographical Review*, vol. 87 (2), pp. 259–74.

Waters, R.C. (1997), 'Tiptoeing Through Technology's Graveyard on the Way to the 21st Century: The Internet as the Backbone of Court Access Programs', paper presented at the Fifth National Court Technology Conference (CTC5), available at http://www.ncsc.dni.us/ctc5/ctc5arts.htm.

Waugh, P. (1991), 'The Use of Computers in the administration of Justice in the United Kingdom', *Yearbook of Law, Computers and Technology* vol. 5, Butterworths, London, pp. 26–35.

Webber, M. (1968), *Explorations into Urban Structure*, University of Pennsylvania Press, Pennsylvania.

Whiteley, P., Seyd, P. and Richardson, J. (1994), *True Blues: The Politics of Conservative Party Membership*, Clarendon Press, Oxford.

Widdison, R. (1997), 'Beyond Woolf: The Virtual Court House', *Web Journal of Current Legal Issues*, issue 2, available at http://www.webjcli.ncl.ac.uk/1997/contents2.html.

Widdison, R. (1997), 'Electronic Law Practice' *Modern Law Review,* vol. 60, pp. 143–63.

Willetts, P. (1996), 'From Stockholm to Rio and Beyond: The Impacts of the Environmental Movement on the United Nation's Consultative Arrangements for NGOs', *Review of International Studies*, vol. 199 (22), pp. 57–68.

Wood, D (1999), 'The International Campaign Against the Multilateral Agreement on Investment: a Test Case for the Future of Globalization?' in J. Pickerill and M. Duckett (eds), *Radical British Environmentalism: Theory into Practice*, workshop proceedings at University of Newcastle-upon-Tyne, Department of Geography, 19 February 1999, pp.32–52.

Woolf, Lord Justice (1996), *Access to Justice: Final Report*, HMSO, London.

Worrall, L. (1995), 'Managing Information in Complex Organisations: A Local Government Perspective', *Local Government Studies,* vol. 21 (1), pp. 115–29.

Wray, S. (1998a), *Transforming Luddite Resistance into Virtual Luddite resistance: Weaving a World Wide Web of Electronic Civil Disobedience*, available at http;// www.gn.apc.org/pmhp/dc/activism/swray.htm, New York University.

Wray, S. (1998b), *Electronic Civil Disobedience and the World Wide Web of Hacktivism: A Mapping of Extraparliamentarian Direct Action Net Politics*, available at http://www.nyu.edu/projects/wray/wwwhack.html, New York University.

Young, J. (1993), 'Global Network: Computers in a Sustainable Society', World Watch Paper 115, Washington DC.

Zuurmond, A. (1998), 'From Bureaucracy to Infocracy: Are Democratic Institutions Lagging Behind?' in W. van de Donk and I. Snellen (eds), *Handbook of Public Administration for the Information Age*, IOS Press, Amsterdam.

Index